OHIO STATE FOOTBALL 2002

THE IMPROBABLE NATIONAL CHAMPIONSHIP

To Rick
Go Bucks!

Steve Basford

Book Design & Production:
Columbus Publishing Lab
www.ColumbusPublishingLab.com

Copyright © 2023 by
Steve Basford
LCCN: 2023916373

Cover photo courtesy of Buckeye Sports Bulletin

Paperback ISBN: 978-1-63337-746-2
E-Book ISBN: 978-1-63337-747-9

Printed in the United States of America
1 3 5 7 9 10 8 6 4 2

OHIO STATE FOOTBALL 2002

THE IMPROBABLE NATIONAL CHAMPIONSHIP

STEVE BASFORD

TABLE OF CONTENTS

INTRODUCTION

THE SCENE: SUN DEVIL STADIUM in Tempe, Arizona, January 3, 2003. The Bowl Championship Series National Championship game between undefeated Ohio State and undefeated Miami, in its second overtime.

The clock had struck midnight about 17 minutes earlier in the eastern time zone, but the carriage had not turned back into a pumpkin.

Moments earlier, it appeared that the magical season had come to a heartbreaking end, as a fourth-down pass to Chris Gamble in tight coverage fell incomplete in the end zone. Orange and green fireworks celebrating an apparent Miami Hurricanes win in overtime over my Ohio State Buckeyes had filled the air.

For about three seconds.

Then, a yellow object fell to the turf in the orange-colored end zone, a penalty flag that kept the dream season alive. The Buckeyes would score the tying touchdown and force a second overtime.

A few minutes later, it was the Hurricanes at the Ohio State one-yard line on fourth down, needing a touchdown to stay alive. As the Hurricanes came to the line of scrimmage, Gamble, now on defense, trotted to his position on the far side. How much gas did he have left in the tank after having participated in over 100 plays?

Like the other 77,501 in attendance, I was on my feet, as I had been for most of the previous (almost) four hours. I had prime seats on the 45-yard line in the upper deck, the home side of the field on the north end of the stadium. I had scored tickets at the priceless price of $145 through a lottery as an Ohio State employee. Before kickoff, I had looked up to my left into the VIP section and seen Ohio Governor Bob Taft and his wife, Hope, waving to the fans. Since their seats were on about the 40-yard line, how did I get a better vantage point than the most important person in Ohio? On second thought, perhaps the most important person in Ohio, at least on this date, was on the sidelines, wearing a scarlet sweater vest and a headset.

The word to describe the Buckeyes' record would also pertain to the environment—perfect. The weather had been warm enough to allow for swimming in the hotel pool, if I had been prepared. The game-time temperature was 70 degrees. The official game notes described the weather as "beautiful".

At the festivities outside the stadium a few hours before the game, I had spotted Jack Tatum—a mainstay of Ohio State's last consensus national championship team in 1968—sporting a white mustache, and had a photo taken with him. I was surprised to find out that I was taller than the legendary Buckeye defender.

If this were a movie, the scene would freeze on that fourth-down play, and I would think back to the last four months of the magical season. I had made the road trips to the Cincinnati game, sitting in the sun on a day so hot that an associate of mine said that he drank six bottles of water, and the Northwestern game, though in Evanston, without having a ticket in advance and having trouble finding a place to park, I almost gave up, before finally finding a school that had a parking spot available. I'd like to brag that I had experienced all of the close games, but I was on vacation in

Massachusetts during the Wisconsin game, at a conference in San Diego during the Purdue game, and was working the stats for a televised high school playoff game—which, naturally, had a one-point score of 20-19—during the Illinois game.

Cut back to Tempe, with the Hurricanes at the Ohio State one-yard line on fourth down and the Buckeyes ahead, 31-24. Cie Grant explodes off the left side of the Buckeye defense and grabs the quarterback to force a fluttering pass, which Donnie Nickey knocks down at the goal line.

National champions!

CHAPTER 1

The Background

A SECOND-YEAR COACH who had a 7-5 record in his first season and who had a record of 14-20 in his first three seasons at his previous job at a Division I-AA college.

A team coming off a season where they won one fewer game than the year before.

A senior class that had a record of 21-15 (13-11 in the Big Ten) over the past three seasons, had won only 10 of its last 19 games, had lost half of their last 14 games, and had lost two of its last three games.

Players who had 76% of the rushing yards and scored 25 of the 40 touchdowns were not returning.

Returning quarterbacks had only 16% of the passing yards and 17% of the passing touchdowns. The starting quarterback had career numbers of 339 passing yards and four interceptions, compared to one touchdown pass.

A kicker who had made only seven of 14 field goals the season before, missing on six of seven kicks from 40 yards or longer.

A freshman running back replacing one who had rushed for 1,294 yards.

An athletic player who had only five receptions in the 2001 season as a freshman.

Based on these, what were the expectations for the 2002 Ohio State Buckeyes?

First, some perspective.

This wasn't just any second year coach; this was Jim Tressel, a coach who had won four Division I-AA national championships at Youngstown State and was regarded highly enough in 1995 to be considered to coach the Miami Hurricanes, the team that the Buckeyes would face in the Bowl Championship Series (BCS) national title game in the 2002 season. He was five years removed from his last national championship in 1997, the same year that Michigan won its most recent one, sharing it with Nebraska. That 1997 championship game was a 10-9 win over McNeese State, an outcome which definitely qualified him to lead the 2002 Buckeyes. His three other championship game wins were by 14, 12, and 8 points—relative breathers that were, thankfully, not held against him in the hiring process. He had been an Ohio State assistant from 1983 through 1985, when the Buckeyes won 75% of their games, won two bowl games by a total of eight points, and played in the Rose Bowl. Appropriately, his last game as an assistant was in the 10-7 win over Brigham Young in the Citrus Bowl, in which the only Buckeye touchdown was on an interception return and the defense snuffed out the last Brigham Young drive with an interception in the end zone with three seconds remaining. He would spend all but two years of his life in the state of Ohio, including his playing and coaching career. He was the son of Lee, a Hall of Fame college coach who had won a national championship at Baldwin Wallace University. He was the All-Ohio Athletic Conference quarterback while playing under his father in 1974.

One can imagine five year-old Jim sitting on his father's knee on New Year's Day in 1958—after shoveling the family's driveway and all the other driveways in the neighborhood—watching the Buckeyes beat Oregon in the Rose Bowl, 10-7 on a field goal in the fourth quarter, and saying,

"That's what I want to do when I grow up, win college games by one score where we pull it out in the fourth quarter and win a national championship!" Lee was the coach at Massillon Washington High School at the time.

This wasn't just any quarterback; this was Craig Krenzel, who had led the Buckeyes to a 26-20 win at Michigan as a sophomore in his first career start, the first Buckeye win in Ann Arbor in 14 (a mystical number that would carry into the 2002 season) years. He had been a *USA Today* honorable mention All-American in high school. That 1987 game was the last game for coach Earle Bruce, who was inducted into the College Football Hall of Fame in 2002; could this be an omen?

This wasn't just any kicker; this was Mike Nugent, who would set Ohio State records and play 16 years in the NFL. In 2002, he would become the first Buckeye place-kicker ever to capture All-America honors. A report on www.espn.com has, "As a kid, Tressel often visited Browns camp with his father. A young Jim Tressel once held the ball for Lou 'The Toe' Groza as the Hall of Famer [playing for the Cleveland Browns] practiced kicking field goals." In two years, Nugent would win the Lou Groza Award. Could this be an omen?

This wasn't just any freshman running back; this was Maurice Clarett, who was the *USA Today* Offensive Player of the Year, selected by the Associated Press as Mr. Football in the state of Ohio, the Associated Press co-Offensive Player of the Year, and a Parade Magazine All-American, who would set the Ohio State season rushing record and touchdown record for a freshman, and who would come within nine yards of the Ohio State freshman single game rushing record at the time, set by the legendary Archie Griffin.

This wasn't just any sophomore athlete, this was Chris Gamble, who would set franchise records for interceptions and pass deflections with the Carolina Panthers.

Yes, the 2001 team had a 7-5 record following the 8-4 record of the 2000 team, but they rebounded from every loss in the regular season with a win, and four of the five losses were by seven points or less; in the fifth loss, they trailed by five points with under six minutes remaining. In the last four of those games, they either led or were tied in the fourth quarter. Against Wisconsin, they lost a 17-0 lead, and against Penn State, they lost a 27-9 lead.

To paraphrase the lines from the movie "For Richer or Poorer", which had Tim Allen saying, "All we gotta do is pretend to be people that we're not to fool people we don't know in a situation we've never been in. We're from New York. How hard can it be?", this version was "All we gotta do is win all 14 games—with seven of those by seven points or less, including the last four games—with a second-year coach, a quarterback who entered the season with career numbers of 339 passing yards and four interceptions compared to one touchdown pass, a freshman running back, a defensive back converted from wide receiver in the fourth game of the season; play in the national championship game against the defending national champions, who were on a 34-game winning streak and have two Heisman Trophy-worthy players; face fourth down twice on offense in overtime while trailing by seven points, and prevent a touchdown on four plays inside our two-yard line on defense in the second overtime. We're from Ohio State. We had a surprising national championship in 1968 with inexperienced players, improving our win total by four over the previous season and beating the defending national champions. How hard can it be?"

How to describe this national championship journey?

The Impossible Dream? No, that was already taken by the 1967 Boston Red Sox, who improved from a 72-90 record in 1966 to reach the seventh game of the 1967 World Series.

The Impossible *Something-Else*? To use the word *Impossible* at all would short-change the program that had a storied history, a solid senior class, and a highly successful coach.

Inconceivable? Already associated with *The Princess Bride*.

Imperfect? What is imperfect about a perfect record?

Unbelievable? That word bounced in my head several times during the season. First, the Cincinnati comeback win—did that really happen? Then, close game after close game—did that really happen? Finally, the win over Miami in the BCS championship game—DID THAT REALLY HAPPEN?? After a few games, the season became very believable.

No, I needed a more descriptive word.

Improbable.

CHAPTER 2

Setting the Stage

FROM THE 2000 SEASON to the 2001 season, the Buckeyes were not exactly trending in an upward direction; they had scored fewer points, given up more points, and had one less win in 2001, compared to the 2000 season.

Going into the 2002 season, using the baseball analogy of being "strong up the middle", on offense, they needed a new center, quarterback, fullback, and tailback. However, the defense fit the bill, returning tackle Tim Anderson, middle linebacker Matt Wilhelm, and safeties Mike Doss and Donnie Nickey.

As Todd Jones of the *Columbus Dispatch* pointed out on the day to kick off the 2002 season, the Buckeyes' 15 losses the previous three years were the most they had suffered in a three-year period since dropping 17 from 1896 to 1898.

The Buckeyes finished the 2001 season outside the Top 25 of the AP poll, in the category of "Others Receiving Votes", behind Marshall, Fresno State, and Hawaii. Jeff Sagarin's ratings had the Buckeyes at #35.

However, going into the 2002 season, they were ranked #13 in the Associated Press poll and #12 by *Sports Illustrated*.

What did the voters know? Why should Buckeyes fans have high expectations?

Why? On defense, the Buckeyes returned five of their top six leaders in tackles, all seniors, and eight players who had started against South Carolina. They returned six players who had started on offense against South Carolina.

Why? They returned players who had 77% of the receiving yards, including their top receiver, Michael Jenkins, who averaged 20.2 yards per reception in his 988 receiving yards.

Why? They had the returning player in charge of the most important play in football, in Coach Tressel's mind—the punt. Andy Groom had averaged 45 yards per punt in the 2001 season. He had ranked third in the nation in 2001, and the two ahead of him were not returning. As a footnote—no pun intended—had had no tackles in the 2001 season, but had six in the 2000 season. In the 2002 season, he would be involved in the most crucial tackle of the season.

Why? Take a look at Coach Tressel's history. In his first year at Youngstown State, his team had a 1-9 record going into its last game against its rival Akron, which had a 7-3 record, and pulled the upset, 40-39. Ironically, Akron would be the first opponent of his OSU career in 2001. He had recorded a 14-0 season (with one tie) in 1994. He had improved his record by six wins from his first to his second year at Youngstown State. Could he improve his record significantly from his first to his second year at Ohio State?

Why? Coach Tressel had already delivered on the promise that he made when he spoke at halftime of the men's basketball game against Michigan on January 18, 2001, the day of his hiring: "I can assure you that you will be proud of your young people in the classroom, in the community, and most especially in 310 days in Ann Arbor, Michigan." He had come from a lower division college, but, as the *Chicago Tribune* pointed out on Tressel's hiring date, several coaches have made the transition successfully, including Frank Beamer, who went from Murray State to Virginia Tech in 1987, which was 14 years prior to Tressel's hiring.

On the day of his hiring, Bob Hunter of the *Columbus Dispatch* wrote: "From the day the OSU job opened, the stream of e-mails from Tressel supporters has been constant, more so than for any other candidate. And the message has been just as constant: Don't overlook this guy or you'll be sorry ... he will be every bit as successful at Division I-A as he was in Youngstown."

Another omen in the *Dispatch* was the comment: "Tressel also does well in Florida, recognized as the nation's top state for high-school talent. He had 11 Floridians this year and 36 in his tenure."

Steve Blackledge's column in the *Dispatch* mentioned glowing praise of Tressel from high school coaches Darrell Mayne of Upper Arlington, which produced Simon Fraser in Tressel's first recruiting class, and Gregg Miller of Brookhaven, which produced Maurice Hall, likewise a freshman in 2001.

Based on key personnel returning, the coach, the history, and how the Buckeyes finished the 2001 season against Michigan and South Carolina, their fans had good reason to expect something big in 2002.

Even the Illinois game on the next to last weekend had signs of good things to come. They entered the game one game behind first place Illinois and had the lead in the fourth quarter against the Illini. A win would have given the Buckeyes a three-way tie for first place at the end of the season. The 34-22 loss to Illinois was their worst loss of the season and their only loss by more than seven points. Illinois would finish the regular season with a 10-1 record before losing to Nick Saban's LSU team in the Sugar Bowl.

Tressel had planned to use both Scott McMullen and Krenzel in the Illinois game, in place of suspended Steve Bellisari, who was a captain and Krenzel's roommate. McMullen started both halves, Krenzel played in the last two possessions of the first half, then re-entered the game during the first possession of the second half with the Buckeyes down, 21-10—their largest deficit of the season to that point. He had nine career pass attempts, none in the season, before the game. He wasn't even with the team for the San Diego State game on October 20, due to attending his sister's wedding. His first three plays were inauspicious—a sack for seven yards and two incompletions. However, the next possession had signs of things to come. His first completion was a 13-yard pass to another sophomore, Michael Jenkins, a combination that would work fairly well in the two seasons to follow. In the same drive, he connected for 35 yards to Jenkins, but Nugent missed a 40-yard field goal attempt. He led the team to a touchdown on each of the first two drives of the second half to give the Buckeyes a 22-21 lead, but he gave up a pick-six interception with 5:19 remaining when the Buckeyes were trailing by only five points. On the first possession of the second half, he connected with Chris Vance for 19 yards on third-and-17, and his first career touchdown pass was 17 yards to Jenkins on a third-and-16 play. His last possession of the game also ended with an interception. The first Illinois score, in the first minute of the game, was on a blocked Andy Groom punt.

What was the level of optimism going into The Game as a nine-point underdog and an unranked team against the Number 11 ranked Wolverines?

THE 2001 MICHIGAN GAME

Three Hundred and Ten days after Tressel became the coach, the Buckeyes upset Michigan, 26-20 in Ann Arbor for the program's 400th Big Ten win. Jonathan Wells ran for three touchdowns in the first half—giving him five against Michigan in the last two years—including a 46-yard run on a fourth-and-one play. Wells had 23 of his 25 carries and 122 of his 129 yards (outgaining the Michigan team by 12 yards) in the first half, having to leave the game for good when cramps flared up early in the second half. If he had stayed 100%, the outcome may have been more decisive, and he may have finished with more than 200 yards. A 200-yard game would have initiated the success that Buckeye running backs have had in Ann Arbor; Chris Wells in 2007, Carlos Hyde in 2013, Ezekiel Elliott in 2015, and J.K. Dobbins in 2019 all topped the mark. It was his fifth consecutive 100-yard performance.

In the second half, the Buckeyes managed only 74 yards total, with 15 yards rushing and one first down. In the 2002 season, they would manage only 80 yards in the first half of a major (understatement) game.

In front of a crowd of 111,571—the second largest crowd in Michigan Stadium history—Krenzel made his first collegiate start and played the entire game, after playing a little more than half the game the week before against Illinois. The year before, he had watched as Drew Henson led the Wolverines to a 38-26 win in Columbus. Henson had foregone his senior season of football in 2001 to pursue his baseball career; otherwise, the 2001 game could have matched him against Krenzel. They had competed against each other in high school. The *Chicago Tribune* had a story about Krenzel, in his sophomore year, coming on in the fourth quarter of Henry Ford High School's game against Henson's Brighton High School and nearly rallying his team with a 140-yard passing performance in one quarter. They would compete against each other in 2004, when Krenzel was with the Chicago Bears and Henson played for the Dallas Cowboys. Henson would play baseball for the Columbus Clippers, the AAA affiliate of the New York Yankees.

The Buckeyes had only one turnover, compared to five by the Wolverines. The defense had four interceptions, including two by Doss with returns of 35 and 36 yards inside the Michigan ten-yard line, and freshman Dustin Fox ended the game with his first career interception. For Doss, these were two of his three interceptions for the year; Tim Anderson had the fourth one, also his only pick of the year.

The Buckeyes benefited from Michigan mistakes. The Wolverines botched a snap to the quarterback in the first half, which gave the Buckeyes two points on a safety. With the score 23-7 and the ball at the OSU 10-yard line in the third quarter, quarterback John Navarre threw a perfect pass to Marquise Walker—who set Michigan records for career and single season receptions—but he dropped the ball. Michigan then missed a 27-yard field-goal attempt; this was in the Wolverines' longest drive of the game.

The defense stopped Michigan on downs at the Ohio State 14-yard line in the fourth quarter. The Buckeyes' only turnover was an interception that Krenzel threw into the end zone on a first-down play, but the safety occurred shortly after it. Could a similar sequence of events happen again in a big game of the 2002 season?

Navarre had lost a fumble at the Ohio State 21-yard line before Krenzel's interception. Both Krenzel and Navarre were sophomores playing in their first Ohio State-Michigan game. Neither was representing his home state; Krenzel is from Michigan, and Navarre is from Wisconsin.

The score at halftime was 23-0, and Michigan scored on its first possession of the second half to make the score 23-7. Were the Buckeyes confident? In two other road games, they had a 17-0 lead and lost 20-17 at Wisconsin, and had a 27-9 lead in a 29-27 loss at Penn State.

The last time that the Buckeyes had a 23-point lead over Michigan at any point of the game was the 50-14 win in 1968, the year of their last consensus national championship with a 10-0 record. The last time that the Buckeyes had a 23-point lead over Michigan at any point of the game in Ann Arbor was the 50-20 game in 1961, the year that they had an 8-0-1 record and received a national championship from the Football Writers Association of America.

In the kicking game, Mike Nugent kicked a 33-yard field goal to make the score 26-13 with 5:58 remaining, which broke a streak of three straight misses and started his record-breaking streak. The field goal was set up when Mike Doss had his second interception of the game, returning it 36 yards. Most of Doss's interceptions in his career would take place without contact with receivers, but on this one, he wrestled the ball away from a receiver.

Andy Groom had a 66-yard punt, his second longest (by one yard) of the season. His shortest punt of 23 yards on the Buckeyes' last possession was effective, too, as it was downed at the Michigan 20-yard line with nine seconds remaining. He avoided getting it blocked, unlike the situation in the fourth quarter that allowed the Wolverines to score on a nine-yard drive. The Buckeyes punted 11 times, including on six straight possessions to open the second half. Coach Tressel said that the punt was the most important play in football, but even he may have agreed that this was overdoing it.

Chris Vance was the second-leading receiver on the team, but his biggest catch of the season may be the one that he made on Michigan's onside kick late in the game. Like the Fiesta Bowl win over Miami, the Buckeyes scored 17 points off of turnovers.

Krenzel was 11 for 18 in his passing for 118 yards (59 in each half) to seven different receivers, six of whom had a catch of at least ten yards. On the 20th anniversary of this game, I interviewed Krenzel and asked him about his mindset going into the game. He said that he had always had confidence in himself and was not the least bit rattled by getting his first start in the biggest rivalry game in all of college football, in a hostile environment—in his home state, no less.

Each team had an incredible 18 possessions in the game. The average possession for the Buckeyes lasted 1:54, and for the Wolverines consumed 1:27.

This was the first win in Ann Arbor since 1987. In that 1987 win, they also gave up 20 points and had their last score on a field goal in the fourth quarter. The Buckeyes came into the 2001 game with a 6-4 record, compared to Michigan's record of 8-2 overall and 6-1 in the Big Ten; in 1987, their record before the game was 5-4-1, and Michigan's was 7-3 overall and 5-2 in the Big Ten. As in 1987, the Buckeyes came into the game off a loss; actually, the 1987 team was coming in on a three-game losing streak.

THE BOWL GAME AGAINST SOUTH CAROLINA

The Buckeyes matched up with South Carolina for the second straight season in the Outback Bowl, fell behind 28-0 in the third quarter, tied it up at 28 with 1:54 remaining, but lost 31-28 on a 42-yard field goal that was barely good on the final play. The Buckeyes had some significant comebacks from 10-0 deficits in their bowl history under Woody Hayes—the 1969 Rose Bowl, the 1977 Orange Bowl (a 27-10 win), and the 1971 Rose Bowl (a loss)—but nothing like this 28-0 hole to dig out of.

Coach Tressel must have been experiencing *deja vu*; in 1992, his Youngstown State team lost the national championship game to Marshall, 31-28, on a field goal with 10 seconds remaining. That game was also a rematch from the season before, and, like the South Carolina game, Youngstown State had trailed, 28-0. In 1987, Youngstown State lost at Northern Iowa, 31-28, in the first round of the playoffs. In 1985, he was an assistant at Ohio State when the Buckeyes trailed 14-0, came back to take a 28-14 lead, only to lose at Illinois, 31-28, on a field goal on the last play of the game. Those South Carolina and Illinois games were the only two games in Ohio State history where they lost by a score of 31-28. All four of those 31-28 games for Coach Tressel were not home games. Referring to that Marshall game, Coach Tressel was quoted in the *Columbus Dispatch* after this bowl game: "If you're in this game long enough, everything happens to you … I guess if you're in it really long, everything happens to you twice." Since this was the third occurrence on a late field goal for him, he must have been involved in football for a long, long time.

Interviewed at halftime, when the Buckeyes trailed 14-0, Tressel said, "We're going to play better in the second half." They had 108 yards in the first half and 280 in the second half, and scored four touchdowns in the span of 13:06.

The Michigan game had ended on an interception. With the score tied at 28 with 1:54 remaining, both teams threw an interception, the only two of the game, in the span of 49 seconds. South Carolina returned Bellisari's interception 37 yards to the Ohio State 29-yard line to set up its winning field goal. Cie Grant, playing at cornerback, had given the Buckeyes a chance to pull out a win when he intercepted to put the ball at the Buckeyes' 18-yard line with 1:12 remaining.

Andy Groom had a 67-yard punt, his longest of the season, and Mike Doss recovered a fumble inside the South Carolina 25-yard line to set up the Buckeyes' third touchdown.

If Coach Tressel had a crystal ball to foresee his success in overtime games in the next two years, would he have played that last possession more conservatively? He did have a running play on first down before the interception on second down.

Krenzel started, but he played only one series and gave way to Bellisari. Krenzel had a seven-yard run for a first down and had his only completion, a four-yard pass to Ben Hartsock. Bellisari passed for 320 yards (269 in the second half) and two touchdowns to Darnell Sanders, and ran for another. Spoiler Alert: the next time that Krenzel would play in a losing game as a starting quarterback would be in October of 2003. In the third quarter, Krenzel had a brief appearance in the drive for their first touchdown and contributed a six-yard run. That drive was aided by a pass interference call on a fourth-and-four play from the five-yard line. In the bowl game a year later, the Buckeyes would be facing a fourth-and-three situation from the five-yard line and be helped by a pass interference call.

Michael Jenkins had eight receptions for 152 yards, with 118 yards in the second half. Chris Gamble had two receptions for 32 yards on the drive for the tying touchdown; he had three of his five receptions on the season in the Michigan and South Carolina games.

South Carolina's coach Lou Holtz may have had a crystal ball; leading up to the game, he was quoted in a story on www.theozone.net with, "... I think Jim Tressel is laying the foundation for some championships at Ohio State."

How would you describe an end-of-season that had one game that broke a sequence of two wins, ten losses, and one tie in the previous 13 games against Michigan, using a quarterback listed as the third string the previous week, and another game that had a rally from a 28-0 deficit in the bowl game and having a chance to win?

The seeds of improbability had been sown.

LOOKING AHEAD

The Michigan game ending on an interception ... Craig Krenzel's solid play in a big game ... Mike Doss returning interceptions to inside the red zone in a big game ... A running back gaining over 100 yards against Michigan ... The Michigan quarterback throwing interceptions and losing a fumble ... Coach Tressel's ability at halftime of the bowl game to predict the remainder of the game ... Cie Grant making a big play late in the bowl game ... Scoring four touchdowns in the bowl game ... A field goal by the opponent that was barely good on the last play of regulation in the bowl game ... Andy Groom booming punts in key games ... Chris Gamble emerging as an offensive threat late in the season ... The defense forcing five turnovers in a big game ... Scoring 17 points off turnovers in a big game ... Opponents failing to catch passes in the end zone in a close game ... Were these omens for the next season?

Mike Doss must have had a crystal ball. In a press conference on January 9—his mother's birthday—Doss, in tears, said that he was returning for his senior year to finish his education and "one more year of college and playing hard and trying to win the Big Ten championship and trying to win a national championship." For a second straight January, a speech by an Ohio State football figure would serve to inspire Buckeye fans. If he had said, "... and most especially, in 358 days, in Tempe, Arizona ...", Buckeye fans may have lost their minds.

How important was the 2001 win over Michigan? The November 21, 2018 *Sports Illustrated* issue had the comment, "Doss says if the Buckeyes had lost to Michigan in '01, he would have left school early and turned pro."

In April, Doss was quoted in the *Columbus Dispatch* with, "Right now I am just concentrating on my senior season, helping us to be the best we can be and make a run for the Big Ten championship and the national championship." Eight years earlier, Joey Galloway had decided to return instead of opting for the NFL, and one of his rewards was to play in the first Buckeye win over Michigan since 1987 and the first win over the Wolverines at home since 1984. Could we have a repeat situation in 2002?

The Buckeyes had four of their five losses in 2001 by seven points or less, which meant that one more play in each of those games could have made the difference between a 7-5 record and an 11-1 record.

The preseason issue of *Sports Illustrated* picked Oklahoma first and Miami second. Two of the observations of the Hurricanes were: "The secondary that held opponents to 138.2 passing yards per game (second fewest in the nation) is gone, replaced by a jumble of underclassmen who collectively have zero starts." and "Slippery sophomore tailback Frank Gore (9.1 yards per carry), who shredded his right ACL in a March practice, should be back on the field by Oct. 1. In his absence, capable backups Willie McGahee and Jarrett Payton will share the running duties." Unfortunately, Gore would not return in 2002.

Sports Illustrated placed Michigan at #20, describing the defense as "dominating" and "elite", Illinois at #24 (they would finish with a 5-7 record), and Penn State at #25.

For the Buckeyes, *Sports Illustrated* had, "Defense will separate the Buckeyes from the rest of the Big Ten this season—that is, assuming coordinator Mark Dantonio has addressed his unit's glaring weakness. Ohio State had the best pass defense in the conference (holding opponents to an efficiency rating of 107.6) yet still finished next to last in third-down conversions allowed (87 of 189, 46%). With three losses coming by a total of eight points, a few more stops could have made a big difference.", and "the secondary is the team's strength, since they have the best defensive back in the country in Mike Doss. The kid is phenomenal. He hits like a Mack truck. His energy on the field seems to get the team's engine running." It also mentioned the potential of Cie Grant, who returned from playing at cornerback in 2001 to the weakside linebacker. Dantonio was in his first season as the defensive coordinator and had been a graduate assistant for the Buckeyes in 1983 and 1984, when Tressel was an assistant coach.

The Ohio State 2002 Football Media Guide had these observations and predictions, most of which were eerily on-target:

- "On the surface, this is, at the very least, another solid team. Scratch beneath the surface, though, and there is the potential for much more. In fact, some pundits have announced the Buckeyes as the team to beat in the 2002 Big Ten title chase."

- They need to replace the entire starting backfield, three linemen, and two linebackers.

- The defense is "potentially lethal."

- The freshman class is "one of the two or three best in the country."

- Coach Tressel said that "Our goal is to win the Big Ten title. But to get there, it is going to take lots of hard work and dedication, and probably a little luck in terms of staying healthy and getting a few breaks along the way."

- "The sky is the limit for the talented Gamble."

- Of Mike Nugent, "His continued improvement and consistency will be key to the Buckeyes' fortunes in the fall."

- Regarding the schedule, "a season that concludes Nov. 23 when Michigan comes to town. Only time will tell what happens after that."

Could the Buckeyes execute one more play successfully in close games?

Could a quarterback with one full game of experience lead the offense?

Could a freshman running back be a factor?

Could the kicker improve his accuracy?

Could defensive end Darrion Scott and linebacker Matt Wilhelm perform well after off-season surgery?

Could the defense hold the lead in close games, once they had it?

Before the 2001 season, Coach Tressel had compared Chris Gamble to Cris Carter. Could Gamble have a breakout season?

Better yet, Gamble would experiment as a defensive back in practice, and Coach Tressel would return Cie Grant from cornerback to weakside linebacker and had moved Dustin Fox from safety to cornerback for the Outback Bowl. Would these moves pay off?

This isn't a Whodunit. You already know the answer.

CHAPTER 3

The Regular Season

THE LEAD-UP

THE SPRING INTRA-SQUAD game gave a glimpse of things to come. The defense dominated, and Mike Nugent's second field goal of the game, a 41-yarder with 4:37 remaining, was the deciding score in the 6-3 victory for the Gray over the Scarlet. That was a good sign for Nugent, who had made only one of seven attempts from 40 yards or longer in 2001.

Will Smith had four sacks in the game, and Doss had an interception. Coach Tressel was quoted in the *Columbus Dispatch* with, "I think our defense could be very, very good.", but he wondered, "How will they handle it when they're back against the wall?"

After Miami's spring game, their quarterback Ken Dorsey was quoted on the www.miamihurricanes.com website as saying the Hurricane defense was "the best defense we will have to face." Of course, he had no way of knowing who the team would face in its bowl game.

At the Big Ten media meeting gathering in Chicago on July 25, the media picked Michigan to win the conference title, with Ohio State second. Perhaps many Buckeye fans were taking a wait-and-see approach;

15,000 tickets for the season opener in less than four weeks went on sale on July 31.

Matt Wilhelm had motivation; he told the *Columbus Dispatch*, "The feeling that I have is if we don't go out this year and beat Michigan, or if we don't go out and win the Big Ten championship or compete for the national championship, I'll feel I'm missing out on something, missing out on greatness."

On August 15, Todd Jones of the *Dispatch* wrote, "Jim Tressel's second OSU team should be better than the 7-5 squad of a year ago, if for no other reason than the defense should be fire-breathing nasty."

Ten days before the opener, Krenzel knew his mission, as he was quoted in the *Dispatch* with "... minimize mistakes. Play solid. Make good decisions." He also had a message for those not familiar with himself and Scott McMullen: "I think those people are going to be in for a surprise."

On the day before the opener, Tim May of the *Dispatch* predicted that the Buckeyes would have a 6-2 record in the Big Ten; he would be correct in picking the Buckeyes to tie for first place. Bob Baptist of the *Dispatch* predicted that the Buckeyes would have a 6-2 record in the Big Ten; he would correctly predict that road games at Wisconsin, Purdue, and Illinois would be stiff tests. The *Dispatch* quoted the predictions of eight sportswriters in Big Ten territory, and their predicted finish for the Buckeyes ranged from second to fourth, with the consensus opinion that the quarterback play was the biggest question mark. Dave Jones of the Harrisburg, Pennsylvania *Patriot-News* was one who predicted a fourth-place finish, and added, "You're not going to win championships with defense anymore."

On the opening day of the 2002 season, Todd Jones of the *Dispatch* wrote, "[The Buckeyes have] more freshmen (11) than seniors (10) in their two-deep chart. They're probably a year away. The seniors don't have a next year. They need to win now. It's time to show a national TV audience that Ohio State is more than just an average team."

TEXAS TECH

The Buckeyes had an eighth home game for the first time in its history and had an extra game added to their schedule, the Pigskin Classic against Texas Tech. Both teams had a 7-5 record in the 2001 season, and the Red Raiders would also play a 14-game schedule, finishing with a 9-5 record. The Buckeyes were favored by only six points.

On August 24, the earliest start in OSU history (other than the very first game on May 3, 1890), the 45-21 win over the Red Raiders on an 83-degree "pleasant" (according to the official account) day was Maurice Clarett's debut. He ran for 175 yards and three touchdowns, two of them 59 and 45 yards, adding four receptions to lead the team. The Buckeyes could have been penalized for having 12 men on the field on one of his scoring runs; the TV camera caught Coach Tressel trailing Clarett down the sideline, in the field of play.

The *Columbus Dispatch* story the next day included a line that the fans were yelling, "Maurice! … or was it 'more ice!'?", due to the warm temperatures. He ran for only nine yards on four carries in the first drive, but he was just getting warmed up. His first carry on the next possession gained one yard, but he exploded for a 59-yard touchdown run on his next carry.

Freshman Bobby Carpenter had the first tackle of the season, on the opening kickoff, causing the Red Raiders to start on their own eight-yard line. The defense registered a three-and-out after a Will Smith sack, and Mike Doss returned the punt 14 yards—his longest return of the season—to the Texas Tech 32-yard line. Doss also had his longest kickoff return of the season for 24 yards. Smith only had four solo tackles, but all four were for negative yardage, including two sacks. Carpenter had another tackle on a kickoff, and freshman Nate Salley also had two tackles.

The Buckeyes scored on their seventh play, a two-yard run by Lydell Ross on his first carry of the season. As a nod to Woody Hayes, the offense lined up in a full-house T formation. Mike Nugent made the tackle on the ensuing kick return, then was done for the season in that category; it was his only tackle. Ross's second carry of the season produced another touchdown.

As a sign of things to come, Texas Tech had a first-and-goal from the Ohio State eight-yard line late in the first half, but was stopped on fourth down at the one-yard line. Another omen was the fact that the Buckeyes scored their most points in an opening game since 1996, the last season in which they had a dramatic win in the bowl game. Dustin Fox had an interception in his second straight regular season game, intercepting in the end zone.

Other omens were the recurring themes of the numbers 14 and 34; the Buckeyes scored 14 in the first quarter and gave up 14 in the fourth quarter, and Krenzel, making his first start in Ohio Stadium, had 14 passes and 34 yards rushing. His first pass of the season was a 17-yard pass to Jenkins on the right sideline going toward the south end zone. That sequence would occur again at a critical point late in the bowl game. His last completion of the season would also be to Jenkins.

Krenzel had two scrambles for 23 and 16 yards on two different touchdown drives, and was quoted in the *Columbus Dispatch* after the game with a scenario that would be repeated throughout the season in key situations: "I'm not the greatest athlete, but I'm a good athlete. I can get moving." Like the opener 14 years previously, the Buckeyes had no turnovers.

Texas Tech scored a touchdown on the last play of the first half and on a pass with 12 seconds remaining in the game. The Buckeyes' defense held the Red Raiders to 31 net yards rushing, with 29 coming on one play. In 1968, to kick off the Buckeyes' last consensus national championship season, Southern Methodist threw 76 passes, 67 by Chuck Hixson, for 437 yards. On this day, Kliff Kingsbury threw 44 passes—he had predicted at least 50—for 341 yards. In the 1968 Southern Methodist game, the visitors had a receiver with over 100 yards, Jerry Levias with 15 catches for 160; in this game, the visitors had a receiver with over 100 yards. Wes Welker—who would have a 12-year NFL career and be named First Team All-Pro twice—had five catches for 117 yards and two touchdowns.

The Red Raiders' average of 5.8 yards per play would turn out to be the highest for an opponent in the season, but their best starting position was their own 39-yard line. Their defense would give up more than the 45 points that they allowed in this game three times in the season.

Ohio State's first play on offense was stymied by a five-yard penalty; the game against Miami in over four months would start the same way. Clarett had the first official play of the season, a five-yard gain, and would have the last one of the season, a five-yard gain for the winning touchdown against Miami.

Matt Wilhelm did not start, due to the Buckeyes respecting Kingsbury with a nickel defense, but led the team with 10 tackles in the game. The Ohio State defense recorded a sack on the first series of the season and would end the season with a quarterback hurry.

Coach Tressel had made a prediction about Chris Gamble, as quoted in the *Columbus Dispatch* before the game, "He is going to make some big plays for us this year." Gamble had punt returns of 27 (returned to the Texas Tech 33 to set up a Clarett touchdown) and 13 yards. Luke Fickell, the Buckeyes' special teams coordinator in his first season on the staff, was probably pleased. Gamble's 27-yard return would be the Buckeyes' longest of the season.

The Buckeyes had almost 12 more minutes of possession time. Their third-down conversion rate of 67% (10 of 15) would be their highest of the season; the next-highest would be 42%. Krenzel had 11 completions for 118 yards, the same numbers that he had in his last full game, the win over Michigan. You can't make this up.

The Red Raiders' coach was Mike Leach, who would continue his successful career at Washington State and Mississippi State before passing away in 2022 at the age of 61. In his typical humor, he was quoted in the *Columbus Dispatch*: "There were points out there where we just took turns drawing straws as far as who was going to foul up."

The Buckeyes defense sacked Kingsbury, the eventual head coach at his alma mater and for the Arizona Cardinals, seven times, a season high. It had a total of nine tackles for a loss. Kingsbury was prophetic in a quote in the *Dayton Daily News* after the game: "The way they ran the ball and the way they play defense, they're going to be hard to beat." If Kingsbury was impressed with the Buckeye defense after one game, he should have been more impressed when the season ended; this game would have the most points given up by the defense in regulation and would be the only time that the defense gave up more than two touchdowns in regulation.

It was only the second meeting between the two programs, with the other one in the 1990 opener. That 17-10 win was befitting of a 2002 game; the winning score was on a 50-yard punt return in the fourth quarter by Jeff Graham, and the other touchdown was by freshman running back Robert Smith.

Clarett was the first Buckeye freshman to score three touchdowns in his debut since Howard Cassady accomplished it 50 years previously. He was the first true freshman to start at running back for the Buckeyes in an opener since Dean Sensanbaugher in 1943, playing for Paul Brown. The front page of the *Columbus Dispatch* on September 26, 1943 had a photo of the most thrilling run of the day, Sensanbaugher's 27-yard touchdown run in his debut, a 28-13 loss to the Iowa Seahawks. He led the team with 89 yards on 13 carries. More similarities to events that would involve Clarett during the season were that a story on the game noted that Sensanbaugher "suffered what is believed to be a broken right hand in the fourth quarter", and that Sensanbaugher was involved in a play where a Seahawk stole the ball from him, although the officials "failed to note [it]". Coach Paul Brown said that Sensanbaugher "did very well" and "is a fine football player". The Seahawks were coached by Don Faurot, who would go on to coach Missouri and turn down an offer to coach Ohio State, an offer that Woody Hayes did accept.

Fifth-year senior guard Mike Stafford, a former walk-on, made his first start and continued to start the next three games while the starter last season, Adrien Clarke, recovered from a lower back strain.

After one game, what were Buckeye fans thinking? "Great offense, but the defense can't continue to give up touchdowns in the fourth quarter"? Response: "Hold on, it's a small sample size, but you're right about the defense."

The Buckeyes' next game would be 14 days later, when they would play on 12 consecutive Saturdays. The Miami Hurricanes would kick off their season the next week, have two bye weeks during the season, and a 12-day and a nine-day break. Their first game was a 63-17 win over Division I-AA Florida A&M, whose coach was Billy Joe. Joe's previous coaching stop was a highly successful one at Central State in Ohio. Miami's record-breaking quarterback Ken Dorsey had a light day, as the Hurricanes used five quarterbacks, finishing 8-of-13 passing; likewise for record-breaking tailback Willis McGahee, who ran six times for 60 yards. Backup tailback Jason Geathers ran for 199 yards.

KENT STATE

The Buckeyes had moved up to Number 8 in the rankings. In the 51-17 win in the first-ever meeting between the two teams, Clarett had only 66 rushing yards, but he had a rushing and a receiving touchdown. After a season-best 10 of 15 third-down conversions the game before, the Buckeyes had a season-low five third-down plays, converting once. They had only four possessions in the second half.

The defense scored as many touchdowns as Kent State's offense did. Mike Doss and freshman A. J. Hawk had pick-six interceptions, with Hawk spiking the ball as he scored, breaking one of Coach Tressel's rules.

Hawk said later that Tressel reminded him to hand the ball to an official if it should happen again; we will never know if it registered, as Hawk would not have another opportunity in his remaining four years as a Buckeye.

Chris Gamble had six receptions to lead the team, and Andy Groom took the day off from his punting duties. The Buckeyes had a season-low 47 plays. They scored on each of their first four possessions and three of their four in the second half. Their average of 8.8 yards per play was a season high. They went from a season-high 57 rush plays the week before to a season-low 22 in this game.

Kent State had 33 more plays and a 22-17 edge in first downs. Their quarterback was future Cleveland Brown Joshua Cribbs, who had 254 yards in total offense. Cribbs played quarterback at Dunbar High School in Washington, D.C., the same high school that produced Ohio State's Cornelius Greene. He had 94 yards rushing, and the other 13 quarterbacks the Buckeyes faced in the season had a combined negative-98 yards net rushing, with a high game of positive seven. He had run for over 1,000 yards as a freshman in 2001.

Maurice Hall (#28) scored his first career touchdown, on a 28-yard run. Krenzel tied an Ohio State record by completing 12 straight passes, spanning the first two games. The defense gave up two touchdowns in the second quarter, the last time that they would give up multiple touchdowns in a quarter this season. Nugent kicked three field goals, two of them at least 40 yards long.

After two games, Krenzel was 23-for-28 in passing. With the score 28-0, Scott McMullen finished the first half at quarterback. When Ryan Hamby caught a touchdown pass from McMullen in the fourth quarter, it gave Ohio State freshmen four of the six touchdowns in the game. Along with Hall and Hawk, Hamby made it three players who scored his first career touchdown.

Another flashback to 1996 was the fact that this was the first game where the Buckeyes had scored at least 50 points since that season.

Coach Tressel—Gasp!—was not wearing his iconic sweater vest; he did his Woody Hayes impersonation with a white, short-sleeved shirt and a tie. On his TV show after the game, he said that his goal on offense was to have at least 200 yards rushing and at least 250 yards passing in each game. When the season was over, the Buckeyes would not achieve that in any game.

Perhaps Buckeyes fans were not yet totally convinced of the greatness of this team; the Texas Tech game had the first non-sellout out since the 1997 opener—which was played on a Thursday night against Wyoming—a streak of 31 games, and this game against the Golden Flashes had more than 5,000 fewer fans than the Texas Tech game.

Miami beat Number 6 Florida in Gainesville, 41-16, in a game that matched two head coaches who had been assistants at Ohio State—Miami's second-year coach, Larry Coker, and the Gators' first-year coach, Ron Zook. A record crowd at The Swamp saw the first regular-season meeting between the two teams since 1987. The Associated Press recap mentioned that Miami actually came into this game as a 2-point underdog. Ken Dorsey threw four touchdown passes, but had three interceptions, including one that was returned for a touchdown in the third quarter. In the same quarter, Maurice Sikes of Miami also had an interception return for a touchdown, on a return of 97 yards. McGahee ran for 204 yards, a career high at the time, but it was the only game of the season where he would not score a touchdown.

WASHINGTON STATE

The *Sports Illustrated* season preview issue had placed Washington State at Number 7, the highest ranked team in the Pac-10. They had the reigning conference coach of the year in Mike Price and 12 returning starters.

The 6th-ranked Buckeyes trailed the 10th-ranked Cougars at halftime, 7-6, before winning, 25-7. Clarett ran for two touchdowns and 230 yards on 31 carries against the defense that would finish as the seventh best in the nation. His total was nine yards short of Archie Griffin's freshman record, set 30 years earlier against North Carolina, and his last two carries both gained no yards. This also meant that Coach Tressel had been on the staff in two of the top six single-game rushing performances by a Buckeye in Ohio Stadium; when Keith Byars ran for 274 yards against Illinois in 1984, his position coach was Jim Tressel.

Washington State scored a touchdown on its first possession, going 80 yards, but was done scoring for the day. The Buckeyes defense held the Cougars to 17 yards on the ground, with a long of 18. The Cougars came into the game averaging 40 points and 443 yards in its first two games. Their quarterback, Jason Gesser, completed 25 of 44 passes for 247 yards. The Cougars would finish the season with a 10-3 record, win the Pac-10 Conference, give USC—which would finish the season ranked Number 5—one of its two losses, and play in the Rose Bowl.

Lydell Ross actually had a better first half than Clarett, gaining 44 yards. Clarett had only 11 yards in his first five carries. With Clarett gaining 194 of his yards in the second half, Krenzel passed only three times after halftime, with one completion. After three games, Clarett had 471 yards and a 7.5 average. His 31 carries against Washington State nearly matched his combined 32 in the first two games.

Nugent kicked field goals of 43, 43, and 45 yards to give him five of at least 40 yards, after making only two of that length in all of the 2001 season. After three games, he had equaled his seven made field goals of his freshman season.

Nugent, on his improvement: *A lot of guys who come into Ohio State or a big football school go through, I need to admit it, you almost kind of question yourself. You see all these people and big crowds and you're playing with like these guys who are seniors, you're going from playing with high school kids to playing with these extremely talented, mature college guys, and you almost feel like you don't belong there. And I remember having moments like, oh my gosh, what am I doing here? Like, am I good enough for this? And I really just put a lot of work in in the offseason. And, it was probably a combination of that, I moved out of the dorms and into an apartment and just, more to kind of back on track to just more comfortable living, having a few more roommates and guys you know really well. I like being off campus and getting into quiet and stuff like that. I kicked a ton in the offseason because I knew I didn't have the games to get ready for until the Fall. So I knew that was the time I could really work on the craft.*

The Buckeye offensive line would give up an average of a little over two sacks per game, but the Cougars sacked Krenzel four times in the first half. The Cougars came up empty twice inside the red zone—once on an interception by Tyler Everett and once on a botched snap on a field goal attempt—and gave up a safety on a bad snap to the punter. After Everett's interception at the four-yard line, the offense ran the ball 12 straight times to consume the last 7:10 of the game,

Coach Tressel again went with the Woody Hayes attire. Buckeye fans finally got the memo that this team could be special; the crowd of 104,553 was the largest in Ohio Stadium history. The win was OSU's first over a top-10 opponent since the 1998 season, going back to January 1, 1999, when the Buckeyes beat Number 8 Texas A&M in the Sugar Bowl, 24-14. After this game, the Buckeyes had something that they had not had in almost two years—a three-game winning streak.

With a nod to the Buckeyes' last consensus national championship, one of the inductees into the Ohio State athletic Hall of Fame was John Brockington, who was a sophomore on the 1968 team.

The Buckeyes ran their all-time record against the Cougars to 8-0. Bob Baptist reported in the *Columbus Dispatch* that a rematch between the two teams was scheduled for 2009 in the state of Washington but not on Washington State's campus, due to the size of its stadium. The hope was to play at the new Seahawks Stadium in Seattle, but a rematch would fail to take place.

On this same day, Willis McGahee of Miami ran for 134 yards and tied a school record with four rushing touchdowns in a 44-21 victory over Temple. Miami had a 21-0 lead early in the second quarter, but Temple was able to cut it to 21-14 later in the quarter. Dorsey passed for 314 yards and two touchdowns, but threw three interceptions. The crowd at Philadelphia's Franklin Field (33,169) was a bit smaller than the one in Ohio Stadium. The *Miami Herald* quoted defensive tackle Matt Walters with, "... we had a chance to put this team away and made two turnovers. They had the ball inside the red zone, scored twice on us and came right back into the game. That kind of stuff will come back and kill us later in the season."

CINCINNATI

An injury in the Washington State game followed by arthroscopic surgery on the Tuesday before the Cincinnati game forced Clarett to sit out the 23-19 win over the Bearcats, a game played at Paul Brown Stadium in Cincinnati, the home of the Bengals. Krenzel scored the winning touchdown on a twisting six-yard run with 3:44 remaining. There were six Bearcat defenders within a few yards of Krenzel on the play. Krenzel did not carry the ball often in high school, but picked the perfect time for his first Ohio State touchdown on the ground.

Krenzel, on adapting to the running aspect: *You do what you've got to do.*

Krenzel was quoted in the *Dayton Daily News* as saying that he saw Chris Vance, who was waving his arms in the end zone, "But Coach Tressel always says throwing the ball over the middle, 95 percent of the time, bad things are going to happen." The Buckeyes had two of their five third-down conversions in the winning drive.

Lydell Ross filled in for Clarett and ran for 130 yards. Krenzel and Nugent, who combined to score the Buckeyes' last 10 points, most likely were not envisioning at the time that they would eventually be members of the Bengals.

It was a hot day, but not hot enough for Coach Tressel to shed his gray sweater vest. Cincinnati Coach Rick Minter matched him, style-wise, with a red sweater vest. Usually, Tressel wore a scarlet one for road games and a gray one for home games so that the players on the field could find him more easily by contrasting with the uniform colors.

It was a big weekend in Cincinnati; with the Reds' final series in their old ballpark and Oktoberfest going on, the city was expecting a half million people in the downtown area. The game notes show that the game set attendance records for Paul Brown Stadium, for any sporting event in the Cincinnati area, and for any game hosted by a Conference USA team. Buckeye fans should have known that this was a good omen, playing in a stadium named for the coach who brought OSU its first national championship, 60 years previously—a coach also in his second year at OSU and with a Massillon Washington High School connection.

The Buckeyes went three-and-out on offense on their first three possessions, with a net of minus-six yards combined. Their next two possessions in the first quarter resulted in a lost fumble and an interception, giving them 16 plays for a total of five yards. They trailed 9-0, the only time all season that they would trail by two scores. For the second straight week, the opponent went 80 yards on its first possession for a touchdown. Gino Guidugli passed on each of the first five plays and completed all five. On their second possession, Demarco McCleskey had a 46-yard run, the longest for an opponent in the season, to the 18-yard line, but Matt Wilhelm had a sack and another tackle for a loss to force Cincinnati to settle for a field goal.

Matt Wilhelm making a sack to force the opponent to settle for a field goal in a four-point win on the road … could that possibly happen again this season?

It took the Buckeyes six possessions before getting their first score, a 20-yard pass to Ben Hartsock—his longest reception of the season and the Buckeyes' longest of the game—in the second quarter. The pass was a surprising one on a third-and-two play. Krenzel had a five-yard touchdown pass to Chris Vance in traffic in the third quarter on a play where he had to scramble to his left.

The Buckeyes had all three of their turnovers in the first half, and the Bearcats had all three of theirs in the fourth quarter, in consecutive possessions. Two interceptions and a fumble in three consecutive possessions by the opponent in the same quarter … could that possibly happen in a close game again this season? The Buckeyes also had two interceptions and one fumble; for the Bearcats, both interceptions were picked off in the end zone.

In the fourth quarter, the Buckeyes had a defensive back wearing number 7, which had many of the fans reaching for their program to learn, *Who is number 7?* They were not alone, as the broadcasters were surprised, too. This was the first appearance of Chris Gamble as a defensive back, and he picked off a Bearcat pass in the end zone. Gamble would have no tackles in the game, but had one of the most important defensive plays. Little did we know at the time that Gamble would become a magnet for significant plays in the end zone throughout the season. Rob Oller of the *Columbus Dispatch* wrote that Gamble had not played defensive back since high school. The offense was not able to capitalize, as they lost three yards in three plays.

Krenzel had a 29-yard run, his longest run of the season, to set up Nugent's field goal to cut the deficit to 19-17. David Thompson recovered a fumble on a sack by Darrion Scott to set up Krenzel's winning touchdown; the Buckeyes had a three-man defensive front on Scott's play.

On the Bearcats' last possession, they advanced from their own 20-yard line to the Ohio State 15 in seven plays without facing a third down. The *Dayton Daily News* pointed out the next day that Guidugli already had engineered four come-from-behind, fourth-quarter victories in the 13 previous games he had played for Cincinnati. They had four passes into the end zone from the OSU 15, but they misfired on all four, including a drop on third down. The first three passes were along a sideline, and the last one was over the middle. What did Coach Tressel say about throwing the ball over the middle? Will Allen intercepted on fourth down to seal the win.

It had the exact same yard line and sequence—three incompletions and an interception—as in the Buckeye loss to Michigan State in 1998. Allen had missed the Kent State game with an injured shoulder and had no defensive stats in the Washington State game. The Buckeyes had a three-man front and did not blitz on the last play. Matt Wilhelm, who had four tackles for a loss in the game, tipped the pass that Allen secured. Allen turned slightly to his right, and the ball fell into his hands. The Bearcats had scored the first nine points of the game, and the Buckeyes scored the last nine.

The *Columbus Dispatch* reported that Mike Doss had knocked down the Bearcat receiver LaDaris Vann on the pass play where Allen intercepted, and Vann pleaded for a penalty, to no avail. Pass interference in the end zone in this game? Not on this play, but, four months later, such a penalty would occur in perhaps the most significant play of the season. The fact that Wilhelm tipped the pass may or may not have been a factor in the non-call, if the officials had seen the contact by Doss.

The *Dayton Daily News* quoted Ben Hartsock with "I tell you what, we're definitely the luckiest team in college football." Would reporters seek him out again this season?

Groom's 48.8 yard average on five punts was instrumental; the Bearcats started every possession on their side of the field, except for the one when they recovered a fumble. That possession ended with a missed field goal. All four scores by the Buckeyes came on possessions where they started on the Bearcats' side of the field; they scored four out of five times that they were in Cincinnati territory. The Bearcats were in Ohio State territory eight times but scored only four times.

Richard McNutt started at cornerback, but was injured and replaced by true freshman E.J. Underwood, who had played at nearby Hamilton High School. He finished the game tied for the third-most tackles—five, his career high—and tied Mike Doss for the most pass break-ups (two). On the first-and-ten play from the Buckeye 15-yard line in the last series, he broke up the pass intended for Jon Olinger in the far right corner of the end zone.

E. J. Underwood: *I should have had three picks in the game!*

The Buckeyes came into the game as a 17-point favorite. They avoided losing to an in-state foe for the first time in 101 years; in 1921, they lost to Oberlin, 7-6. It had been 68 years since the Buckeyes had played on the road against another Ohio school (beating Western Reserve in 1934 by the score of 76-0), and 91 years since OSU had last made the trip to Cincinnati (winning 11-6 in the last game of the 1911 season).

The Ohio State seniors had experienced the 1999 game against the Bearcats, who led by two scores in that game, 17-3, before the Buckeyes prevailed, 34-20. In that game, the Bearcats had a 525 to 496 edge in total yards. Donnie Nickey started and had seven tackles, Doss had three tackles, and Cie Grant, Matt Wilhelm, Kenny Peterson, and Fred Pagac, Jr. also played in both meetings. For Cincinnati, LaDaris Vann had a 75-yard touchdown reception, and Jonathan Ruffin had a 23-yard and a 46-yard field goal; both would be prominent in the 2002 game. The Buckeyes also played the Miami Hurricanes in the 1999 season.

In this game, the Bearcats had a 415 to 292 edge in total yards. Their missed extra point was the only miss of the year by a Buckeye opponent;

Jonathan Ruffin had made a nation-leading 65 consecutive PAT kicks, a school record, before the miss. With the Bearcats up 9-0 in the first quarter, he was short on a 49-yard field goal attempt; he had kicked a 44-yard field goal earlier and added a career-best 49-yarder in the second quarter. He had won the Lou Groza Award, College Football's Top Kicking Award, in 2000, and Nugent would win it in 2004.

Krenzel had been 23-for-28 for 308 yards in passing in the first two games, but was only 18-for-39 for 200 yards combined against Washington State and Cincinnati. After four games, the defense had faced two quarterbacks who would finish in the top eight in passing yards for the season—Kliff Kingsbury finished first, and Guidugli finished eighth. Guidugli completed 26 of 52 passes for 324 yards; the 52 attempts were a career high for him, which would be tied in the 2004 season.

How was Buckeye Nation now assessing the team's prospects after this game, after winning its first three games at home by an average score of 40-15? They need Clarett in order to win? No, the ground game seemed sound, as Ross gained 130 yards. Avoiding turnovers would be paramount? Absolutely; in the first three games, the Buckeyes had a 5-2 advantage, but in this game, each team had three. Once the Buckeyes managed to hang on to the ball, the game turned; they went the last 34 minutes without one, while the Bearcats turned it over three times in the last 11 minutes, resulting in the go-ahead touchdown and the game-sealing interception. Fortunate to win, or displaying toughness to make big plays in critical situations? The Buckeyes had shown that they could dominate at home, what about on the road? Time would tell.

On this day, Miami beat Boston College, 38-6, a game that was scoreless in the first quarter and had only a 10-6 score at halftime. A huge play for Willis McGahee was his 77-yard gain on a screen pass to the right side of the field. Speaking of Miami in the Associated Press recap, Boston College coach Tom O'Brien said, "I think they're more explosive on offense [than last year], especially with that tailback. That tailback is a difference-maker. When he gets in the open field, he accelerates. He takes off."

INDIANA

Things seemed to be back to normal in the 45-17 win; the Number 6-ranked Buckeyes were back at home, they had no turnovers, the passing game regained its sharpness—18 of 23, with Krenzel 11-of-16—and Clarett returned and ran for 104 yards and three touchdowns, all in the first half. Referring to his knee that had required surgery and had required stitches at halftime, and perhaps looking ahead to a possible championship matchup, he was quoted in the *Columbus Dispatch* with, "I try to be one of the toughest people on the team because people winning games have got to be tough. If you saw Miami last year when they won the national championship, they were a tough team."

The oddsmakers must have been feeling pretty good about themselves; the Buckeyes were 27 1/2-point favorites. But, the score was only 14-10 before Clarett scored with :38 remaining in the first half. After punting on their first possession, the offense scored on seven of its next eight.

Gamble had the longest run of the game on a play that started with a fake handoff to Clarett, 43 yards for a score, the longest of his three carries on the year. It was his first career touchdown. The second-longest run of the game came from another non-running back, when Donnie Nickey ran 28 yards on a fake punt in the first series.

The defense held the Hoosiers to 56 yards on the ground. Yamar Washington, who had gained 163 and 129 yards in his two previous games, was held to 15 yards in 10 carries.

Jenkins caught a touchdown pass from both Krenzel and McMullen, who was a perfect seven-for-seven in his passing. McMullen maintained his perfect day by catching one of his own passes off of a deflection. Nugent kicked a career-long 51-yard field goal, and Dustin Fox blocked a punt to set up a touchdown that made the score 35-10.

Ohio State's 1942 national championship team, coached by Paul Brown, held its 60-year reunion this weekend, with 26 of the 43 members still surviving.

The Miami Hurricanes were idle on this day.

NORTHWESTERN

The Number 5-ranked Buckeyes won in Evanston, 27-16, coming in as a 25-point favorite. Clarett ran for 140 yards and two touchdowns, over-coming three fumbles—two of them in the first quarter. Clarett had a rough end-of-the-week; he had a fear of flying and had only one previous flight. To his credit, he would not fumble again in the season.

The 27 points would be the second-lowest scored against the Wildcats in the season, who had been giving up 40 points per game coming in, but the Buckeyes did enough to beat the Wildcats for the 23rd straight time.

Lydell Ross added another 83 yards on the ground, and Krenzel chipped in with 62 yards, a career high at the time. Wildcat fans felt that they were robbed when an apparent touchdown pass to Mark Philmore, a Reynoldsburg High School grad, was ruled a no-catch. If video review had been in place, it may have been a different story. The Wildcats had to settle for a field goal.

Gamble had the team's longest kickoff of the season with a 56-yard return to open the second half, setting up a field goal by Nugent. Gamble also had the longest reception of the game, 48 yards, which led to a Clarett touchdown. Gamble's stats on defense consisted of one pass breakup, on a third-and-one play from the one-yard line, after which Northwestern missed an 18-yard field goal attempt. The Wildcats hurt themselves by missing two of their five field goal attempts. Their rushing average of 4.2

yards per play turned out to be the highest of any Buckeye opponent. They also had the longest kickoff return by an opponent, 67 yards.

In the second quarter, Northwestern had a 46-yard punt return, with Andy Groom making his first tackle of the season. The Wildcats were penalized 15 yards on the return, but Groom would get some practice for his second, and last—and most important—tackle of the season in three months, on another lengthy punt return.

In each of their two road games, the Buckeyes were shut out and trailed in the first quarter. In each game, they committed two turnovers in the first quarter and three turnovers in the game. They recorded their only two takeaways of the game in the last 3:33, an interception by Cie Grant and a fumble recovery by Donnie Nickey.

Both coaches had spent time at Miami of Ohio. Tressel was an assistant in 1979 and 1980, and Randy Walker played there and was the head coach from 1990 through 1998.

The game featured the three most recent recipients of the Mr. Football award for Ohio high school players—Maurice Clarett (2001), Northwestern's Jeff Backes (2000, from Upper Arlington and a teammate of Simon Fraser), and Bam Childress (1999, from Bedford St. Peter Chanel). In addition, Buckeye quarterback Justin Zwick—who was from Massillon Washington and was being redshirted—shared the Associated Press Division I Offensive Player of the Year award with Clarett in 2001.

This game would turn out to have the most points scored in regulation and the biggest winning margin in games away from Columbus for the Buckeyes. At the end of the day, the Buckeyes were the only remaining undefeated team in the Big Ten. It was the Buckeyes' first 6-0 start since 1998.

The last Buckeye touchdown was Clarett's 20-yard run. In the last eight games of the season, the longest touchdown run would be nine yards.

Miami beat Connecticut, 48-14, as Dorsey passed for 216 yards and three touchdowns, and McGahee ran for 107 yards and three touchdowns.

The Associated Press recap quoted UConn coach Randy Edsell with, "That's the No. 1 team in the country, far and away. I think they'll run the table again and be the national champion." However, the *Miami Herald* would prove to be slightly off-target in its prediction that Miami's future schedule included "... a few who don't appear to rate a chance, West Virginia, Rutgers, Pitt and Syracuse."

SAN JOSE STATE

The total offense was 567-265 in favor of the fifth-ranked Buckeyes in the 50-7 win. San Jose State had averaged 43 points per game in their three previous games, all wins. For the Spartans, it was their sixth road game out of seven, with another road game the following week. It was the first meeting between the two teams.

Clarett ran for 132 yards and two touchdowns and added a third on a seven-yard reception, giving him 15 on the season to break the previous OSU freshman record of 13. He would have no more until the last two games, missing significant action due to injuries.

Krenzel passed for 241 yards and three scores to three different receivers—Clarett, Jenkins, and Vance. Jenkins had seven catches for 136 yards. Eight Buckeyes had at least one carry, and nine had at least one reception.

San Jose State had a nine-yard run on the first play of the game, but finished with zero net yards rushing on 13 carries, the lowest number of carries ever against Ohio State. The Spartans' quarterback, Scott Rislov, was 31-of-37 for 257 yards in the first half, but only five-of-seven for eight yards in the second half. The Spartans had a 250 to 235 edge in total offense in the first half, but trailed 24-7. They managed only 30 yards in the second half.

The Spartans reached Ohio State territory in all six possessions of the first half and in none of their six possessions of the second half. They failed to convert on fourth down in two of their first three possessions, missed a field goal, and fumbled at the Ohio State 24-yard line twice. Their first punt came with 4:49 remaining in the third quarter. While the Spartans were punting on their last four possessions, Andy Groom had one punt on the afternoon, for 58 yards, and that came on the Buckeyes' second possession.

The Buckeyes defense recorded four fumbles—San Jose State fumbled on four straight possessions, straddling the second and third quarters—and an interception; ironically, San Jose State had entered as the Number 1 team in the country in takeaways. The offense would have duplicated its 51 points from the Kent State game, but a bad snap on a PAT attempt caused Nugent to have his streak stopped at 51. He kicked three field goals to make his streak 15, tying Vlade Janakievski for the longest in school history. More irony: the San Jose State kicker missed his only attempt, extending the streak by opposing kickers to three.

With this game, the Buckeyes had faced two of the three Division I-A head coaches who held a doctorate degree—Fitz Hill of San Jose State and Mike Leach of Texas Tech. The third, Rick Neuheisel of Washington, was fired two months before facing the Buckeyes in the 2003 opener.

The 2002 team had already accomplished something that the high-powered 1998 team had not and that the high-powered 2006 team, which would play for a national championship, would not—score at least 50 points in two games. It would take another eight years for an Ohio State team to accomplish it—in Coach Tressel's last season. The attendance in this homecoming game set a record at Ohio Stadium.

You would think that a team with a Cinderella year would have at least one one-point win to make the narrative totally magical. The Buckeyes' closest margin of victory would be four points, but, ironically, Miami had a one-point win. While Ohio State was recording its biggest margin of victory of the season, Miami had its closest game of the regular season, a 28-27 win over Number 9 Florida State where they trailed 17-7 and 27-14, but scored two touchdowns within three minutes in the fourth quarter. While Ohio State would benefit in two games by having opposing receivers fail to secure passes in the end zone, the Hurricanes used their tried-and-true formula for beating their rivals—having the Seminoles kicker miss a field goal in the last minute. With three escapes from Florida State in their recent history—in 1991, 1992, and 2000—where the Seminoles missed field goal attempts "Wide Right", this time, the Hurricanes survived a missed field goal attempt, wide left, on the last play of the game. As an omen, Ken Dorsey threw two interceptions and lost a fumble, actions—along with a field goal attempt on the last play of regulation—that would repeat themselves in just under three months, in the most important game of the season. Dorsey completed 20 of 45 passes, his only performance of the season where he completed less than half of his passes, for 362 yards, tying his career high at the time.

Miami coach Larry Coker was quoted as saying, "it's the best football game I've ever seen." Ohio State fans would be saying that perhaps multiple times in the upcoming months, including in a game that *Sporting News* would call the Game of the Decade. This game had a record crowd in the Hurricanes' home stadium against their rival, something that Ohio State would duplicate in six weeks.

Number 2 Oklahoma beat Number 3 Texas to reduce the number of undefeated teams by one. This marked the half-way point of the Buckeyes' season, and it would be the last game where they never trailed. Things were about to become very interesting.

WISCONSIN

The fourth-ranked Buckeyes had their second nail-biting win, 19-14 in Madison. The game-winning drive was 88 yards, capped by a three-yard pass to Ben Hartsock (wearing jersey #88) with 9:59 remaining. On his television show following the game, Tressel said that Hartsock had been engaged to his future wife during the week. The touchdown came on a first-and-goal play to Hartsock on the right side of the field. A first-and-goal pass to Hartsock on the right side of the field in a little less than three months later on the road would turn out to be one of the most critical plays of the season. Krenzel scrambled for 16 yards on a third-and-two play on the drive.

Gamble had an interception in the end zone on the Badgers' next possession, with 7:09 remaining; that was his only stat on defense in the game. Groom had his longest punt of the season, 74 yards for a touchback on their next possession. After a three-and-out by the Badgers, the Buckeyes were able to run the ball nine times and consume the last 4:29 of the game. Groom averaged 50.2 yards per punt; his shortest of 35 was just as effective, as it was downed at the one-yard line. He had another of 50 for a touchback and another of 53 that went out of bounds.

It took the Buckeyes only three plays to score their first touchdown, thanks to a 25-yard run by Clarett and a 47-yard touchdown catch by Jenkins, who caught the ball at the Wisconsin 40 and sprinted to the end zone. Krenzel had looked to his right before the snap; Tressel said on his show that the primary read was to the right, but Krenzel saw that it was overloaded.

It would turn out to be the only touchdown that the Buckeyes would score in the first quarter of the six games away from Columbus, being outscored by a combined score of 16-32, with four shutouts. It was also the only game away from Columbus where they scored on their first possession. Nugent's second field goal came after Doss recovered a fumble at the Wisconsin 32-yard line.

Clarett ran for 133 yards, his sixth game of at least 100 yards to set an Ohio State record by a freshman.

The defense recorded five sacks, with four in the first half and three of those in the same possession. All five sacks occurred on possessions when the Badgers reached the 50-yard line or deeper. Will Allen had his only sack of the season. The Badgers had given up 10 sacks in a 24-21 home win over Northern Illinois earlier in the season. Doss had a season-high 14 tackles.

The game featured big plays by both teams. For Wisconsin, Anthony Davis ran for 144 yards, the only 100+ effort by an opponent in the season, with a long of 41. Jonathan Orr had a 42-yard reception for a touchdown.

Jenkins had 114 yards in receptions, including a 45-yard catch on a third-and-six play in the winning drive, where he was double-covered. The play had started from the Wisconsin 16-yard line, and the ball was in the air for about 53 yards, as Krenzel launched it from the eight-yard line. Krenzel's 204 yards passing would be his most in a road game this season, a week after he posted his most of the season. Gamble had the Buckeyes' longest reception of the game, 48 yards, on which he slipped and could have scored for an 80-yard play and the only touchdown catch of his career. In a few months, he would have the team's longest reception of the season. His play set up a 27-yard field goal for a 10-7 lead. Nugent set an Ohio State record with his 16th straight successful field goal, breaking the team record set by Vlade Janakievski.

Wisconsin lost its third straight Big 10 game by five points or less. This was the fourth straight year in the matchup where the visiting team won. The Buckeyes have had two games in their history with a 19-14 score, and both were against Wisconsin; the first was in 1950.

The www.espn.com story on the game had that "Ohio State has just three formidable opponents left—Penn State, Minnesota and Michigan." Apparently, no one had informed Purdue or Illinois that they would be formidable.

The Miami Hurricanes were idle on this day.

PENN STATE

The Miami vs. West Virginia game kicked off at noon, with the Buckeyes' game against the Nittany Lions starting at 3:30. As the color commentator for ESPN's coverage of the Hurricanes-Mountaineers game, Chris Spielman previewed Ohio State with, "Their defense will get their biggest challenge with all the weapons that Penn State has. In my opinion, the best quarterback in the Big Ten is Zack Mills." He listed his candidates for the Heisman Trophy as Maurice Clarett, McGahee, and his front-runner, Ken Dorsey.

In the fourth-ranked Buckeyes' 13-7 win over the 18th-ranked Nittany Lions, Chris Gamble (jersey #7) was responsible for seven points as he intercepted Zack Mills (#7) on a third-and-13 play, zig-zagged 40 yards for a touchdown, and DID hand (more like, flip) the ball to an official. Both of his touchdown plays in the season came down the right sideline to the south end zone of Ohio Stadium. His score came with 13:07 remaining in the third quarter, a time that was a preview of the final score. He would finish the season with 31 receptions without a touchdown, so his second and last touchdown of the year was most timely. He carried the ball on his interception not entirely securely, but he did carry it with his outside arm. A key interception in a few months would be costly when an opponent carried it with his inside arm.

Gamble may also have saved seven points; Krenzel fumbled at the Penn State goal line on the Buckeyes' first possession, and the Lions' Anwar Phillips returned the ball 58 yards before Gamble chased him down, fighting off three Nittany Lions to make the tackle. Gamble picked the perfect time to record his first tackle of the season, and it came on offense. It was also his only tackle of the game. That Penn State possession ended with an interception by A. J. Hawk. Gamble also had his most punt return yards of the year, with 64 on five returns. He also made his first start at cornerback, and played the entire game on defense.

Clarett left the game in the first series with what was determined to be a separated left shoulder. He finished with 39 yards on four carries, with 30 on his first carry. He did eclipse the 1,000-yard mark on the year, running his total to 1,019 and becoming the eighth freshman in Big Ten history to achieve the mark. Due to his exit, the Buckeyes had balanced (at least in 2002 terms) rushing: Ross with 40 yards, and Clarett and Krenzel with 39 each. The offensive line was without the services of right tackle Shane Olivea, who underwent an appendectomy the Tuesday before the game.

Nugent's 37-yard field goal—which glanced through off the right upright—extended the lead to 13-7 with 1:05 left in the third quarter. He had an earlier 37-yard field goal in the second quarter following an interception; ten of the Buckeyes' 13 points came with the help of an interception. After losing the lead on Gamble's interception return, Penn State reached the Ohio State 36-yard line twice in the following four possessions, but elected to punt each time.

Andy Groom had a 53-yard punt in the first half for a touchback, a 59-yard punt out of the end zone with 4:51 remaining, and a 55-yard punt that put Penn State at its own 15-yard line with 3:02 remaining.

Andy Groom: *My favorite game outside of the national championship, selfishly, would be Penn State at home. I was the guy who got to speak at the skull session. Coach Tressel pegged me for that game, and I remember just standing in front of that whole crowd, just talking about how we need that 12th man on the field, this is going to be the biggest game of the year, we need you so loud that they don't want to come back to Ohio Stadium, ever. That's the loudest I've ever heard Ohio Stadium, and that's the loudest stadium I've ever been in, in my entire life. It was pretty cool being part of that, being able to get in the skull session and ask for that, and then being able to have one of the best games of my life. At the end of the game, I have to punt twice. I'm running out on that first one, and Coach Tressel grabs my arm, and he says, "Groomy, show me why I gave you a scholarship, show me why the punt is the most important play in football." So I go out there, and I rock a 60-yarder, we ended up covering it very well, so they're past the 50, they have to punt. And then I have to do it again, and he pulls me aside again and he says "Show me again", and I go out there and rock a 55-yarder. We end up winning the game by six points, and we're in the locker room, and the whole team and coaches are yelling my name and they're all chanting "Groomy", and it was a very special part of my Ohio State life, coming from a walk-on punter freshman year to end up being a small part of a national championship team, and ended up being an all-American.*

The offense had its two longest possessions of the season in terms of number of plays—14 and 15—but they produced only three points. The 15-play possession was the one that resulted in Krenzel's fumble at the one-yard line.

The defense held the Nittany Lions to eight first downs and a season-low 179 yards—58 yards in 28 plays in the second half and 352 fewer than in the 2001 game—with two other interceptions, one by end Will Smith for his only pick of the year. The eight first downs matched the eight that the Nittany Lions had mustered in their 14-10 upset of the Miami Hurricanes in the 1987 Fiesta Bowl for the national championship in Sun Devil Stadium. They had 80 of their 179 yards on their touchdown drive and averaged nine yards per possession in their other 11 possessions. Mills threw three interceptions, just as he had in the 2001 game that the Nittany Lions won, 29-27. The defense could have had a fourth interception—it would have been Donnie Nickey's only one of the season—but it was negated by a borderline penalty for roughing the passer. Dustin Fox, who had strongly considered going to Penn State, led the defense with seven solo tackles and had a tackle for loss and a pass break-up.

The Buckeyes had almost 15 more minutes of possession time; the 14-play, 72-yard drive that resulted in Nugent's second field goal consumed 8:21 of play. Penn State's average time per possession was 1:44.

Larry Johnson, who had four games this season with at least 257 yards rushing and would finish with 2,087 yards to lead all college football running backs, was held to his lowest production of the year—16 carries for 66 yards. In the second half, he had eight carries for eight yards. His school-record 257 yards, which he would break three more times in the season, had come the week before against Northwestern, in just over a half of play. Amazingly, Penn State had rushed for 1,317 yards as a team in 2001, an all-time low for the program. Johnson and Joshua Cribbs of Kent State, OSU's opponent in the second game, would finish tied for the highest gain per rush in Division I-A college football at 7.7 yards. Johnson would win the Maxwell Award in 2002; Ken Dorsey of Miami had won it in 2001.

This would be the only home game where Krenzel had an interception, and he had two, part of a season-high four turnovers by the offense. The defense recorded three turnovers, all of them interceptions. The attendance set another record for Ohio Stadium.

Penn State had now lost all five games in Ohio Stadium since joining the Big Ten in 1993 and had not scored more than one touchdown or more than nine points in any of the games. They had entered the game averaging 36.9 points per game.

The 13 combined points scored by the offenses were the lowest at Ohio Stadium since the Buckeyes lost 6-0 to Wisconsin in 1982, a season in which the Buckeyes won their last seven games. The last time that Ohio State had won a game without scoring an offensive touchdown in the regular season was in 1974, the 12-10 win over Michigan, as Tom Klaban kicked four field goals. The last time that they had scored 13 or fewer points and won a Big Ten game was a 13-6 win at Minnesota in 1988. That was 14 years previously, but it would be matched 14 days after this win over Penn State.

Referring to Gamble, the *Columbus Dispatch* reported that, "It's believed Paul Warfield, an OSU star from 1961 to 1963, was the last

Buckeyes player to start a game on offense and defense." Substitution rules changed dramatically in 1964, with a return to two-platoon football that reduced the need for two-way players. In 1963, Warfield led the team in minutes played, and his high of the year was 54.5 minutes (out of 60) against Penn State in a home game where he scored the only Buckeye touchdown and which the Buckeyes lost, 10-7. In that season, like Gamble, he had one rushing touchdown and led the team in punt returns. He also threw two passes, led the team in receiving and kickoff returns, and had two interceptions. He had played on the undefeated (8-0-1) Ohio State team in 1961 that received a national championship from the Football Writers Association of America, and would play on the winning side in three NFL championship games—in his rookie year of 1964 with the Cleveland Browns, in 1972 with the 17-0 Miami Dolphins, and in 1973, another Super Bowl champion.

Gamble had made another change from 2001, changing his jersey number from 83 to 7. Tressel may have had a soft spot in his heart for #7, as that was his jersey number as a quarterback at Baldwin Wallace.

Since Warfield's playing days, a few Buckeyes have made the switch. Tom Campana had a combined 19 receptions in his first two years, but his 1971 stat line resembles Gamble's. He had one reception, three kickoff returns, 34 tackles, and two interceptions, and led the team in punt returns—including one for a touchdown against Michigan. He had 447 of the team's 481 punt return yards. Rick Middleton switched from tight end in 1971, when he had a touchdown reception, to linebacker for the 1972 and 1973 seasons. He was drafted in the first round by the New Orleans Saints in 1974 and also played for the San Diego Chargers. Bruce Elia switched from linebacker to fullback in the third game of 1973—the Buckeyes had a 10-0-1 record—when Harold Henson was injured. He scored a touchdown in the Rose Bowl, and led the team in touchdowns with 14 and in scoring, after recording 13 tackles on defense. Returning to linebacker in 1974, he led the team in tackles. Jay Koch had two touchdown receptions in the 1987 season as a freshman tight end and had a combined 82 tackles as a linebacker in his last two seasons.

At the end of the day, the Buckeyes were one of eight major-college teams still undefeated. The Buckeyes had entered the game ranked sixth in the first Bowl Championship Series standings.

Ken Dorsey threw for a career-high 422 yards and two touchdowns in the 40-23 Miami victory over West Virginia, giving him 784 yards in his last two games. With the score 10-7 in the second quarter, the Hurricanes benefited from another missed field goal, by the opponent, wide left. Miami lost a 17-7 lead, and the score was 17-17 in the third quarter after West Virginia capitalized on a Miami fumble inside its 15-yard line. Miami had only a 24-23 lead in the third quarter. The Hurricanes gave up a season-high 363 yards on the ground to the Mountaineers' ground-oriented offense, under coach Rich Rodriguez.

In the third quarter, Glenn Sharpe of Miami was called for a "halo rule" penalty on a punt. In a few months, he would be involved in a monumental penalty call.

MINNESOTA

In the 34-3 win, the 6th-ranked Buckeyes—they had dropped from fourth, apparently not impressing the voters in the Penn State win—held the 23rd-ranked Golden Gophers to no points in the last 55 minutes of the game, 53 net yards on the ground in 36 attempts—after 51 yards in losses were factored in—and 59 passing yards, giving up a total of 291 yards and 15 first downs combined in the last two games. Minnesota had just seven first downs and 112 yards of offense, an average of two yards per play, with only seven yards in the second half.

The Buckeyes failed to score on their first five possessions, extending their streak to 19 straight without an offensive touchdown, scoring only on the Gamble interception return against Penn State in that span.

However, they scored four touchdowns and had two field goals in the next seven possessions.

The Gophers had 390 rushing yards the week before. Terry Jackson came into the game with consecutive games of 159, 239, and 238 yards. Thomas Tapeh came into the game with consecutive games of 113, 176, and 147 yards. The Buckeye defense held them to 49 and 32 yards, respectively.

The Gophers entered the game with a 7-1 record. They came into the game leading the Big Ten in rushing offense and in total defense, and were fourth against the run.

Clarett was in uniform but was not used, due to the shoulder stinger injury suffered in the Penn State game. Hall ran for a touchdown and 93 yards, his highest output of the season. Ross ran for 89 yards, his highest output against a Big Ten team in the season, and two touchdowns.

Chris Vance, who had learned in the morning that his brother had been killed the night before in their home town of Fort Myers, Florida, had a touchdown reception against Minnesota for the second straight year.

Gamble finally recorded his first tackle on defense, tied for the team lead in solo tackles with five, and tied for second in total tackles with six. He also led the team in receptions with three, and led the team in punt returns and kickoff returns. He had three interceptions in the season before he had a tackle on defense. He had created a new position in football, the Designated Interceptor, except that, unlike the designated hitter in baseball, he was not idle during the rest of the game.

It was the only game of the season where Krenzel had negative rushing yards, due to a season-high five sacks.

The last time that an opponent had scored three points in a game had been in 1997, when the opponent had also been Minnesota. The Buckeyes could have posted their first shutout in four years; the Gophers' only score came on a field goal after they blocked an Andy Groom punt on OSU's first possession. Each team had a punt blocked and had a bad snap on another. The defense would finish the season giving up an average of 243 passing yards per game, but they gave up a total of 157 in the consecutive games against Penn State and Minnesota.

Defensive end Darrion Scott was quoted in the *Columbus Dispatch* with, "All we want is for our offense to put up seven to 10 points." Technically, the offense had not done that the week before against Penn State, but his prophecy would come true a week later.

Tressel and Minnesota coach Glen Mason had been assistant coaches at Ohio State during the 1983 through 1985 seasons, and both left in 1986 to become a head coach in northeast Ohio—Mason at Kent State. In 1986, as a future Ohio State national championship coach was leaving the staff, another was joining it—Urban Meyer as a graduate assistant. Meyer would also be the next Ohio State coach after Tressel to have a perfect season, 12-0 in 2012.

The two most lopsided wins for the Buckeyes in the Big Ten were against Indiana and Minnesota, whose coaches Gerry DiNardo and Glen Mason would become members of the studio talent on the Big Ten Network.

On the same day, #3 Virginia Tech, #4 Notre Dame, and #5 Georgia all lost by seven points, allowing Ohio State to move to Number 3.

In New Jersey, the Miami Hurricanes trailed a Rutgers team—that would finish with a 1-11 record—going into the fourth quarter, but posted four touchdowns to win, 42-17. The Associated Press quoted Ken Dorsey with a foreshadowing comment, "When you're not ahead in the fourth quarter, that's a pretty good indication that you're in danger of not winning." He threw for 192 yards and had two touchdown passes, giving him 78 for his career, a BIG EAST Conference record that eclipsed the 77 thrown by Donovan McNabb at Syracuse. Willis McGahee ran for 187 yards and two touchdowns. The Associated Press account had an ironic statement, "The Miami Hurricanes are making a habit of playing close games." Equally ironic was the quote from Miami center Brett Romberg, "We always seem to pull things out at the end of games." Larry Coker said, "There's no doubt we're the No. 1 team in the country. We played a close game, but a lot of teams play close games."

More foreshadows for a major game in the next two months were that Dorsey had a minor injury to his non-throwing hand, Willis McGahee re-injured a toe on his right foot, the Hurricanes had a 17-14 deficit after three quarters, and their opponent had an unsuccessful fake field-goal attempt where the holder tried to run for the first down. After this game, the Hurricanes dropped to second in the Associated Press media poll and third in the BCS standings.

Before the Rutgers game, the www.miamihurricanes.com website had these points that would prove to be short-lived:

- Miami is 11-1 against ranked opponents with Dorsey as a starter, including 6-0 against teams ranked in the top 10.

- When Miami scores first, it is nearly a lock to win. Beginning with the 1983 season, the Hurricanes have gone 160-14 (.920) when scoring first. [Note: they would score first against Ohio State.]

- Coker's start at Miami is the best of any first-time head coach in the "modern era" of college football (post-1950) for wins without a tie or loss. Oklahoma's Barry Switzer started out 21-0-1 in 1973-74, but suffered a tie in his second game as head coach. Coker's unbeaten/untied start is the best by a first-time Division I-A head coach since Walter Camp of Yale led the Bulldogs to 28 consecutive victories before a loss in the 1888-89 seasons.

PURDUE

Like Minnesota the week before, Purdue was coming off a bye week. The 10-6 Buckeyes win at West Lafayette was a matchup between the third-ranked Buckeyes with their Big Ten-leading defense and Purdue's Big Ten-leading offense. It had the Craig Krenzel-to-Michael Jenkins "Holy Buckeye" play, as called by Brent Musburger. Musburger had exclaimed "Holy Toledo!" in the 2000 Purdue win when Drew Brees connected with Seth Morales on a 64-yard play for the winning score with 1:55 remaining. That game helped Purdue end a 34-year drought without a Rose Bowl appearance. The 2000 game was also decided by four points, 31-27.

The 37-yard pass into the wind came with 1:36 remaining, with Jenkins (#12) beating Purdue's defender #12 (Antwaun Rogers). Rogers, who grabbed Jenkins's jersey sleeve early in the route (no penalty was called) and held it as Jenkins ran for about five yards, and Jenkins had played youth football together when both lived in Cincinnati. The play came on a 4th-down-and-1 situation—they actually needed a yard and a half—and the odds were that the Buckeyes would not try to gain the first down on the ground, as Clarett had left the game with a shoulder stinger, and they had only four rushing first downs in the game, which was their lowest mark of the season by three. Even when Clarett seemed to be sound, he had been stopped on a third-and-1 play and a third-and-2 play. Their final tally of 94 rushing yards was a season low. Purdue blitzed two linebackers, but Lydell Ross and Branden Joe picked them up with blocks. Jenkins and Gamble were the only two wide receivers in the formation.

Coach Tressel said that Hartsock was the primary target and that Gamble actually ran the wrong route on the play. Gamble had keyed the drive with a 22-yard punt return, and Krenzel had completed a 13-yard pass to Hartsock on third-and-14, with Rogers making the tackle, before the game-winning pass. Rogers had broken up a pass intended for Jenkins in the first quarter.

Jenkins wasn't tackled by a Boilermaker on the touchdown, but he was shoved to the ground by Gamble out of celebration and after fulfilling his obligation of flipping the ball to an official. In a Big Ten Network program highlighting the play, Jenkins said that he improvised from a post route to a "go" route, and Tressel said that the play "… certainly wasn't designed that way." The play ended a streak of 11 straight possessions, going back to the Minnesota game, without a touchdown.

Did any Buckeye cynics at the time scream, "You scored too soon! You left too much time on the clock for the opponent!"? They would have been thinking back to the loss to Iowa in 1987—Earle Bruce's last home game—when they scored with 2:45 remaining, and to the loss to Michigan in 1988, when they scored with 2:02 on the clock. In both cases, the opponent scored for the win after the Buckeye scored to take the lead. No, they knew that this year's team, with its superior defense, was different. Note that in the Fiesta Bowl of the 2008 season, played in the Phoenix area, the good fortune would run out, as the Buckeyes scored with 2:05 remaining, only to see Colt McCoy lead the Texas Longhorns to the winning score.

Wilhelm recorded a sack shortly after a 58-yard pass play—the longest by an opponent in the season—and Purdue had to settle for a 32-yard field goal and a 6-3 lead with 7:50 remaining in the game. Wilhelm had made a key sack in the Cincinnati game to force the Bearcats to settle for a field goal. The Krenzel-to-Jenkins heroics took place two series later. Purdue's field goal accounted for the first second-half points against Ohio State since a touchdown by Northwestern on October 5.

Both of Purdue's field goals took place after they had reached the Ohio State four-yard line. The Boilermakers would enter the red zone four times and score a total of six points. The Buckeyes offense had only one series in the red zone, and that culminated in the Nugent field goal on the last play of the first half.

Purdue entered the game averaging 30 points per game. The Buckeye defense held the Boilermakers—who were coming off a game where they ran for 407 yards—to 56 yards on the ground, with a long of seven yards by quarterback Brandon Kirsch. Gamble had an interception at the OSU 11-yard line with 45 seconds left to seal it; Kyle Orton's pass was in the air for about 57 yards. A graphic on ABC's telecast had shown that Purdue was the worst team in the Big Ten for turning the ball over. The Buckeye defense ended the first and last Purdue possessions with an interception of a pass, which, if caught, could have led to a score. Dustin Fox had a pick in the far corner of the end zone on Purdue's first possession. On that play, Mike Doss gave a nudge to the intended receiver in the end zone, sending him to the ground. No penalty was called ... Was the pass uncatchable? Did the officials even see the contact? We will never know.

Jenkins and Gamble combined for 138 of the team's 173 receiving yards and for all 46 of the team's punt return yardage, with Gamble having the longest of the game, 22 yards to start the winning drive, and the most yards, 35. Jenkins's punt return of 11 yards came on a punt that he blocked, his only punt return of the season and his only defensive stat of the season. It was the second straight week that the Buckeyes had blocked a punt.

In the first quarter, a Krenzel pass was deflected and intercepted by Niko Koutouvides, a first-team All-Big Ten middle linebacker. It led to Purdue's first field goal, but at least Krenzel made the tackle on the play, his only tackle of his four-year Buckeye career.

Nugent kicked a 22-yard field goal, his shortest of the season, on the last play of the first half. Krenzel had a key 15-yard run in the drive, the longest run of the game for either team. Matt Wilhelm had set up the field goal with an interception. Krenzel had tried to run for a first down, but was stopped at the five-yard line with no timeouts. Calling that game, Musburger swore that the Buckeyes did not get the kick off in time as the first half wound down for the field goal, but he ate his words when he saw the replay. This was the fourth straight game where the Buckeyes trailed in the first half.

Nugent: *That's another situation that the coaches do a great job pre-paring us for. And everyone knew exactly what needed to be done, what we had to do. And, luckily we got out there and snuck it in, and you could tell everyone in the crowd at Purdue, they were all mad because they're like, no, they didn't get the play off. A lot of people were thinking, "oh, the time ran out when I kicked the ball." But it doesn't matter when the ball is kicked, it matters when it's snapped. Once people saw that replay, they're like, oh shoot, they're right, it was snapped before the clock was up. That's a tough one to be able to execute, because you've got all the lineman on the field who were so focused on a series that they just had. And they're just like, what are we doing? But everyone knew exactly what to do.*

The Buckeyes had to punt in all five possessions in the second half, before the possession that produced the winning touchdown. Other than the Holy Buckeye play and the field goal drive, their deepest penetration was the Purdue 40-yard line. On the five possessions before the winning drive, they had 19 plays that gained a total of 46 yards.

The two scoring possessions for the Buckeyes had started with 3:15 remaining in the first half and with 3:10 remaining in the game and ended, respectively, with no time on the clock and with 1:36 on the clock. This almost matched the tension of the game in 1990 against another Black and Gold team, the 27-26 win at Iowa. In that game, the Buckeyes scored a touchdown as time expired in the first half—on a Greg Frey pass deflected into the hands of Jeff Graham—and a touchdown from Frey to Bobby Olive with one second remaining in the game. That game would have been befitting of the 2002 Buckeyes.

Having beaten Purdue in 2001 by the score of 35-9, the defense had given up a total of 15 points and one touchdown to the Boilermakers over the past two seasons. Purdue would prove to be a thorn in the side of the

Buckeyes in upsets in 2004, 2009, 2011, and 2018, but the Buckeyes survived this upset attempt.

After the game, Boilermaker fans serenaded the team with "Overrated!", to which the team responded, "Undefeated!" The Buckeyes moved to 11-0 for the first time since 1995; in that season, they also had an extra game added to the schedule as the opener, a 38-6 win over Boston College in the Kickoff Classic, played in Giants Stadium in New Jersey.

The three-game streak of giving up a total of 16 points was the program's best since 1979, when they had three different streaks that were better—6, 7, and 13. That was Earle Bruce's first season, when the Buckeyes had an 11-0 record in the regular season and lost to USC in the Rose Bowl, 17-16.

The Buckeyes had won by four points, and Texas A&M beat Number 1 ranked Oklahoma by four points on this day to leave the Buckeyes and Miami the only two remaining undefeated teams. The state of Ohio entered the weekend with two undefeated teams, but Number 20 Bowling Green, coached by Urban Meyer, also lost for the first time.

OSU fans may disagree, but this game did not have the most exciting finish in college football on this date. Devery Henderson caught a deflected 75-yard touchdown pass from Marcus Randall as time expired to lift Nick Saban's LSU team to a stunning 33-30 victory over Kentucky, also on the road.

Miami won a non-conference game at Tennessee, 26-3, in their best defensive effort of the season. They had dropped to second in the AP media poll and third in the BCS rankings before the game. Dorsey, playing with a shell cast on his left wrist, passed for 245 yards, McGahee ran for 154, and Andre Johnson had five catches for 105 yards. Todd Sievers was successful on four out of five field goal attempts, all in the first half, to tie the team record for the third time. As an omen for two months later, Don Soldinger, the Hurricanes' special teams coordinator, was quoted in the *Miami Herald* with, "He's a money kicker. He's going to make the kicks when you need him." And, referring to the hostile environment, Sievers said, "I like this kind of atmosphere, it gets you fired up, it gets you focused." The defense recorded seven sacks. The Hurricanes did not score in the last 20 minutes of the game. They scored only two touchdowns in the four quarters, an event that would be duplicated in a memorable game away from home in two months.

ILLINOIS

Going into the game at Illinois, Ohio State was ranked first in the BCS rankings, but was only a nine-point favorite. They were also the last team in the Big Ten not to have played in an overtime game. They would need overtime to beat the Illini, 23-16.

For the second straight week, the Buckeyes had no touchdowns in the first half and only one in regulation, on a pass to Jenkins down the left sideline into the south end zone in each case. The Illini's John Gockman (wearing jersey #13) kicked a 48-yard field goal as time expired to force the overtime, a kick that was barely inside the left upright. Interestingly, the kick went through the uprights with three seconds on the clock, but the clock continued to run to zeroes. Gockman had made another with 31 seconds remaining in the first half. With the wind at his back in the fourth quarter, he attempted another one, from 59 yards with 2:17 remaining, that fell short. If he had made it, it would have been the longest in Illinois history. The *Chicago Tribune* reported that Gockman "... is Illinois' designated long kicker. The junior from Coal City, Ill., and Joliet Junior College is the guy coach Ron Turner calls on for field-goal attempts of 42 yards or more." Gockman's three successful field goals had an average length of 45 yards, and Nugent's three field goals had an average length of 39 yards. Gockman had just three field goal attempts coming into the game.

Andy Groom, on the wind: *You've got Illinois, you've got Northwestern, you've got Purdue, Purdue is probably the worst. Illinois is always known to be one of the worst places to punt, and actually I punted it in the first half really well into the wind. If you don't turn it over, it's going to come down rather quick. I know I had to punt to Eugene Wilson, and he ended up running one back, and I had to cut it off. It's super challenging, but the Big Ten overall can be absolutely horrendous.*

The Buckeyes were unable to pick up a first down after Gockman's miss, allowing the Illini to complete the drive that started with 1:04 remaining and ended with the tying field goal.

Maurice Hall had the winning eight-yard run for a touchdown in overtime, as Clarett was in uniform again but had no action due to his ongoing shoulder injury. It was the only designed run of the five plays in the winning drive. On second-and-ten, Krenzel threw a pass to Vance, who juggled it in the end zone but could not secure it. In a few minutes, it would be Illinois with a similar situation. Krenzel had a 14-yard scramble on third-and-ten, as the Illini blitzed one linebacker, to set up Hall's score. In the fourth quarter, Krenzel had a sneak for a first down on a third-and-one play and an 11-yard run on a third-and-nine play where he broke out of the grasp of two tacklers 11 yards behind the line of scrimmage.

Maurice Hall: *Coming into the season, I expected to start. So, mentally, I had already expected I'm the man, so when that didn't happen, it did, mentally, hit me kind of hard, but my dad always used to say, when you do get that opportunity, make sure to take advantage of it. In the Illinois game, I was kind of a feature back, but then, I ended up actually starting against Michigan that year at that game as well. I knew physically, I was good. Mentally, I just wanted to make sure*

I was ready at all times, that whenever the game came my way, that there was no disappointment on my end mentally that would cause me to not have the focus I need to have in a moment like that.

The Illini had a first-and-ten at the 11-yard line in their attempt to even the score in overtime, but, similar to the Cincinnati game, their receivers could not secure passes inbounds in the end zone. On the second-down play, they completed a pass to a leaping receiver in the end zone on the sideline; if he had landed vertically, it would have been a touchdown. But, Dustin Fox, who had been defending on some major pass gains earlier in the game, grabbed the receiver in the air and pushed him out of bounds, nullifying the catch. On third down, the receiver had the ball and took three steps in the end zone, but was juggling it before falling out of bounds, with Gamble defending him. Tim Anderson knocked down the Illini's last pass to seal the win.

For the second straight week, the home fans were vocal when the game ended. Illini fans, unhappy with the officiating calls on the last two passes, voiced their displeasure.

As a foreshadow for the future, the *Columbus Dispatch* had three crystal ball-like mentions:

Illini coach Ron Turner wasn't sure if his receivers were inbounds or not. But if officials did blow the calls, it's time to implement instant replay, he said. "I'd like to have instant replay all the time," Turner said. "It's a crying shame for those kids, if the game was decided by the officials."

And this overtime is a full-fledged hoot. More, please.

"Overtime? I don't want to go through that anymore," Gamble said.

Illinois had converted on a fourth-and-five play from their own 30-yard line to keep the drive alive for the tying field goal, and completed an 18-yard pass on second-and-19 in overtime.

In the first quarter, Krenzel stretched the ball to the end zone pylon, but he was not given the touchdown. ABC's analyst, Gary Danielson, said that it should have been a touchdown. After three false start penalties, they had to settle for a Mike Nugent field goal. The Buckeyes reached Illinois territory in all five possessions of the first half, but managed only two field goals. Illinois went three-and-out on their first three possessions and on their fifth possession. They punted in each of their first five possessions, but scored in four of their last seven. Punting into the wind, their first three punts netted just 21, 25, and 18 yards. On their fourth possession, two penalties and a sack produced a third-and-42 and a fourth-and-40 situation.

Leading 6-3 at halftime, Coach Tressel elected to take the ball in the third quarter, which meant that Illinois would have the wind at its back in the fourth quarter.

Nugent missed two field goals in the game, ending his consecutive streak at 23 for the season and 24 overall. His second miss, a 41-yard attempt in the fourth quarter, came on the Buckeyes' longest possession of 12 plays and 67 yards.

Nugent: *It was a really tough wind. I was pretty bummed out, because you don't go into any season thinking about records or anything like that. But, I started breaking a few consecutive field goal records for Ohio State. As much as I didn't want to think about that, I was like, honestly, that would be pretty cool to be able to build up a national collegiate record. And I think I came up short like one or two, something like that. And I hit the ball well in that game. I think I had a couple field goals early. And then, going the other direction, I still feel both kicks that I missed, they were almost the exact kick.*

I was on the right hash and being almost outside the right upright, but you never want to aim outside it. You just feel like the ball is not going to move that much. And sure enough, both kicks, I started off on the right and ended up missing left. So it ended up being a tough one, but at the end of the day, we won the game, and I can't go back and say I would want to change anything about not only that game, but the whole season.

Nugent's streak of 24 was over, but Jenkins extended his streak of games with a reception to 24. Jenkins (#12) had the only Buckeye touchdown in regulation, a 50-yard reception in the third quarter, in win #12 on Krenzel's 12th touchdown pass of the season. Jenkins said that he lost the ball in the lights and saw it only when it fell into his hands. To that point, it was Krenzel's longest completion of his career and Jenkins's longest reception of his career. Before this play, the Buckeyes had scored only one touchdown in their last 20 possessions. A flag was thrown for the defender getting a hand on Jenkins's chest, but the Buckeyes obviously did not need the penalty.

The two touchdowns in regulation came 1:13 apart in the third quarter; Illinois connected on a 19-yard touchdown pass before the scoring pass from Krenzel to Jenkins. The 23-yard scoring drive for the Illini was set up by a 52-yard punt return by Eugene Wilson, the longest punt return by an opponent in the season. On Illinois's next possession, they reached the Ohio State 18-yard line, but Will Smith forced a fumble that Tim Anderson recovered for the only turnover in the game.

Jenkins had six catches (of the team's 10) for 147 yards (of the team's 176), Walter Young of Illinois had 144 yards receiving, and both of the 6'5" receivers had a touchdown catch. After halftime, Jenkins had 127 of his yards, and Young had 138 of his yards. In the 2001 game between these two teams, they had 155 and 133 yards, respectively, and each had a touchdown catch.

For Krenzel, it was his last touchdown pass of the season. It was also redemption for him when considering the loss to Illinois in 2001. In that game, he came in after Scott McMullen had started; he threw his only touchdown pass of the season, but gave up a pick-six interception with 5:19 remaining when the Buckeyes were trailing by only five points.

For Jenkins, it was his last touchdown reception of the season. His last three touchdown receptions of the season came in games decided by a total of nine points in regulation, against Wisconsin, Purdue, and Illinois. His next two touchdown receptions would also come in an overtime game, the three-overtime game against North Carolina State in 2003.

The defense gave up a net of 53 rushing yards on 34 carries, with a long of ten. The defense had its streak of 13 straight quarters without giving up a touchdown snapped in the third quarter, but it recorded six sacks of quarterback Jon Beutjer; David Thompson, starting in place of the injured Darrion Scott, had three-and-a-half sacks. When Beutjer played for Iowa in 2000, the Buckeyes defense had sacked him three times. Like Beutjer, Gockman had spent some time at Iowa, where he redshirted as a walk-on in 1999.

Like the Wisconsin series, the road team had won the last four games in this series. This was the second straight trip to Illinois that had a field goal at the end of regulation; in 2000, Dan Stultz had kicked a 34-yard field goal to give the Buckeyes a 24-21 win. In the 1985 game at Illinois, the Illini kicked a 38-yard field goal, also on the last play and through the south uprights, to defeat the Buckeyes, 31-28.

The 23-16 score meant that OSU had given up 16 points twice in 2002 to the two Big Ten teams based in Illinois, with both games played in the state of Illinois and in the two lowest attended games of the year. They had a 12-0 record for the first time in their history. Oddly, Iowa concluded its regular season this day with a win to clinch at least a tie for the Big Ten championship.

After sweeping Wisconsin, Penn State, and Illinois, winning by a combined 18 points in the span of five games, the Revenge Tour of the three Big Ten teams that had beaten the Buckeyes in 2001 was complete.

Miami was idle, but they beat the Pitt Panthers at home on the following Thursday, 28-21. Miami trailed 14-7, and the game was tied at 14 at halftime. The Panthers, coached by former OSU assistant Walt Harris, had a fourth-and-5 situation that ended on an incomplete pass from the Miami 20-yard line that sailed just beyond a receiver in the end zone on their last possession. The account on www.espn.com mentioned that Dorsey was wearing a soft cast on his left wrist. He finished 14-of-26 for 163 yards, his lowest output of the season against a Division I-A team. Willis McGahee ran 19 times for 159 yards and scored two touchdowns, breaking the Miami single-season record. Sean Taylor had a touchdown on a reverse in a punt return, taking the handoff from Roscoe Parrish. The Hurricanes had two significant season-ending injuries in the game— defensive end Cornelius Green (no relation to the Ohio State quarterback of the 1970s) was among the team's top 10 tacklers, and receiver Kevin Beard, who was fourth on the team with 23 receptions and tied for third with four touchdown catches.

MICHIGAN

With the Buckeyes' 14-9 win in the 99th meeting between the teams, they clinched a spot in the BCS championship game.

The Wolverines came in ranked Number 12 with a 9-2 record and had spoiled perfect season opportunities for the Buckeyes with a tie in 1973 and with defeats in 1969, 1995, and 1996. They had also given the Buckeyes their only loss in the 10-1-1 season of 1993.

The Buckeyes entered the game having won five games by seven points or less; the Wolverines came in with a 5-1 record in games decided by seven points or less. None of the Buckeyes' wins were by less than four points, but the Wolverines had two wins by two points each and two by three points each.

Michigan had three possessions in the first half and kicked a field goal in each one. They entered the game making only eight of 20 field goal attempts, using three kickers. In the second half, they would come no closer to the Buckeyes' end zone than the 24-yard line, where they had their last two plays of the game. Will Allen, who attended Huber Heights Wayne High School in Ohio, intercepted on the three-yard line on the last play to seal the win, as Dustin Fox had done the year before.

The 9-7 halftime deficit marked the third straight game in which the Buckeyes had no touchdowns in the first half. In the 1996 Michigan game, it was Ohio State who settled for three field goals in the first half in a 13-9 loss. That 1996 game also ended with an interception by an Ohio native, Marcus Ray of Columbus Eastmoor High School.

With the Buckeyes ahead 7-6 in the second quarter, Wolverine quarterback John Navarre completed a pass in the end zone to Braylon Edwards, but the Michigan receiver was called for offensive pass interference. The Field Judge took a few seconds to throw his flag, and Chris Gamble was defending the play in the southwest corner of the end zone. In the Buckeyes' following game, a pass interference call involving the Field Judge and Gamble in the southwest corner of the end zone would also prove to be critical.

In ABC's pregame segment, color analyst Gary Danielson said, "I think that Maurice Clarett is going to have to play to beat Michigan." He had not played since the third play of the second half against Purdue, two weeks prior. He made his first appearance in the Buckeyes' second possession, and his first three plays were a nine-yard reception, a seven-yard run, and a 28-yard run. The drive ended with his two-yard touchdown run and a 7-3 lead. He accounted for 47 of the 78 yards gained on the drive, and actually had to leave the game for two plays before his touchdown run, after a blow to his left shoulder.

In game #13, Clarett (#13) had the first touchdown, and Hall had the winning one, a three-yard run. The Buckeyes kept the first drive alive thanks to Ryan Hamby recovering a fumble by Jenkins on a rare screen pass, in Ohio State territory. On second-and-nine from the Michigan 10-yard line, Krenzel ran to the five-yard line, where he took a hard hit, which led to a delay of game penalty. The Buckeyes were helped by a pass interference penalty by the Wolverines on the next play, the play before Clarett's touchdown. He had not scored since the San Jose State game, six weeks previously.

This was the third straight game in which all of the touchdowns were scored by Jenkins or a player named Maurice, with Hall scoring the winning touchdown for the second straight game, on a three-yard option pitch with 4:55 remaining. The ball had been on the right hashmark, with the option play to the short side of the field. Hall finished the game with only four carries for three yards, though he had a season-high 61 yards in kickoff returns. Michigan's Cato June gave Hall a hard hit about three yards deep in the end zone.

Maurice Hall: *Cato June, man. I'm like, come on, I'm already in the end zone. The funny part is, until I actually saw it with my own eyes, I don't even remember him hitting me, because I knew I was in the end zone. And it was so crazy, because, when you're playing, you never hear any of the crowd. But after I scored that touchdown, I've never heard a crowd so loud in my life. Obviously, that was special, something that I'll never forget.*

On the first play of the winning drive, Krenzel had a 15-yard completion to Brandon Schnittker, a pass that was actually intended for Jenkins. If Schnittker had not made the grab, he would have finished the season with a total of one carry and one reception, for a total of 13 yards. His other reception of the season gained a first down and set up a Nugent field goal in the five-point win at Wisconsin. Four plays later, Krenzel had a sneak for exactly the one yard that he needed on fourth down at the Michigan 33-yard line. The conversion on fourth down matched the total that they recorded successfully in eight third-down tries in the game. They ran the sneak instead of trying a 50-yard field goal, which would have been Nugent's second-longest of the season. The next play was a 26-yard pass to Clarett on a wheel route, which the Buckeyes hadn't shown before in the season, and Hall scored the winning touchdown two plays later on the only option play of the season. Two defenders converged on Krenzel, which allowed him to make the toss to Hall. He passed or ran for 53 of the 57 yards of the drive.

On their next possession, Michigan reached the Ohio State 30-yard line, but Navarre was sacked by Darrion Scott and fumbled, with Will Smith recovering. On the season, Scott led the team with 8.5 sacks and tied for the lead with three forced fumbles; one of them was in the fourth quarter of the Cincinnati game.

In the previous week, the Buckeyes had the ball with 2:17 remaining in regulation, but could not pick up a first down, allowing Illinois to start their game-tying drive with 1:04 remaining. In this game, the Buckeyes had the ball with 2:02 remaining, but could not pick up a first down—it was only their second three-and-out of the game, with the first one coming on their first possession—letting Michigan start their last drive from their own 20-yard line with 58 seconds remaining. John Navarre converted on 4th-and-ten in the first set of downs, and the Wolverines had a first-and-ten on the Ohio State 24-yard line with nine seconds remaining. Navarre spiked the ball on first down, then his pass with Edwards as the target sailed out of the end zone, leaving one second on the clock.

Buckeye fans were wishing that the clock operator at Illinois had been assigned to the game. This was the first year that required independent clock operators, so the Buckeyes had no home-field advantage. In November of the previous year, Michigan State had beaten Michigan in

Spartan Stadium with a touchdown pass on the last play. In that game, Wolverine fans protested that the clock should have expired on the play before, instead of stopping with one second remaining. In hindsight, leaving one second on the clock would produce one of many iconic moments in the season.

On the last play of the game, Will Allen intercepted at the three-yard line. Navarre's previous pass was too long, and his last one may have reached the goal line, at best. Allen's interception was the only one for either team in a combined 62 passes. His two interceptions on the year that sealed the wins over Cincinnati (picked off in the end zone) and Michigan netted no return yards. The only two turnovers of the game were Michigan's fumble with 2:02 remaining and Allen's interception. In the 2001 and 2002 Michigan games, the Buckeyes' edge in turnovers was a combined seven to one.

The Wolverines dominated the stats, especially in the first half. In the second quarter, Michigan ran 30 plays to five for the Buckeyes, including a drive of 8:24 in 19 plays. They were the only opponent to score on its first three possessions. Michigan had 89 plays to 48 for Ohio State, but the Buckeyes averaged 5.5 yards per play, compared to 4.1 for the Wolverines. The 89 plays were the most by any opponent in the season. In the first half, the Wolverines had 47 plays, including their three field goals, to 17 for the Buckeyes; nine of the 17 came on the touchdown drive. The Wolverines were a very efficient 12-for-22 on third down, which included eight-for-11 in the first half. They had an edge of 211 yards to 102 for the Buckeyes in the first half, but the Buckeyes were plus-five in the second half.

For the fourth straight year in the rivalry, the losing team had more total yards. Krenzel was 10 (as in Big 10) for 14 (as in 14 points in the game and 14 wins on the year) in passing.

Tressel's 155th career win as a college coach equaled the number that his dad, Lee, had in his career.

This was Clarett's 10th game of the year. He rushed for 119 yards, exactly 10% of his 1,190 yards to that point, in the game to earn a tie for the Big 10 championship. He had 82 yards in the second half and had the longest run for either team, 28 yards, and the longest reception for either team, 26 yards on a wheel route that led to the winning score. His 154 yards on rushes and receptions were more than half of the team's 264. His 35 receiving yards were his high for the season. The Buckeyes had 13 first downs, one of them on a penalty; Clarett accounted for eight of the other 12 first downs. He broke Robert Smith's Ohio State rushing yardage record for a freshman. His touchdown was in the south end zone, just as Archie Griffin had done 30 years previously as a freshman in the win over Michigan, when the team also scored 14 points. Both Clarett and Griffin had the team's longest reception in those games; Archie actually had no competition in his game, as he had the only reception.

Michael Jenkins also broke the 1,000 mark for receiving yards for the season in the game.

Krenzel had none of his ten completions in the third quarter, but had four in the fourth quarter, to four different receivers. It was the only game of the season without a field goal attempt by Nugent; the deepest advance that the Buckeye offense made other than for their two touchdowns was the Michigan 35-yard line. The Buckeyes had only nine possessions, their fewest of the season. For each team, none of their nine possessions started on the short side of the 50-yard line.

This was the first time that the Buckeyes had beaten Michigan in consecutive years since the 1981 and 1982 seasons. Krenzel became the first Buckeye quarterback since Mike Tomczak in 1982 and 1984 to have two wins over Michigan, and the first to have consecutive wins over the Wolverines since Cornelius Greene in 1974 and 1975. Krenzel's two wins were by six and five points, and Greene's two wins were by two and seven points. None of the three quarterbacks is from Ohio; Tomczak is from Illinois, and Greene is from Washington, D.C.

Coach Tressel became the first Ohio State coach to win his first two games against Michigan since Francis Schmidt accomplished it in 1934 and 1935; Schmidt went on to win his first four against Michigan. Michigan in 1934 was the defending national champion. The Buckeyes had lost nine of the last twelve in the series when Schmidt was hired, and had lost 10 of the last 13 to Michigan when Tressel took over. In 1934, Schmidt was another first-year Ohio State coach who expressed optimism about playing Michigan, saying that their players "put their pants on one leg at a time, same as everybody else."

In regulation of the last three games of the regular season, the Buckeyes had only four touchdowns in 32 possessions, but it was the fifth time in the last seven games of the regular season that the defense had pitched a shutout in the second half. The attendance broke the Ohio Stadium record again.

For the seniors, it was the fewest points scored against Michigan in their careers. Even the 1999 team with a 6-6 record had scored 17 in Ann Arbor. It was the fewest points that the Buckeyes had scored in a win against Michigan since the 1981 game had the same score, and the fewest points that the Buckeyes had scored in a home win against Michigan since the 12-10 game in 1974. The only two games in Ohio State history with a 14-9 score are against Michigan. The 1981 game had the same scoring pattern: Michigan up 3-0, OSU up 7-3, OSU up 7-6, Michigan up 9-7, OSU wins 14-9 with a touchdown in the last five minutes. The Buckeyes were +2 in turnovers in that 1981 game, too. The Buckeyes were outgained by 100 yards in the 1981 game and by 104 yards in the 2002 game. Braylon Edwards's father, Stanley, played for the Wolverines in the 1981 game. As an omen, the Buckeyes scored 31 points in the Liberty Bowl win (31-28) over Navy in the 1981 season.

This was the only game of the season where the Wolverines failed to score a touchdown. They also scored only nine points against Iowa, the Big Ten co-champions, but they had a touchdown in that game. Michigan had also kicked three field goals in the 1998 game, which was the last home win for the Buckeyes over the Wolverines.

For the second straight meeting, John Navarre had at least 47 passes. For the second straight meeting, Michigan had at least one receiver with over 100 yards—Marquise Walker with 160 yards in 2001, and Edwards with 107 and Ronald Bellamy with 101 in this game. In the two wins over Michigan in 2001 and 2002, the Buckeyes had been outgained by a total of 519 yards to 691.

Since the 2002 game, the only time that the Buckeyes and Wolverines combined for less than the 23 points scored in the 2002 game was in 2007, a 14-3 Ohio State win played in a downpour in Ann Arbor. On the day of this 2002 game, Tim May of the *Columbus Dispatch* had pointed out that Michigan held a 5-4 edge in the games played on this date, so this win evened the score at five each.

On the night before the Michigan game, the OSU men's basketball team, in an exhibition game, beat a team that was familiar with winning streaks, the Harlem Globetrotters.

Ohio State's regular season was over, and the team was officially invited to the BCS championship game after the game, but Miami would play on the next two Saturdays, scoring a combined 105 points; their 49 and 56 points in those games would be their two highest outputs against Division I-A teams in the 2002 season, and their 565 and 556 yards of total offense would be their two highest outputs of the season.

Donnie Nickey was already thinking ahead to Miami; he was quoted in the *Columbus Dispatch* with, "They're beatable ... There is not one totally dominant team this year ... I think on any given day, the team that wants it more is going to win it." Matt Wilhelm was quoted in *Sports Illustrated* with, "They're beatable."

Michigan would also play a team from the Sunshine State—the Florida Gators—in a bowl game, and win, 38-30, in the Outback Bowl in Tampa, where the Buckeyes had played the last two seasons.

The following week, Miami beat Syracuse on the road, 49-7, leading only 21-7 at halftime. Dorsey passed for 345 yards and was sacked twice, and the Hurricanes had 565 yards of total offense. Willis McGahee ran for 134 yards, which allowed him to break the Miami single-season record. He had touchdown runs of 61 and 51 yards. Sean Taylor had an interception for a touchdown, and Andre Johnson finished with six catches for 181 yards.

On December 7, Miami beat Virginia Tech at home, 56-45. McGahee ran for a school-record six touchdowns and a career-best 205 yards, one yard more than he had against Florida. It was his tenth game in the season with at least 100 yards rushing; his two games that fell short of 100 were the six-carry game against Florida A&M and the 95-yard effort against Florida State. His 39 carries tied the school record. Dorsey passed for 300 yards, and Andre Johnson had six catches for 193 yards. The Hurricanes had 556 yards of total offense, following their 565-yard effort the week before. The 56 points were more than the Buckeyes had scored in their last three games combined. This game had several foreshadows:

- Early in the game, ABC's color commentator, Bob Griese, said that Miami ranked 92nd in college football in turnover margin, after ranking first in 2001.

- ABC's play-by-play broadcaster, Brad Nessler, said of the Miami offensive line, "They don't give up sacks."

- In the third quarter, Nessler had a phone chat with Jim Tressel. One of Tressel's keys to the upcoming match against Miami was, "who takes care of the football."

- Miami's Roscoe Parrish had punt returns of 29 and 43 yards. He would finish the season with 392 yards, more than Ohio State had as a team.

- Virginia Tech's quarterback, Bryan Randall, ran 25 times for 132 yards.

- Speaking of the Hurricanes, Virginia Tech coach Frank Beamer was quoted with, "They are real good. The offense is great, and the defense is solid. They just sit there and pound you."

- The Associated Press quoted center Brett Romberg with, "We've still [got] one more game, and that's when we'll celebrate—when we win that game."

- The *Miami Herald*, referring to Dorsey's Heisman potential, had "How are these voters going to feel when Dorsey is standing there after the Canes have squashed Ohio State like a bug in the Fiesta Bowl and UM is holding its second consecutive national championship?"

- The *Herald* also had, "... Andre Johnson, who cannot be covered by anyone in college football ..."

- Kellen Winslow was quoted with, "We're way too fast for Ohio State ... Nobody can hang with our speed."

CHAPTER 4

The Miami Game

BETWEEN THE MICHIGAN GAME and the Fiesta Bowl, Krenzel and Gamble were selected by their teammates as Co-Most Valuable Players of the 2002 season. Cie Grant was a unanimous choice as the recipient of the Bo Rein Most Inspirational Player award. How is that for omens? Gamble was the first sophomore to be named MVP since Archie Griffin in 1973, which was the last season with no losses.

The Buckeyes were the first Big Ten team to play in the BCS national championship game. In the Tostitos Fiesta Bowl in Tempe, Arizona, they beat the defending champions Miami Hurricanes—who were on a 34-game winning streak—in a 31-24 win in double overtime. The Buckeyes were 11½-point underdogs; Miami had been a 13-point favorite about a week before the game. The table was set for the Buckeyes; this was the fifth BCS championship game and an opportunity for the fifth different conference to win it, following Tennessee (Southeastern Conference) in 1998, Florida State (Atlantic Coast Conference) in 1999, Oklahoma (Big 12) in 2000, and Miami (BIG EAST) in 2001. In fact, from the 1998 season through the 2022 season, Ohio State played in the championship game five times—in the 2002, 2006, 2007, 2014, and 2020 seasons—and no other Big Ten team played in a championship game.

In the Buckeyes' history, playing an extra game had not been a predictor of the season-ending success. In 1986, they lost to Alabama, lost to Michigan, but won the bowl game over Texas A&M. In 1994, they beat Fresno State, beat Michigan, and lost the bowl game to Alabama. In 1995, they beat Boston College, lost to Michigan, and lost the bowl game to Tennessee. In 1997, they beat Wyoming, lost to Michigan, and lost the bowl game to Florida State. In 1999, they lost to Miami, lost to Michigan, and did not have a bowl game.

THE HISTORY

It was the third time in 25 years that the Buckeyes and Hurricanes had met, and in the third different venue, and in the third different month, and on the third different day of the week, with the Fiesta Bowl on a Friday. The others were in Ohio Stadium in 1977 (on a Saturday in September) and in Giants Stadium in 1999 (on a Sunday in August), with both of them in the first game of the season.

Miami in those two meetings had Ohio connections. Their first-year coach in 1977 was Lou Saban, who played for the Cleveland Browns and had been the coach at Case Institute of Technology in Cleveland, which evolved into Case Western Reserve University. Since 1951, Saban was Miami's sixth coach, while Ohio State had one in that span. The game had several similarities to the 2003 Fiesta Bowl. The Buckeyes lost two of its top running backs, Jeff Logan and Ricky Johnson, to injury during the game. Miami quarterback E.J. Baker threw for 210 yards, but the Buckeye defense recorded two interceptions and a fumble, and held Miami to minus-13 yards on the ground, including minus-63 by Baker. The *Columbus Dispatch* quoted Saban with, "And I am sorry that the officials had to get into the game. A couple of calls sure did not do anything for us." The British Broadcasting Corporation produced a documentary on Woody Hayes that year, and it had extensive footage from the Miami game. The host, Desmond Wilcox, reported that the Buckeyes won, "10 points to nil", and that the marching band was nicknamed the "Grandest Band in the Land."

The 1999 game—won by Miami, 23-12—was the Kickoff Classic, and the Miami coach was Butch Davis, who would leave to coach the Cleveland Browns in 2001. Its assistant coaches in 1999 included Larry Coker and first-year defensive coordinator Greg Schiano, a future Ohio State assistant. Ironically, the Miami coach that day could have been Jim Tressel, who was considered for the job in 1995. Rob Oller of the *Columbus Dispatch* reported that Tressel had also drawn interest from Maryland (whose athletic director was Andy Geiger and who would join the Big Ten in 2014), Michigan State (whom the Buckeyes lost to in 1999), and Pittsburgh. Brent Musburger and Dan Fouts called the game for ABC.

That 1999 game, which had a game-time temperature of 85 degrees and matched the Number 9 Buckeyes and the Number 12 Hurricanes, was the first season-opening loss for the Buckeyes in 13 years, going back to the 16-10 loss to Alabama in 1986, in another Kickoff Classic in the same stadium. The Hurricanes' quarterback was another Ken, Kenny Kelly, and he ran for one of his two career touchdowns in his first start. He would later spend time in Ohio as a member of the Cincinnati Reds in 2005. The Buckeye offense generated only 220 yards of total offense. Their only touchdown drive reads like those from the 2003 Fiesta Bowl— two plays for seven yards, following a fumble recovery on a quarterback sack. The Buckeye defense gave up a 67-yard touchdown pass to Santana Moss with eight seconds remaining in the first half, a 44-yard touchdown run by James Jackson, and another run for 42 yards, but could take some solace in the fact that they blanked the Hurricanes in the second half and that the Hurricanes would score fewer points in only two other games that season, against Number 1 Florida State and Number 2 Virginia

Tech. The defense recorded two fumbles by Kelly, two interceptions, and three sacks—similar numbers compared to what they would do in the 2003 Fiesta Bowl—but Miami had the same numbers by its defense. The *Columbus Dispatch* reported that the "... clear majority of the 73,037 in Giants Stadium were Ohio State fans." Dorsey would start the last three games in 1999 to kick-start his brilliant career, leading the Hurricanes to the highest three-game point total (155) in school history.

Mike Doss and Donnie Nickey each saw his first action as a Buckeye against Miami and would see his last action as a Buckeye against Miami. Like Dorsey, Doss would finish his 1999 freshman year with a bang—29 tackles in the last three games, starting the last two. In this game, he had one tackle, and Nickey had seven.

Donnie Nickey: *They were so fast, I was shocked by the speed. I lost containment a few times, because I misjudged the speed, I wasn't used to it. The running backs, James Jackson and Najeh Davenport, and Santana Moss.*

It is conceivable that neither the 1999 nor the Fiesta Bowl matchups would have taken place; the 1999 matchup was arranged on December 8, 1998. The *Columbus Dispatch* reported on December 9, 1998 that the Kickoff Classic had pursued Ohio State for one of its teams in 1998, but the Buckeyes declined.

Entering the Fiesta Bowl, both programs had had a six-loss record within the past five seasons; Ohio State had a 6-6 record in 1999, and Miami had a 5-6 record in 1997 while on probation.

Similar to the fact that the 2002 season had its earliest opening game for the Buckeyes—other than the very first game in 1890—January 3 was the latest date in a season for the program to this point.

Ironically, Miami had won its first national championship in the 1983 season with a quarterback from Youngstown, Ohio—Bernie Kosar—and had Archie Griffin's brother, Keith, as a running back. They had entered the season unranked, scored 31 points in the championship game to beat a Number one-ranked team (Nebraska) that would join the Big Ten, and made a crucial stop on a pass play (a two-point conversion) with 48 seconds remaining. In Dick Fenlon's story in the *Columbus Dispatch,* he described Miami coach Howard Schnellenberger as having a "calm and determined manner", and had a quote from Griffin, who ran for 41 yards in the game, on Kosar, "He's always calm. He never panics". That game took place on the same day as Ohio State's last-minute win in the Fiesta Bowl.

THE LEAD-UP

Ironically, the Fiesta Bowl took place in Sun Devil Stadium, the home venue of John Cooper's head coaching stint at Arizona State. An extra bonus for the fans was that they were treated to all-you-can-eat Tostitos and salsa. The Buckeyes had lost to Penn State in the Fiesta Bowl of the 1980 season, 31-19, despite leading 19-7. They had beaten the Pitt Panthers in the Fiesta Bowl of the 1983 season, 28-23, scoring the winning touchdown in the south end zone on a 39-yard pass from Mike Tomczak down the left sideline to Thad Jemison with 39 seconds remaining. The *Columbus Dispatch* reported that "the play ... was designed to go nowhere near him", and Earle Bruce said that "We were supposed to throw the outlet (to Cedric Anderson on the other side of the field)." Holy Buckeye, anyone? The assistant coach in charge of quarterbacks in that 1983 season was Jim Tressel, in his first of three seasons. Tomczak would later become an Advisor to the Head Coach at Youngstown State after Tressel returned to Ohio State.

Miami was #1 in the BCS poll, and OSU was #2. The game matched two second-year coaches—Tressel, who had interviewed for the Miami job in 1995, and Larry Coker, who had been an assistant at Ohio State.

Coker was the defensive backs coach for the Buckeyes in 1993, when they had a 10-1-1 record and won the Holiday Bowl, and in 1994, for John Cooper's first win over Michigan. He was an assistant coach at Oklahoma State when they played at Ohio Stadium in the season opener in 1989, which the Buckeyes won, 37-13. He had won the national championship in his year #1 (2001), and Jim Tressel would win his in his year #2 (2002). They were named the head coach of their team 16 days apart in 2001. Coker won the Bear Bryant Award and the American Football Coaches' Association (sharing with Ralph Friedgen of Maryland) Coach of the Year awards in 2001, and Tressel won these two awards in 2002. Coker won his first 24 games as a head coach; Walter Camp, "the father of football", holds the record with a 28-0 start in 1888-1889 at Yale. The *Ohio State Lantern*, the student newspaper, wrote that Tressel had met with Coker in Miami during a Hurricanes' spring practice session.

The Hurricanes had scored a school-record 503 points in the regular season, breaking the record that they had set the season before. Their average of 41.9 points per game was almost identical to their 42.7 of 2001, but they were giving up almost twice as many points per game as in 2001 —18.1, compared to 9.8.

The Hurricanes' 34-game winning streak matched the one that Penn had—before losing to Lafayette in October of 1896—for the sixth-longest in Division I-A history. It was the longest since Toledo won 35 straight from 1969 through 1971. Oklahoma's all-time record 47-game was within reach; that streak by the Sooners was broken in 1957, a year in which Ohio State won a national championship.

This was the third straight year where the opposing coach in the Buckeyes' bowl game was a former OSU assistant coach, following two against Lou Holtz of South Carolina in the Outback Bowl.

Miami's defensive backs coach was Mark Stoops, whose brother, Bob, won the national title in his second year at Oklahoma—improving on a 7-5 record the season before—15 days before Tressel's hiring, and had removed himself from consideration for the Ohio State job. Mark and Bob's uncle, also named Bob, had coached on Tressel's Youngstown State staff.

There were positive omens for a Buckeyes win. Opposing quarterbacks who could use their legs had been effective against Miami. West Virginia's Rasheed Marshall ran for 93 yards and a touchdown. Pittsburgh's Rod Rutherford ran for 69 yards and a score, and Virginia Tech's quarterback, Bryan Randall, ran 25 times for 132 yards.

Predictions in publications were encouraging to Buckeyes fans. Greg Boeck in the *USA Today* wrote that, "McGahee calls the Buckeyes' defense the best he's faced."

Matt Hayes—how's that for a last name?—in *Sporting News* wrote of Ohio State, "They're gonna win. The Ohio State Buckeyes will beat the defending national champion Miami Hurricanes in the Fiesta Bowl national championship game. That's right—they're going to take care of the big, bad Canes in a game that means everything. So what if the Buckeyes play like PBS on Prozac and their coach reminds you of Mr. Rogers?" And, "How do you stop someone that no one has all season? Get physical and be patient." He quoted a BIG EAST defensive coordinator with, "I know this sounds strange, but you have to put the game in Dorsey's hands. You've got to stop the run." However, Willis McGahee was confident—"You'd have to be crazy to pick against us." McGahee's two games with the lowest average gain per attempt were in the one-point win over Florida State and the 40-23 win over West Virginia, which had a 24-23 score late in the third quarter.

In the *Miami Herald*, referring to Miami's speed, Donnie Nickey said, "I think we've got the athletes that can match up", and Willis McGahee agreed, saying, "Their speed is good enough to stay with us." Dan Le Batard of the *Herald* wrote, "Miami has proven vulnerable to the run, the quarterback draw especially."

The December 27 *Columbus Dispatch* quoted Miami's assistant coach Art Kehoe with, "If you think Ohio State beating us would be the shock of the century, you're mistaken."

In the December 30 *Dispatch*, Ken Dorsey said of Matt Wilhelm, "He's a great player. He's somebody we've got to account for. He's all over the field. He's very active, and he gets a lot done." It would turn out that Wilhelm would give Dorsey a rude awakening late in the game. Dorsey, like Krenzel, was a *USA Today* Honorable Mention All-American in high school.

Even Trev Alberts of ESPN, a perceived Buckeyes-hater, was quoted in the *Dispatch* with, "Ohio State matches up quite well with Miami."

However, in another quote in the *Dispatch*, Dorsey said, "We feel comfortable being in close games where we have to pull it out." Kelly King wrote in *Sports Illustrated* that Miami had the nation's best offensive line.

If the Buckeyes' defensive coordinator, Mark Dantonio, had read the *Dispatch*, he would have perked up at the comments of Miami's center Brett Romberg: "I wouldn't want to be a defensive coordinator going against our football team." and "I don't think anybody is comparable to our speed and strength." However, in the *Gainesville Sun*, Romberg said. "We could easily get knocked off. People are downplaying the whole deal of Ohio State not rising to the occasion, but we know, we watch film. It's going to be as hard a game as we've had this year, probably the hardest we've ever played."

Dean Sensanbaugher, the 1943 freshman running back—who was living in Florida, fittingly, at the time of the Fiesta Bowl—referred to Clarett's injuries as he was quoted in the *Lakeland Ledger* with, "... if he plays the whole game, there's a possibility that Ohio State will win."

Sensanbaugher had played in an improbable game as a freshman for Paul Brown in 1943, a game that had a, putting it mildly, delayed penalty call and is termed the game that had a "fifth quarter". The game was played on the 13th (naturally) of November. The *Columbus Dispatch* story mentioned that the official—one of four in the game—who detected the penalty was from Michigan. The Ohio State media guide describes the finish as "With a game apparently ending in a 26-all tie, Ohio State and

Illinois left the field. But the teams were called back 20 minutes later when it was discovered the Illini were called for a penalty on the Buckeyes' final play. With little of the crowd remaining, John Stungis kicked a 27-yard field goal—the first of his career—for a 29-26 OSU win." Paul Walker of the *Dispatch*, a high school and college football official, wrote, "The ball didn't clear the cross bar by more than two feet. It just barely went over and there for a second while the ball was at its peak, those of us on the sidelines thought it would fall short." A caption for a *Dispatch* photo used the term "overtime". Like the opportunistic Buckeyes of 2002, this team recovered an Illinois fumble on the 23-yard line with 10 seconds remaining. They had an incomplete pass into the end zone on the apparent last play of the game. Sensanbaugher scored a touchdown on a five-yard run earlier in the game, and the Ohio State website shows him as gaining 170 yards on 33 carries. Another *Dispatch* story had, "Illinois was a team built on speed", while, "Ohio's emphasis was on power, on making short but sure gains. In short, on retaining possession of the ball." On the following day, a *Dispatch* story mentioned that Illinois coach Ray Eliot was "more incensed about the timing ... than he was about the offside or calling his boys back on the field from various stages of undress." Interestingly, the game program lists the title for Brown and Eliot as "Director of Football".

Given that a freshman (Stungis) had recorded the winning points against a team whose colors include orange—while the Buckeyes were dressed in white uniforms—and that the game had a combined 55 points, and that a field goal was barely good with no time on the clock, and the delayed penalty call, could history repeat itself?

The Fiesta Bowl would match two running backs who had over 1,000 yards and had games of over 200 yards in the regular season. The *Gainesville Sun* reported that, "If not for his fear of flying, Maurice Clarett might well be battling Willis McGahee for playing time in the Miami backfield.", and quoted Clarett with, "I wanted to go to Miami. I'm not going to lie ... Coach (Jim) Tressel knew I wanted to go to Miami, but

I was too scared to fly." McGahee's bio on the www.miamihurricanes. com website mentions that he chose Miami over Florida, Florida State, Alabama, LSU … and Ohio State. The December 28 *Columbus Dispatch* mentioned that, "McGahee seriously considered going to Ohio State. But he didn't like the cold weather, and his mother didn't want to move to Columbus. So he stayed home and signed with Miami." It quoted him as saying, "I wanted to go to Ohio State, but things change as you go along." He had runs of 61, 68, and 69 yards in the season, while Clarett's longest was 59 yards.

The bio on the www.miamihurricanes.com website for Kellen Winslow, their tight end, lists that he chose Miami over Michigan State, Washington, UCLA, Texas, Michigan, Southern California … and Ohio State. The bio on receiver Ethenic Sands, who would have three receptions in the Fiesta Bowl, shows that he chose Miami over Florida State, Ohio State, and Temple.

The December 10 *Columbus Dispatch* reported that Miami's center Brett Romberg, a native of Windsor, Ontario, said that his favorite teams growing up were Ohio State and Michigan and that he had narrowed his choices to OSU and Miami. The *Dispatch* also reported that offensive guard Sherko Haji-Rasouli considered only Miami and Ohio State.

The two quarterbacks were noted for their work in the classroom, in addition to on the field; Dorsey was a three-time BIG EAST All-Academic Team member. Rusty Miller of the Associated Press reported that Krenzel was seventh among Division I-A quarterbacks with an efficiency rating of 148.1, and Dorsey was eighth at 148. Dorsey came into the game with a 38-1 record as a starter, and Krenzel had a 14-1 record, although in the one loss, the Outback Bowl, he played in only two full series. In that game, when South Carolina scored their four touchdowns, Krenzel had not played in the preceding Ohio State possession.

The game also matched two receivers who had over 1,000 yards— Michael Jenkins, who attended Leto High School in Tampa, and Andre

Johnson, who attended Miami Senior High School. Interestingly, Johnson was only the second player in Miami history to gain 1,000 or more yards receiving in a season, while Jenkins was the fourth Buckeye to achieve the mark, following Cris Carter, Terry Glenn, and David Boston. The *Tampa Bay Times*, reporting on Jenkins's commitment to Ohio State out of high school, wrote that he was "... arguably the most versatile high school football player in Hillsborough County last season," and had, "Jenkins, who played running back, quarterback, wide receiver, cornerback, linebacker, both safeties and returned kicks for Leto, chose the Buckeyes after visits to Notre Dame, Virginia Tech and Georgia Tech."

Note: as I was researching the Columbus Dispatch archives for this book, I did a double take when I saw two headlines in the Faith and Values section of the newspaper from the day of the game: PARISH'S ROOTS RUN DEEP and URBAN MINISTRY OFFERS MEALS AND OPPORTUNITIES.

While the Buckeyes were preparing on January 2 for a team from Florida that had the number four and number five finishers in the Heisman Trophy voting—Willis McGahee and Ken Dorsey—Iowa was in Florida for the Orange Bowl, which they lost to USC in a game that had a combined 55 points, 38-17. That game featured the Heisman Trophy winner, Carson Palmer of USC, and the runner-up, Brad Banks of Iowa.

The Hurricanes elected to wear their green jerseys for only the third time in the season, having worn their orange jerseys four times. The last time that they wore green was in the Pittsburgh game, when they survived a late incomplete pass to win, 28-21.

The honorary captain was someone who was familiar with streaks, Cal Ripken Jr.

In the pregame interview for ABC, Coach Coker told Lynn Swann that one of the keys for the Hurricanes was to "Not turn the ball over." He would prove to be right in his prediction but would be disappointed in his team's execution.

THE FIRST QUARTER

The Buckeyes had the ball first. When they kicked off the season against Texas Tech, the starting left tackle was Ivan Douglas, and the starting left guard was Mike Stafford (the only senior starter on offense). In this game, they were Rob Sims and Adrien Clarke, respectively. The Buckeyes' offensive line consisted of four juniors and a freshman. Nick Mangold, another freshman, would see significant time in the game, while Miami's defensive front four were all seniors.

The first possession of the game started inauspiciously, as the Buckeyes had a penalty on the first play for having 12 players in the huddle—Chris Gamble had raced onto the field, thinking that he was supposed to be in on offense—and Clarett lost two yards following the penalty. However, the next play was a sign of things to come, as Krenzel had an 11-yard run. He would later have another 11-yard gain, the two longest runs of the game for either team.

A five-yard penalty on the first play, which was the first of nine penalties that the Buckeyes would finish with in the game ... that formula had worked well in the Michigan game of 2001, so why not again?

On the Buckeyes' punt on their first possession, Keith Jackson, calling the game for ABC, informed how dangerous Miami's Roscoe Parrish was as a punt returner; he would prove it on the last punt of the game. Cie Grant left with a bruised rib on the first possession on defense, replaced by A. J. Hawk, but he returned after a short rest. Spoiler Alert: He would make a big play with the game on the line. In the previous bowl game, he also was shaken up in the first half and came back with a big play near the end.

Conversely, the Hurricanes' first play was a positive one for the Buckeyes, as Will Smith came in off the left side of the Miami offensive line untouched and sacked Ken Dorsey with one hand, for a loss of three yards. It was only the ninth sack of Dorsey in the season. The

Buckeyes' last play of the game would also entail pressure on Dorsey by an untouched defender. Kenny Peterson also sacked Dorsey on the seventh play of their first possession.

The Hurricanes scored on their second possession, going 52 yards in five plays, with two of those plays a 28-yard pass to Kellen Winslow and a 25-yard touchdown pass to Roscoe Parrish, thanks to a block by McGahee on a blitzing Donnie Nickey. Nickey came about 17 yards from his safety position on his blitz, as Dorsey launched his pass from the 34. The 165-pound Parrish dragged Doss into the end zone for the last five yards. During the drive, Will Smith and Winslow had a minor skirmish that Winslow felt that Smith had instigated; Dan Fouts said on ABC's telecast that the Buckeyes should have been penalized.

Dustin Fox took part of the blame for the touchdown. In a *Sports Illustrated* online story, he was quoted with, "A few plays earlier I had I blitzed off the edge and McGahee almost knocked me out. I'm pretty sure I had a concussion. I don't remember too much about the game after that hit, but I do remember I was supposed to be on Roscoe. I told Doss, 'I don't know what's going on. I don't know where I am.' So Doss took Roscoe." Fox also wrote in a Twitter post: "When Roscoe scores that first touchdown, I didn't know the play call and hung [Mike Doss] out to dry because I was still woozy. Doss wasn't too happy with me." You can see Fox moving from the left side to the right side as the play begins, and he was not near any Hurricane as the play developed. It was Parrish's second career touchdown reception and his first against a Division I-A team, having had the other one against Florida A&M in the opener.

On the Buckeyes' first play following the touchdown, Krenzel launched a pass that was in the air for about 57 yards as he was pressured back to his eight-yard line, but Sean Taylor tipped and intercepted the ball at the Miami 35-yard line. The Hurricanes then reached the Buckeyes' 44-yard line for the second time, but had to punt each time.

Krenzel's only completion in the first quarter was 12 yards to Jenkins (#12) and gave the quarterback exactly 2,000 yards on the season to that point. Troy Smith, redshirted in his first season but in uniform, on the sideline congratulated Jenkins on the catch. It was the Buckeyes' first first down of the game, and it came with less than 30 seconds left in the quarter.

On the last play of the quarter, it appeared that Clarett's run to the right side was supposed to be a reverse hand-off to Gamble, but he kept the ball and was met by four defenders for no gain.

At the end of the quarter, the Buckeyes had run 10 plays that gained 33 yards, had started two of their four possessions with a five-yard penalty, and had thrown an interception in another.

THE SECOND QUARTER

Groom had a 63-yard punt that forced Parrish to retreat 20 yards to inside his 10-yard line and allowed the coverage to hem him in for only a six-yard return, with the tackle by Steven Moore, one of Moore's three tackles in the season. Moore was lined up on the right side of the formation but ran to the left side to make the tackle near the opposite sideline, fighting off two blockers. Moore was playing in his 13th game of the season and attended St. Charles, a Catholic high school in Columbus. Another graduate of a Catholic high school in Columbus would make a key tackle on a Parrish punt return late in the game.

In the Miami possession, Gamble was called for defensive holding that may have prevented a big gain to Andre Johnson. He would have a similar situation on Miami's last possession of the game.

The Hurricanes turned the ball over three times in the quarter on two interceptions and a fumble. Dorsey had only three interceptions in the previous six games, in which he had 173 passes. The Buckeyes scored two touchdowns in the span of 78 seconds, one after an interception that Mike Doss returned 35 yards to the Miami 17-yard line, and the other after a sack/fumble caused by Kenny Peterson on a blind-side tackle; the fumble was recovered by Darrion Scott at the Miami 14-yard line. Doss returned his interception when it went off the hands of Andre Johnson. Ironically, Doss (jersey #2) was tackled by Willis McGahee (jersey #2) on his return; a Buckeye running back would record a tackle on a Miami interception return in the third quarter. Doss had also played as a tailback in high school, so his athletic return was no surprise. After his interception, the Buckeyes had nearly as many yards from interception returns (47) as they did on plays from scrimmage (56).

Krenzel muscled in for the first touchdown on a one-yard sneak on fourth down following a timeout, and Clarett scored the second touchdown on a seven-yard run. After Clarett's touchdown, Buckeye fans were wondering, who is that guy on the sideline in a red sweater vest, pumping his right fist? It was the left-handed Coach Tressel, but the display of emotion was out of character.

The Buckeyes had not scored any points off turnovers in the previous 11 quarters, and had not had an offensive touchdown following a turnover in the previous six games.

The Buckeyes had forced a third turnover before those two when Dustin Fox intercepted Dorsey and returned it to the Miami 37-yard line. Wilhelm closed in on Dorsey and leaped high to affect the pass. The Buckeye possession was hurt by a delay-of-game penalty, but Krenzel set up a 4th-and-1 play at the Miami 17-yard line with an 11-yard run. The ball was on the right hash mark, and the Buckeyes lined up for a field goal. But, they faked the kick, and Andy Groom, the holder, was stopped short on his carry to the short side of the field. Groom had the option to pitch the ball to Nugent, trailing the play. If Miami had film on the Buckeyes from the 2000 season, they would have seen that Groom had gained 14 yards on a fake field goal attempt against Iowa. In an interview on www.elevenwarriors.com, he said that in that 2000 game, he was supposed to roll out and throw a pass to Dan Stultz, the placekicker.

Both of Dorsey's interceptions were on third-down plays. His bio on www.miamihurricanes.com has, for the 2002 season: "... on third down plays, he completed 78 of 123 (63.4%) attempts with only 4 interceptions."

When Miami had the ball after Clarett's touchdown, there was 1:10 remaining in the first half, but they had only one timeout left. They ran four plays to reach their 42-yard line, then elected to let the clock run out, rather than run a play on fourth-and-one.

The 14-7 halftime lead marked the first time in almost three months, going back to the San Jose State game on October 12, that the Buckeyes had scored two touchdowns in the first half. They had also gone 14 straight quarters, going back to the Minnesota game, without scoring two touchdowns in a quarter. The Buckeyes finished the first half with 80 yards of total offense—their lowest in any half of the season—and a slim 10-second advantage in time of possession, thanks to having 4:20 more than the Hurricanes in the second quarter. Miami had 15 carries for 11 yards in the first half, with McGahee gaining 25 yards on 12 carries, boosted by a 10-yard gain on the last play of the half. He had all 12 of their designed run plays, and seven of the 12 gained one yard or less, with five for a loss.

All of the Buckeyes' plays on offense in the first quarter had been on their side of the field, reaching only the 30-yard line on their best drive, and all of their plays on offense in the second quarter had been on the Miami side of the field, starting on the Miami 37-yard line or deeper.

Coming into the game, Miami had scored an average of 22.7 points in the first half. This was the first time that they had failed to score at least 10 points in the first half. Dorsey completed eight of ten passes for 119 yards in the first quarter, but three of seven for 23 yards in the second. The Buckeyes had converted one of six third-down opportunities in the first half, to run their streak to two of 14 going back to the Michigan game.

When interviewed at halftime by ABC sideline reporter Todd Harris, similar to his halftime prediction in the previous bowl game, Tressel said, "It's going to be a battle. It's going to be down to the final second. We're going to play as hard as we can and see if we deserve it." Like his "310 days" speech, he would hit the nail on the head again. A graphic on ABC's broadcast showed that this Miami team was not as dominant as its 2001 edition. In the previous season, they led at halftime in every game, but this was the third time in 13 games this season that they trailed.

THE THIRD QUARTER

Gamble had the longest play of the game on offense—and the Buckeyes' longest reception of the year—a 57-yard catch in the third quarter on a third-and-15 play. It was Krenzel's longest completion of his career to that point, and the longest pass play of the season that the Hurricanes gave up. Gamble had about a five-yard separation from the defender, who recovered for the tackle. If the pass had not been a tad underthrown so that Gamble did not have to wait on it, he may have scored. Gamble lost the ball as he was tackled, but the Field Judge, Terry Porter, emphatically indicated that Gamble had been down before the ball came out.

> Krenzel: *If that is a better throw, Chris scores. I got it up a little late and underestimated how far downfield Chris was, how fast he was. We got the safety, I think it was Maurice Sikes, to kind of jump the middle route, and in that cover-two, that left Chris over the top wide open. I underthrew it probably by five or seven yards. Chris is just so dang fast that you could definitely see that I underthrew it, but had I not underthrown it, it's a walk-in touchdown.*

On the next play from the six-yard line, Tressel called for a pass play. In a special program on the Big Ten Network, Tressel said that he called the play because Miami was not easy to run on. Actually, Clarett had scored a touchdown in the second quarter on a seven-yard run. Sean Taylor intercepted Krenzel's pass in the end zone and brought the

ball out, but Clarett ripped the ball away on the return to give possession back to the Buckeyes. It was Clarett's only tackle of his Ohio State
career. Branden Joe, coming out of the backfield on the right side, was
uncovered on the play, but Krenzel tried to hit Ben Hartsock in the end
zone. If Hartsock had caught the pass, it might have set a championship
game record for a touchdown pass involving two players with the highest combined Grade Point Average. Add in the fact that they shared the
same Zodiac sign.

It was Krenzel's only interception of the season in the end zone; the
opponents scored a total of only three points following his seven interceptions, with the field goal coming in the Purdue game.

If the pass had been completed to Joe, it would have been his second touch of the year on offense, and his second touch of his Ohio State
career; he had one carry for one yard otherwise. Taylor appeared to have
been covering Joe, but left him to head to the path of the pass to Hartsock.
Clarett's recovery, tackle, and strip was reminiscent of Gamble's tackle on
the return of Krenzel's fumble in the Penn State game. Two of the most
important tackles of the season came by players who were on offense.
Taylor had half of his four interceptions of the season in this game and
tied his career high for tackles with 11.

Clarett hustled to make the play after picking himself off the ground
from making a block, and had a clump of sod in the top of his face mask
as a result of the tackle. Woody Hayes would have scolded Taylor for car-
rying the ball in his inside arm. The Clarett strip was compared to the
similar play 10 seasons previously when Alabama's George Teague stripped
the ball from Miami's Lamar Thomas in the Sugar Bowl, another game
that denied Miami a national championship. Both Clarett and Teague
wore #13. In each case, the Miami player was running from left to right
on the TV screen.

Taylor's 28-yard return was the longest by an opponent in the season.
Nugent kicked a 44-yard field goal (an OSU record 25th in a season) in

the ensuing possession, after the Buckeyes could gain only one yard in three plays. The sequence was eerily similar to what happened against Michigan in the 2001 game—an interception into the north end zone on a first down play that led shortly to points for the Buckeyes. In the last three games of the regular season, the Buckeyes never had a ten-point lead at any point of a game, until now with the score 17-7. For Nugent, the game was in another metropolitan area that he would eventually call home; he would play for the Arizona Cardinals in 2009.

This was the Buckeyes' last score in regulation. Their three scoring possessions in regulation had a total of 12 plays and 25 yards after subtracting the seven penalty yards by Miami.

The scoring run in bowl games the last two years for the Buckeyes was now 45-10, after outscoring South Carolina, 28-3. Miami had beaten Nebraska, 37-14, for the BCS Championship the season before, but was outscored in the second half of that game, 14-3. This 17-7 score meant that the scoring run for Miami's opponents was 31-10 over those two championship games and 25-7 in this season.

McGahee scored on a nine-yard run, where he started to the left but broke it to the wide side on the right, to make the score 17-14. His 28th touchdown was the third-highest for a season at the time, trailing Barry Sanders and Mike Rozier. He had 25 of his 67 yards on three carries in the drive. McGahee and Winslow (35 yards) combined for all of the 60 yards that the Hurricanes gained in the drive. McGahee's 10-yard gain was one of his two longest in the game, but in each of the other games in the season, he had a longer gain than 10 yards. It was the first rushing touchdown given up by the Buckeye defense in 21 quarters, going back to the Penn State game.

The Buckeyes' 87 yards of offense in the quarter was more than what they had in the entire first half. It was the only quarter in regulation where they outgained the Hurricanes, though they were outscored, 7-3.

THE FOURTH QUARTER

It was the third time in the season that Miami trailed in the fourth quarter. The Buckeyes were not impressed; they had trailed four times in the fourth quarter, against Cincinnati, Wisconsin, Purdue, and Michigan. Would the third time be a bad luck charm for the Hurricanes?

A key play of the game occurred when McGahee was knocked out of the game with a knee injury on a tackle by Will Allen. It came on a screen pass to the right side on a third-and-ten play. McGahee had played just five games during his senior season in high school due to a knee injury and had a mid-season knee injury in 2001 at Miami. A screen pass to the right side to McGahee had produced a 77-yard gain against Boston College and a 68-yard gain on Miami's winning touchdown drive against Florida State. The Buckeyes' defense was most likely prepared for it. In a *Sports Illustrated* online story, on the tenth anniversary of the Fiesta Bowl, Allen said, "We knew the screen was coming based on their formation. I was breaking on it before the ball was thrown."

On the next play, Todd Sievers missed a 54-yard field goal; the attempt was not much of a stretch for him, as he had made a 53-yard field goal at Florida during the season, and, as a 17-year-old at Ankeny High School in Iowa, he had made one from 63 yards, an Iowa state record.

The miss by Sievers capped a set of five significant plays. Allen had made a hard hit on Winslow on a catch for a first down, followed by Dorsey overthrowing a pass from the Ohio State 35-yard line to Parrish, who had a step on the defender and was inside the five-yard line, followed by Doss nearly intercepting a pass that he could have taken the distance, followed by the McGahee injury, ending in the missed field goal. That was the only time in the game that Dorsey passed on four consecutive plays.

Miami was now faced with the fact that their next leading rusher on the season had less than one-fourth the yards that McGahee had. That was Jason Geathers, who had considered Ohio State in his recruiting process and had games of 199, 86, and 72 yards in the season. However, Geathers had moved back to receiver after Kevin Beard had a season-ending knee injury in their tenth game. McGahee had 28 of their 33 rushing touchdowns, and Geathers had three. That left Jarrett Payton—who had about one-eighth the yards that McGahee had gained and had no carries in the game—next in line. He was coming off his two best games of the season, a combined 14 carries for 96 yards. Payton, like Kellen Winslow, Jr., is the son of an NFL Hall of Fame member, Walter.

By comparison, Ohio State had more heavily-used running backs due to Clarett's injuries—Lydell Ross, who had one-half the yards that Clarett had, and Maurice Hall—and a quarterback who could run.

On the possession following Miami's missed field goal, the Buckeyes had their only possession where they made three first downs. On the third play, Krenzel was hit by Jonathan Vilma, who had a clear shot at him, and was lifted off his feet and sent to the turf after getting a pass off. *Sports Illustrated* had described Vilma as soft-spoken, and he described himself as quiet and easygoing, so he let his playing do the talking for him. On second-and-12 from the Miami 30-yard line, Krenzel tried to connect with Bam Childress over the middle; a completion would have gained another first down. Miami's defensive back Kelly Jennings disrupted the pass, though it appears that his right hand may have grabbed Chidress's jersey for a moment. Jennings would commit an obvious grab later in the quarter.

Bam Childress: *I think that Kelly Jennings, with his right hand, he grabbed it a little bit.*

Nugent missed a 42-yard attempt—shorter than the one that he had made—to the right with 6:36 left in regulation. He was successful on 25 of 27 on field goals in the season before this one. Nugent and Iowa's Nate Kaeding, who won the Lou Groza Award, finished the season with

120 points each to break the conference record of 111 points set by Neil Rackers of Illinois in 1999, but Nugent came close to holding the record by himself. If the field goal had been good, the final score could have been a 20-14 win for only the fourth time in Ohio State history—previously in 1958, in the national championship season of 1954, and in the very first game in its history, played on May 3, 1890 at Ohio Wesleyan University.

> Nugent: *To be honest with you, there are a few kicks in your career that you sit there and you're just like, I had the same exact kick my senior year. It was almost verbatim on the right hash, like about 42 yards, I think something like that at Northwestern in overtime, the same exact kick, and it's that one kick where you hit it perfect, everything feels great, you look up, and you miss. 99 times out of 100, I know exactly what I did wrong on a kick, but those two kicks I sat there thinking, I don't have a clue, I don't know what I did wrong and ended up watching film, and my steps were incorrect. You want to make sure you have a 90 degree angle, but in college you have such a harsh angle when you're on the right or left hash. I kind of went straight along with the field, not with my angle. So, on both kicks, I was a little too close to the ball where I kind of missed them before I even kicked them, where I was lined up. The ball or my body where I lined myself up, both kicks went exactly where I aimed them, but, mentally I was not even that aiming outside like I did so, but just just incorrect steps on my walk back. It's one I wish I could have back.*

The possessions for each team that ended in a missed field goal were almost identical; Miami had 11 plays for 39 yards, and Ohio State had 11 plays for 38 yards.

The Hurricanes appeared to be headed to the go-ahead touchdown when Dorsey connected with Parrish on a pass from the Ohio State 47-yard line to inside the 25-yard line, but Nickey and Fox jarred the ball loose, and Will Allen recovered it on the 18-yard line for the fifth and last turnover of the game. It was Allen's only fumble recovery of the season, and it meant that all three of his turnover plays took place with under six minutes remaining in the fourth quarter and inside the opponent's 20-yard line. Miami had committed a total of three turnovers in its previous four games. Parrish, a freshman, came into the game with 14 receptions, but had a season-high five in this game. It would take him two more seasons before he had a game with six receptions, in a loss to Clemson.

This meant that Miami's 28-yard return of an interception and Parrish's 26-yard reception, their second-longest of the game, both resulted in turnovers. Earlier, their longest kickoff return of 39 yards resulted in no points.

There was 5:08 on the clock, and Krenzel picked up a first down on third down with a four-yard run, exactly the yards that were needed. The Buckeyes faced another third-down situation at their 32-yard line, third-and-six. Krenzel threw a pass to Gamble that was ruled incomplete. Replays showed Kelly Jennings grabbing Gamble's jersey on the play, that Gamble may have caught the ball inbounds anyway, and that Miami may have committed a late hit on Krenzel. Ohio State appeared to have snapped the ball with the play clock at zeroes; they were draining the play clock consistently in the fourth quarter. If the play had stood, the Buckeyes would have had a first down with Miami having only one timeout remaining. If you are keeping score, the Buckeyes were now oh-for-two on the season on The-Officials-Missed-The-Grab-of-The-Jersey calls, though the one in Purdue did not affect the Holy Buckeye touchdown.

This set up Andy Groom for the last and most important most-important-play-in-football of his career. Up to this point, Roscoe Parrish had been limited to one punt return for six yards. Groom and Mike Doss combined on a touchdown-saving tackle on Parrish's 50-yard return with 2:02 remaining in regulation. For Groom, this was his only assisted tackle of the season. It appeared that A. J. Hawk had been blocked in the back around the Miami 40-yard line, but a penalty was not called.

A. J. Hawk: *It was a big-time hit in the back, a total clip.*

Parrish fielded the ball at his 24-yard line; Doss made a swipe at him at the Miami 30-yard line, and like Clarett's key play of the fumble strip, made up a lot of ground to assist in the tackle. Like Steven Moore earlier, Groom attended a Catholic school in Columbus, Bishop Hartley. The tackles on Parrish's two returns were by a former walk-on (Groom) and a walk-on (Moore).

That play had several similarities to the 1993 Holiday Bowl, where defensive back Ty Howard made a touchdown-saving tackle on a 52-yard pass play on Brigham Young's last possession, to keep the lead at 28-21. Larry Coker was Howard's position coach in that season, his first year as an Ohio State assistant. Both Howard (Briggs) and Groom attended high school in Columbus. That Holiday Bowl win was the first bowl win for John Cooper, and this BCS win would be the first bowl win for Jim Tressel. Both games were decided by seven points where the Buckeyes scored last; BYU had four unsuccessful plays after a first-and-goal at the Ohio State six-yard line on their last possession.

Parrish's return meant that the four longest returns against the Buckeyes in the season had come away from Columbus. Illinois had a 52-yard return, Northwestern had a 46-yard return, and Cincinnati had a 29-yard return. Of those four, only Illinois followed it with a touchdown; the other three produced two field goals and a possession that stalled when the first half ended.

Doss had been covering Parrish on his touchdown catch in the first quarter. Parrish had atoned for his fumble from earlier in the quarter, and his return to the 26-yard line gave the Hurricanes their only starting position in regulation in Ohio State territory, while the Buckeyes had four possessions that started in Miami territory. In the fourth quarter, Parrish had two receptions and the punt return for a total of 84 yards, but the Hurricanes scored only three points in the quarter. In six games in the regular season, Miami had scored at least ten points in the fourth quarter.

Simon Fraser, another central Ohio product—from Upper Arlington High School—recorded his only tackle of the game two plays later, sacking Dorsey. Cie Grant blitzed on the play, and the Miami lineman tried to fend off both Grant and Fraser, which gave Fraser a path to Dorsey. The Buckeyes defense allowed Miami to gain only three yards on three plays. Miami's last offensive play in regulation was a seven-yard pass to Payton, for only his second reception of the season.

Miami took a timeout with three seconds remaining. Michigan had reached the Buckeyes' 24-yard line for the last play with one second remaining and failed. Miami was now on the Buckeyes' 23-yard line for perhaps the last play.

After Miami's timeout, Tressel tried to ice Miami's kicker, Todd Sievers, with two timeouts. After about five minutes of timeouts, Sievers kicked a 40-yard field goal—that was barely good at the right upright—on the last play of regulation to force overtime. The rule change to prohibit consecutive timeouts would come many years later. In the January 18, 2003 *Columbus Dispatch,* Matt Wilhelm was quoted as saying that the kicked ball hit his thumb. He had helped secure the win over Cincinnati by deflecting the Bearcats' last pass in the first of the seven games decided by seven points or less.

One of the officials who signaled the kick as good was the Field Judge, Terry Porter. Sievers led college football in the season with 66 extra points, but had missed his previous four field goal attempts, including one in this game, the 54-yard attempt. He had made 12 of 21 attempts on the season before this kick, but this one was his first in almost two months. His 59% success rate on the season was the worst of his three-year career; he had made 81% the season before. As in the Michigan game, the Buckeyes had the misfortune of having a struggling opposing kicker becoming accurate at the right time for his team. Krenzel, wearing jersey #16, had been the hero up until this point, and Sievers, wearing jersey #16, now had his shining moment.

Mike Nugent: *What was I thinking then? All I thought about was, assume it's going right down the middle, because it's one of those things, you don't sit there and just pray, I hope he misses, I hope he misses, you just don't want that attitude; obviously, you want the guy to miss so we win the national championship, but you have to go in thinking, okay, he's going to make it, I've got to be ready to kick the game winner at the end of this game, you just kind of assume that you're going to be kicking on the next series. That was extremely clutch, what a kick, the last second to tie the game for the national championship, I still to this day don't think it got enough credit. I actually have never met him and haven't seen him since that night, and I just want to tell him, that is a tough kick, what a ball to be able to hit that. That makes that kick even tougher, coming off four misses in a row.*

Andy Groom: *I actually roomed with Sievers at the East-West Shrine game a few days after the national championship. We ended up trading our warm-ups, I still have his warm-up, never worn it, but it's cool, it's up in my attic. He was a great guy, never said anything negative, a very good person. He had his ring from the previous year. Obviously, he wasn't happy with the situation but handled it very well.*

A team that had averaged 42 points per game in the regular season came within a few inches of finishing with only 14 in this game. If Miami had scored a touchdown instead of the field goal, the final score could have been a 21-17 loss for the first time in Ohio State history.

The Buckeyes had made their field goal on a possession in the third quarter that gained one yard, and the Hurricanes made their field goal on a possession that gained three yards. It was the second straight bowl game with the opposing kicker kicking a field goal on the last play of regulation, and the kickers had similar last names—Daniel Weaver had the winning kick for South Carolina. For some reason, the official account shows that the field goal was successful with one second remaining. Keith Jackson was 0-for-2 winging it on his recollection of the Ohio State loss to Oklahoma in 1977, 25 years previously, when he could not recall the Sooners' kicker Uwe von Schamann's name and thought that his field goal was 43 yards. In fact, it was 41 yards. That field goal came with three seconds remaining and was also into the north goal. Ohio State had beaten Miami in that same season, 10-0 in Columbus.

In the last 11:26 of regulation, the game had at least seven game-changing plays—the McGahee injury, two missed field goals, the fumble by Roscoe Parrish that gave the ball to the Buckeyes on their 18-yard line, the missed call of Gamble being grabbed, the 50-yard punt return by Parrish, and the Sievers field goal on the final play.

After four quarters, the Buckeyes had generated 215 yards of total offense. Their 215 yards in regulation were a season-low, with the previous low of 264 in the Michigan game. They had 135 yards in the second half, compared to 80 in the first half, but scored only three points in the second half, compared to 14 in the first half. When the two teams met in the 1999 season, the Buckeyes had 220 yards. In the three games against Miami, the Buckeye defense had recorded a total of 10 turnovers, but the offense managed a total of only six points in the second half. The Miami defense had been fairly on-target; they had given up 18 points per game in the regular season.

Krenzel had completed only five of 16 passes in regulation, the same numbers that Number 2 Penn State had in upsetting Number 1 Miami in the 1987 Fiesta Bowl for the national championship.

THE FIRST OVERTIME

While the Buckeyes had no overtimes in its history before the season, this was Miami's third, and in its third different venue. In 1997, they had a 45-44 win in double overtime at Boston College, and in 1998, they lost to Virginia Tech at home, 27-20. In that game, their quarterback wore jersey #11.

To establish the possessions, referee Randy Christal tossed the coin and caught it in his hands, instead of letting it fall to the turf, not something that you see every game. The Buckeyes won and deferred.

Miami elected to take the ball on offense and scored on a seven-yard pass to Winslow, as Dorsey launched a jump-pass. Will Allen was called for pass interference on the play, which Miami naturally declined. Though it had no impact on the play, the contact appeared to be incidental. Dorsey's 28th touchdown pass of the season matched the 28 that McGahee had scored on the ground. The Buckeyes had scored 17 straight points to take a 17-7 lead, followed by Miami scoring 17 straight points to take a 24-17 lead. It was the only time all season where the Buckeyes trailed by at least seven points after halftime.

The Buckeyes' possession faltered with a five-yard penalty for a false start and a four-yard sack on second down. The offensive line had their worst three-game stretch in the Minnesota, Purdue, and Illinois games with 12 sacks, but gave up only two in the Michigan game, and this one was the only sack of the game. On third-and-14, Krenzel missed on a screen pass to Clarett to the right.

> Krenzel: *You design every play to accomplish the goal, which at that point is/was to get a first down. But, in the event that it didn't happen, in third-and-long in four-down territory, you're really working hard to simply try to make it fourth and manageable. Similarly, when you are not in four-down territory, on second and long, you're trying*

to get to third and manageable. Worst case scenario, that screen pass would have been just to try to get to fourth and manageable, which we obviously didn't do the best job of that, either.

Neither team took a timeout. On fourth-and-14, Krenzel connected on a 17-yard completion to Jenkins on the right sideline in front of both Sean Taylor and Glenn Sharpe to keep the drive, game, and season alive.

On the ensuing second-and-ten play, Miami's Jonathan Vilma and Sean Taylor gave Krenzel a hard hit on his seven-yard scramble to the five-yard line. It was practically identical to the hit that he had taken at the Michigan five-yard line in the first touchdown drive of that game.

On third-and-three, Krenzel's pass to Hartsock in the end zone was incomplete. Again, there was much brain power at work. Krenzel and Hartsock would earn several academic honors, and Vilma earned BIG EAST All-Academic Team honors in 2001 and 2002, and first-team Verizon Academic All-American in 2002. Vilma had a career-high nine assisted tackles in the game.

The Buckeyes now faced another fourth down, fourth-and-three on the five-yard line. Miami took a timeout, during which ABC's analyst Dan Fouts said that Jenkins, the big-play receiver all season, and Ben Hartsock were the first two options. However, Krenzel immediately went to Gamble, the lone receiver on the right side, outside the hash marks—more on hash marks later. Miami blitzed and knocked Krenzel down—it was amazing that he got enough zip on the pass, which wobbled a bit—and Glenn Sharpe was called for pass interference by Field Judge Terry Porter, who waited about three seconds to throw his flag, first signaling defensive holding. The suspense was prolonged as referee Randy Christal consulted with two other officials before announcing the penalty.

If Gamble had caught the pass, it would have been his only touchdown catch of his Ohio State career and the third different way he had scored in the season; he previously had a touchdown on a rush and an interception return. And, he had a touchdown on a kickoff return against Cincinnati called back due to a penalty. A catch would have broken the 500-yard mark for receiving yards; he finished with 499 in the season. He probably would have set a championship game record for being the only player to score a touchdown and participate in over 100 plays. The Buckeyes had good fortune previously in the game when Sharpe, a true freshman, was defending; both of his tackles came on completions for first downs.

The Hurricanes entered the game averaging 10 penalties for 85 yards per game to lead the BIG EAST, and were penalized for more than twice as many yards as their opponents, but committed only six for 30 yards in the game. Their six penalties tied a season low, and their five in regulation were a season low, as were their 30 yards in penalties. They had gone the entire fourth quarter without a penalty. This was a team that had committed 14 penalties twice, against their rivals Florida and Florida State. The Buckeyes had committed the first four penalties of the game.

That was Krenzel's fifth and last pass of the game into the end zone. None of them were complete, but two of them led to positive outcomes, including the interception by Sean Taylor where Clarett stole the ball and led to Nugent's field goal. Krenzel could attribute his oh-fer to rust; since the Holy Buckeye play, which Jenkins caught at the goal line, he had no passes into the end zone in the Illinois or Michigan games, and none until less than four minutes remained in the second quarter of the Fiesta Bowl. The Michigan and Miami games represented the only time in the season that Krenzel would have consecutive games without a touchdown pass.

The full-game replay of the game does not capture the premature fireworks in Miami's orange and green colors. The play was in the orange-colored end zone, with a host of camera operators and photographers behind the end zone, wearing green tops. Krenzel, who was flattened on the play, fetched his helmet and signaled, "first down".

The 1997 Rose Bowl also had a controversial play in the south end zone, but that one went in the opponent's favor, and the Buckeyes also came out with a win. Arizona State's first touchdown was on a 25-yard pass that receiver Ricky Boyer never seemed to control. If video review had been in effect and the play had been overturned, we may not be talking about Joe Germaine's heroics on the winning drive. If the play had occurred in overtime and Ohio State had lost, it would have been Buckeye fans who were screaming for unfairness. It also appeared that Ohio State's Antoine Winfield may have interfered on the play. Pass interference is not a reviewable play, but if video review had overturned the touchdown, it would have been Sun Devil fans doing the screaming.

Terry Porter would be on the field for another monumental Ohio State game that involved the eventual national champions. He was the Field Judge in the 2005 game against Texas in Ohio Stadium, which the Longhorns won, 25-22, on their way to the BCS Championship win over USC, which broke the Trojans' 34-game winning streak. The same referee and umpire from the Fiesta Bowl were also officiating in that 2005 game. Porter made the touchdown signal on the go-ahead scoring catch by Limas Sweed of the Longhorns with 2:37 remaining. Sweed caught the pass near the sideline, and video review confirmed that it was the correct call. Eight Buckeyes who played in the Fiesta Bowl—Brandon Schnittker, Rob Sims, Nick Mangold, Ryan Hamby, Mike Kudla, Bobby Carpenter, A. J. Hawk, and Nate Salley—also played in the 2005 game against Texas.

Regardless of whether Miami fans agree with the pass interference call, it had to be a case of karma, given the questionable ruling on the third-down pass from Krenzel to Gamble on their last possession in regulation. Interestingly, ABC showed two angles on replays, but not from the end zone camera, which had been used on Winslow's touchdown. ABC's color commentator Dan Fouts—who had been the quarterback for San Diego Chargers teams when Kellen Winslow, Sr. was his main target from 1979 through 1987—was more vocal about the pass interference play

("Bad call ... bad call") than he was about the obvious grab of Gamble's jersey previously, when he said, "Little hold there, that should have been called". The first overtime drive took 11 plays to cover the 25 yards.

The September 2007 edition of *Referee* magazine included Porter's decision among the 18 best calls in officiating history. Big 12 Commissioner Kevin Weiberg told the *St. Louis Post-Dispatch*, "Terry Porter has been one of our highest-rated officials."

The *Oklahoman* newspaper on August 29, 2003 had a story on the call, "Porter was ripped for initially signaling defensive holding, then changing the call to interference. But Duncan [Donnie Duncan, the Big 12 director of football operations; the crew was a Big 12 crew] said both calls were correct. The Big 12 office reviewed the play and declared Porter's call right on four counts. On the fourth-down play, Duncan said, Miami cornerback Glenn Sharpe committed four fouls on Ohio State flanker Chris Gamble: holding first, then blocking Gamble's move to the inside (interference), then another hold and finally another interference." Ironically, Duncan had replaced Earle Bruce as the head coach at Iowa State in 1979 and had been an assistant under Barry Switzer of Oklahoma when the Sooners beat the Buckeyes in Columbus in 1977, 29-28, on Uwe von Schamann's field goal.

The same story has: "And for several years, NFL-level evaluators have graded Big 12 officials, and Porter consistently has been the best back judge.", and "... months before, ... Big 12 supervisor of officials Tim Millis issued his annual written report on his troops. About a certain back judge, Millis wrote: 'If the most important game comes down to one call by one official, Tim Millis wants Terry Porter making the call.' "

In a story on https://www.cigaraficionado.com/article/making-the-right-call-8465, referee Randy Christal said, "All anyone cared about on the pass interference call was how late the flag came, but if you watch the play on the tape, it was absolutely the correct call. The man was held three times on the same play."

The penalty placed the ball at the two-yard line. Three plays later, Krenzel scored on a one-yard sneak. He ran or passed for 21 of the 22 yards that the Buckeyes gained in the possession. Clarett gave a great effort on first down by breaking a tackle to turn a four-yard loss into a one-yard gain. Ohio State fans had to sweat out Nugent's PAT kick; it came from five yards further back after a false-start penalty.

THE SECOND OVERTIME

The Buckeyes had the ball first. Lydell Ross started the possession with a nine-yard gain, but was shaken up on the play. His two longest gains of the game of nine and five yards came in touchdown drives. Krenzel converted on a third-and-one play with a five-yard sneak. Krenzel hit Jenkins, running a rare crossing route from right to left, with a six-yard pass to put the ball on the five-yard line. Sean Taylor had tight coverage; an interception would have been his third of the game. Krenzel had been 0-for-5 passing on first down, with two interceptions, before completing the pass, and that gave Jenkins two receptions in overtime to match his two in regulation.

> Krenzel: *That's a play that we had in our repertoire, if you will, but we just hadn't hit him on that, underneath, X shallow route during that game, specifically.*

Maurice Sikes tackled Jenkins on the reception, giving him a career-high 12 tackles. However, it would be the last tackle for a Miami player in the game, as the next play was Maurice vs. Maurice; Clarett scored the winning touchdown on the next play, breaking a tackle by Sikes. His four previous rushes had gained one, one, zero, and zero yards. Earlier in the game, he had a five-rush streak of zero, one, zero, one, and one yard.

It was the third straight game that a player named Maurice scored the Buckeyes' winning touchdown. Maurice Hall had scored the last touchdown of the game against Minnesota, Illinois, and Michigan, also making it four of the last five games where a player named Maurice had scored the last touchdown. Clarett finished with an Ohio State freshman record of 18 touchdowns, but who would have guessed at the time that the winning touchdown would come on his last carry as a college player?

The 15 consecutive plays that the Buckeyes had on offense over the two overtime sessions were four more than in their 11-play possession that ended in a missed field goal. Of their four touchdown drives, this was the only one without a Miami penalty.

Similar to the 1997 Rose Bowl—where it was David Boston—a freshman scored the winning touchdown in the north end zone, it was a five-yard play in each case, and it was his second touchdown of the game. Each player has two syllables in his first and last name. In that Rose Bowl, the defense also gave up 17 points in regulation, and the Buckeyes also beat a previously undefeated team, Arizona State. Both Miami in 2002 and Arizona State in 1996 averaged more than 40 points per game.

On the first play of Miami's possession, Matt Wilhelm stopped Jarrett Payton for a one-yard loss, which would be the defense's 100th and last tackle for a loss in the season. On a blitz on the next play, Wilhelm floored Dorsey and knocked him out of the game for a play. Backup quarterback Derrick Crudup—whose Deerfield Beach High School mascot is The Bucks—completed an eight-yard pass to running back Quadtrine Hill in his only play.

Both teams took a timeout. When Dorsey converted on 4th-and-3 with a pass to Winslow, it seemed as if this was the game that would never end, since it was the fourth time that the game could have ended—following the field goal by Sievers at the end of regulation, the fourth down pass to Jenkins in the first overtime, and the pass interference call against Glenn Sharpe four plays later. In addition, the Buckeyes had nine other plays in the first overtime where they could have turned it over and ended the game, and the Hurricanes had seven other plays in the second overtime where they could have turned it over and ended the game.

On first-and-goal from the six-yard line, Gamble was called for pass interference on Dorsey's pass to Andre Johnson in the end zone. Tressel tried to appeal that the pass was uncatchable. That penalty may have saved the day for the Buckeyes.

The Hurricanes now had first-and-goal on the two-yard line. On first down, Payton gained only one yard, tackled by Cie Grant. On second down, Dorsey missed on a pass to a wide-open Eric Winston. If they had connected, it would have been Winston's only catch of the game, his third of the season, and his first in almost four months.

Miami's Quadtrine Hill—who was from the same hometown in Florida as Gamble, Sunrise—had only six previous carries in the season, his freshman year. Now, on third down, he was called on for his only carry of the game. Wilhelm stopped him for no gain.

Both teams had used their timeout on the previous fourth-down play. Miami had lined up with two tight ends and no wide receivers in the previous three plays, but used three wideouts on the 4th-and-goal play from the one-yard line.

Cie Grant bind-side blitzed Dorsey, throwing him to the turf, and Nickey knocked down the pass to close out the win. Defensive players are coached to knock down passes instead of trying to intercept them in situations like that. Ironically, the 2002 season would be the only one for Nickey without an interception.

Nickey [note that Buckeye fans were definitely not nitpicking]: *I could have caught the ball, but I dropped it.*

Appropriately, in the three biggest games of the past two seasons, including the two Michigan games, an Ohio native had the last touch on defense. The game had gone past midnight in the eastern time zone, but the Cinderella story did not change. The Buckeyes had blitzed on Miami's two touchdown pass plays, but the third time was a charm. They had a sack on Miami's first play of the game and had a near-sack on the last play of the game, with Grant and Will Smith both untouched on their plays. If Dorsey had completed the pass to Winston or to a receiver on the final play, Miami would have had 33 passing and 33 rushing touchdowns on the season. If Payton or Winston had scored, it would have been his only touchdown of the season.

Grant had had a late big play in the bowl game the previous year, an interception with 1:12 remaining, and is from New Philadelphia, Ohio. Woody, who coached there, must have been smiling.

In the span of five plays on their last possession, Miami had plays involving three little-used players—Hill, Crudup, and Winston—all of whom had no touches in the game before the possession. In their last possession, Miami had eight plays, and six of them gained one yard or less. They had three rushes, for minus-one, one, and zero yards. All five tackles on the last possession were by Ohio natives—Fox and seniors Wilhelm, Nickey, and Grant.

The two overtimes had a total of three pass interference penalties in the end zone, one of them declined when Kellen Winslow had the go-ahead touchdown, and Gamble was involved in the last two, one as a receiver and one as a defensive back. They were the only pass interference penalties of the game, and were two of the three penalties in the game that produced a first down.

Dorsey won the Sportsmanship Award for the game, but the scene of Tim Anderson consoling Dorsey, who was on his knees on the field after the last play, is a perfect image of sportsmanship. The Hurricanes' loss dropped their record in Fiesta Bowl games to 0-4. In their 14-10 loss to Penn State in the 1987 game for the national championship, they had seven turnovers and outgained the Nittany Lions, 445 to 162.

RECAP

The *Sports Illustrated* story previewing the game had some of these keys to victory:

- "Don't let Willis McGahee beat you." and "McGahee has been unstoppable all year." The defense held him to 67 yards on 20 carries and five yards on three receptions.

- "Win time of possession." The Buckeyes had almost three more minutes of possession time in the game, including seven more after the first quarter. Larry Coker was quoted in the *Columbus Dispatch* on a prognostication, "When we've gotten in trouble is when we've allowed teams to control the clock."

- "Hit Ken Dorsey often. The one time Dorsey lost as a starter, that Washington game in 2000, the Huskies smacked him around, sacking him three times." That was in reference to the last time that the Hurricanes had lost. The Buckeyes sacked Dorsey four times and forced him to fumble once,

- "Keep it close. Miami is not a great fourth-quarter team." The Buckeyes gave up only three points in the fourth quarter, and that took a 50-yard punt return to get the Hurricanes into field goal territory.

Each team was successful on six of 18 on third downs, although Miami was successful on only three of their last 14 and had a streak of six straight where they failed to convert. Ohio State converted only one of their first six opportunities, but five of their last 12. The Buckeyes were successful on two of three on fourth down (matching their success rate for the season)—scoring their first touchdown on Krenzel's sneak, on the pass to Jenkins in the first overtime, and unsuccessful on the fake field goal play. Miami was successful on one of two on fourth down—successful to keep the drive alive on their last possession and unsuccessful on the last play of the game.

The Hurricanes had more total yards, 369-267, but the Buckeyes had the longest reception and the two longest runs. The Hurricanes' 329 yards in regulation were 143 less than what they had in the previous year's BCS championship game against Nebraska. The Buckeyes' three longest rushes were 10 (by Clarett) and 11 yards by Krenzel twice, and only one of those gained a first down. The longest run for Miami was 10 yards, by McGahee twice. For the second straight bowl game, the longest Buckeye run was by a quarterback, with Steve Bellisari having the longest in the previous season.

The Buckeyes struggled on first down, averaging 2.2 yards per play and throwing both of their interceptions; and, they had penalties on three other first down plays. On other downs, they averaged 4.5 yards per play. Even discounting the 57-yard pass play, they averaged 3.3 yards per play on plays after first down. After their first 18 first down plays, their average was 1.2 yards per play.

For Clarett, other than his touchdown runs of five and seven yards, the Hurricanes defense held him to 35 yards in 21 carries. Interestingly, of the 24 plays that the Buckeyes had for their four touchdowns, Clarett had only five carries (21%). Of the other 49 plays, he either carried the ball or was the target of a pass 21 times (43%). In the four possessions for touchdowns, he had no carries in the seven plays in the first possession, and had one carry—for the touchdown—in the two plays of the second possession. In the third possession, he had gains of one and zero yards, but on the carry for one yard, he broke a tackle to avoid a four-yard loss and allow Krenzel to score on a one-yard sneak. In the fourth possession, he had gains of zero and the five-yard game-winning touchdown. When the Buckeyes had a first-and-goal at the six-yard line following the 57-yard pass to Gamble, Clarett did not have a chance to carry the ball, as Krenzel threw the pass that Taylor intercepted in the end zone. He finished with only 47 rushing yards on 23 carries, but 40 of his yards came after halftime. It was another similarity to one of Archie Griffin's games; Griffin was limited to 46 yards in 19 carries against Michigan in 1975, in another seven-point win for the Buckeyes where they trailed by seven late in the game. Clarett was the only Ohio native to record yards from scrimmage, and his 47 yards accounted for only 18% of the team's 267 yards.

The Buckeyes seemed to get the benefit of the doubt on borderline calls—Gamble's 57-yard catch where the ball popped out on the tackle; Clarett's strip on the interception return that Keith Jackson questioned but Dave Parry, the NCAA national coordinator for football officiating, said was a good call; and the halo penalty on a punt return that Dan Fouts questioned. Buckeye fans would argue that their quota of favorable calls ran out in that game, given the loss in 2019 to Clemson in the College Football Playoff semi-final game, which had a targeting call against the Buckeyes and a fumble return for a touchdown that was ruled no-fumble on video review, and the loss in 2022 to Georgia in the College Football Playoff semi-final game, where targeting was not called as Buckeye receiver Marvin Harrison dived for a pass in the end zone.

Miami's Andre Johnson led the nation by averaging 21 yards per catch and came into the game on a four-game streak that had 549 receiving yards and an average of 27 yards per reception, but was held to four receptions for 54 yards, with three of the receptions in the first quarter. Jenkins matched him with four receptions. It was Johnson's third lowest game of the season in terms of receiving yards and only his fourth game of the 12 that he played in without a touchdown. His longest reception was 20 yards; he had a longer one in ten of the other 11 games. He was the target of five other passes which were incomplete. He had no catches in the second half and one in the first overtime for nine yards. In the BCS championship game the year before, he had seven receptions for 199 yards. Gamble was assigned to Johnson and, ironically, had more receiving yards than Johnson.

Of the seven turnovers in the game, both interceptions by Dorsey and the Parrish fumble came on a third-down play, and both interceptions by Krenzel were on first down.

Both of Krenzel's interceptions were thrown inside the hash marks. All seven Buckeyes receptions were completed outside of the hash marks. What did Coach Tressel say about throwing the ball over the middle? All seven receptions against a team from Florida were by natives of Florida—Jenkins (Tampa), Gamble (Fort Lauderdale, about 30 miles from Miami's campus), and Vance (Fort Myers).

Krenzel did attempt passes to Hartsock, Clarett, Branden Joe, and Bam Childress, but they are from Ohio, so that would have spoiled the story. Several of the incompletions were near-catches; Clarett appealed for pass interference on one, Childress may have been grabbed, and two passes to Hartsock were in the end zone, one of which Sean Taylor intercepted.

The Buckeyes roster listed ten players from Florida, and six of them saw action in the game. In the previous year's bowl game, Jenkins, Vance, and Gamble, playing in their home state, combined for 15 of the 22 receptions; players from Ohio had the other seven receptions. Interestingly, Maurice Hall lived in Miami until age four, went back to visit in the summers, met Dan Marino, Mark Duper, and Mark Clayton at the Dolphins' practices, and had the Hurricanes and Florida State as his two favorite teams growing up, though leaning to the Seminloes. Bryce Bishop, the Buckeyes' starting offensive right guard, is from Killian High School in Miami. The lineman to his left, center Alex Stepanovich, attended Berea High School, the same high school as Coach Tressel.

Four of the five Miami turnovers were claimed by players from Ohio: Clarett, Will Allen, Dustin Fox, and Mike Doss. Fox and Doss, both from Canton, had the two interceptions. The fifth turnover was caused by Kenny Peterson, who was a teammate of Doss at Canton McKinley.

Three of Jenkins's four receptions gained first downs—including the one for 17 yards on fourth-and-14 to set up the score in the first overtime—and the one that did not gain a first down did put the ball on the Miami 5-yard line, with Clarett scoring the winning touchdown on the next play.

Six of Krenzel's seven completions gained first downs, and his two longest completions (57 and 17 yards) came on 3rd-and-15 and 4th-and-14 plays, respectively. The 57-yard play was more than twice as long as the next longest play of the game, a 28-yard completion to Winslow. Krenzel rushed or passed for nine of the 14 first downs; Clarett ran for four of the first downs, and the other first down was from the famous pass interference penalty.

For Simon Fraser, it meant that for the second time in three seasons he had played on an undefeated championship team, adding to his state title at Upper Arlington High School in 2000, that team going 15-0. In Upper Arlington's last two games that season, they had a 10-7 win over undefeated Cincinnati Colerain and the 15-9 championship win over undefeated Solon, secured with an interception at the one-yard line with 46 seconds remaining. That game in Canton had a temperature that was about 50 degrees lower than the one in Tempe.

For Mike Doss, it made three championships in six years, including his two state titles with Canton McKinley in 1997 and 1998; and, his McKinley team was named the Super 25 football champion by USA Today in 1997. The Fiesta Bowl must have also felt familiar to Doss, the Big Ten Defensive Player of the Year and the defensive MVP of the Fiesta Bowl. In the book, "Stark County's Sports Icons & High School Greats", Mike Popovich writes that in 1997, Mike Doss "... drove a St. Ignatius receiver out of bounds at the 1 on the last play of McKinley's 31-24 state semifinal victory." The Bulldogs also scored 31 points in the championship win over Cincinnati Moeller.

Buckeye linebacker Robert Reynolds wasn't the only member of his family to be on a national championship team in 2002. His older brother,

Patrick, was a starting defensive end for Western Kentucky, which won the 2002 Division 1-AA title. Western Kentucky's magical 12-3 season had a start of losing three of their first five games, a win over Youngstown State, and wins in the playoffs against Western Illinois and McNeese State (ranked Number 1, in the championship game) where they avenged regular-season losses. Their coach was Jack Harbaugh, father of Jim, who was born in Ohio, graduated from Bowling Green, coached at high schools in Ohio, was an assistant at Bowling Green, was an assistant at Michigan during the 1979 season—when Ohio State had an 11-0 regular season record—and was the defensive coordinator at Stanford in 1981 when the Buckeyes beat the Cardinal. Harbaugh was named the Coach of the Year in Division I-AA by the American Football Coaches Association in 2002, as Tressel won the award for Division I-A.

Cities named Utica were good to the Buckeyes—Krenzel is from Utica, Michigan, and Will Smith, who tied for the most solo tackles in the game with six, was from Utica, New York. In the previous year's bowl game, Smith led the Buckeyes in assisted tackles with six. Krenzel led all rushers with a career high 81 yards, 16 more than Miami had as a team. He had 19 carries, after averaging eight in the regular season. Miami had given up 114 rushing yards to Nebraska's quarterback, Eric Crouch, in the previous BCS championship game. Krenzel's seven completions netted 122 yards, matching the 122 that Kellen Winslow had by himself, and his 203 total yards (of the Buckeyes' 267) matched the digits of the calendar year of the game. He had 102 of his 122 passing yards after halftime. The story previewing the game in *Sports Illustrated* on December 18, 2002 stated that the Miami pass defense is the nation's finest, giving up just under 120 yards per game.

Winslow's 11 receptions were a Fiesta Bowl record and a record for any Miami bowl game. He had nine receptions after halftime. His 11 receptions were more than what he had in the three previous games combined—his previous high was six—and his 122 yards surpassed his previous high of 84, which came in the one-point win over Florida State. Both his number of receptions and yards gained would be career highs. Only once did a pass intended for Winslow not result in a catch, and that came in Miami's last possession. It marked the third straight game where an opposing receiver had at least as many receptions as the Buckeyes as a team; Walter Young of Illinois had 10 to OSU's 10, and Braylon Edwards of Michigan had 10 to OSU's 10. Parrish was the target of a pass six times, and five of them were completions.

The Buckeye defense gave up five rushing first downs per game in the 2002 season, and held Miami to only three—none in the first half, one each in the third quarter (in their tenth possession), fourth quarter, and first overtime. Miami's two rushing first downs in regulation were a season-low, and their total of three tied their low for the season. The Hurricanes had plays of 20, 23, 25, 26, and 28 yards, and the 50-yard punt return by Parrish, and a 39-yard kickoff return by Andre Johnson. Other than those five plays from scrimmage, they averaged 3.4 yards per play. Dorsey had averaged 15.8 yards per completion in the regular season and 16.5 yards per completion in the previous BCS championship game, but averaged 10.6 in the Fiesta Bowl.

The five Buckeyes scores came on "drives" of 17, 14, 1 (field goal), 25, and 25 yards, with the two longest ones taking place in the overtimes. This was similar to the Buckeyes' second-half performance in their previous national championship game against USC in the 1968 season, where the last two touchdowns came on drives of 21 and 16 yards. As in the win over USC, the defense recorded five turnovers. The five by Miami were a season-high, as were their three lost fumbles.

Six of the seven combined touchdowns were in the south end zone, which had "MIAMI" painted on an orange background; the winning touchdown was the only one in the north end zone, which appropriately had "OHIO STATE" in gray letters on a scarlet background. Both field goals were in the north end zone, and all four interceptions—two by each team—were thrown with the team going toward the north. Miami's four punts were 43, 43, 43, and 44 yards.

Lynn Swann, who had played for USC against the Buckeyes in his last college game, the Rose Bowl of the 1973 season—when the Buckeyes had a 10-0-1 record—did the post-game interviews.

Sadly, on the morning of the game, Sid Gillman—the coach who was successful in the college and professional ranks and was a captain on the 1933 Ohio State team—passed away. He was inducted into the Pro Football Hall of Fame in 1983, along with Ohio State and NFL star Paul Warfield. Coincidentally, Warfield's first year as the analyst on WOSU-TV's delayed broadcasts of Ohio State football games was 1983, the first year for Tressel as an Ohio State assistant.

The Columbus sports scene had other dramatic games on the same day as the Fiesta Bowl and on the two following days. On the day of the Fiesta Bowl, the Columbus Blue Jackets NHL hockey team also played a game that went into overtime against the Washington Capitals, a game that ended in a 2-2 (as in, two goals for each team, compared to two touchdowns in regulation for Ohio State and Miami) tie. On the next day, the Blue Jackets played, naturally, the Phoenix Coyotes, and won, 2-0, recording their only shutout in the midst of almost a three month span. Also on January 4, the day after the win over Miami, the Buckeyes' men's basketball team lost to Louisville, 72-64 … in overtime, naturally. Chris Gamble playing in 120 of 178 plays against Miami? Brent Darby and Sean Connolly did their best Chris Gamble impersonation, playing all 45 minutes for the basketball Buckeyes. On January 5, two days after the Fiesta Bowl, the Ohio State women's basketball team—under first-year coach Jim Foster—had a 70-66 victory over the 17th-ranked Texas Longhorns.

Miami athletics got into the action, too. The Hurricanes men's basketball team opened their on-campus arena on January 4, beating North Carolina, 64-61, in overtime, naturally.

On January 4, the *Lake City Reporter* newspaper in Florida had on its Sports section front page, in addition to its story on the Fiesta Bowl, a photo of a certain high school basketball player in Akron, with the caption "St. Vincent/St. Mary's (Ohio) has been running wild on a national barn-storming tour to show off Number 1 NBA prospect LeBron James (above). The tour continues tonight in Los Angeles." The game against Mater Dei of California, played at UCLA's Pauley Pavilion, would be televised on ESPN2. He had 21 points, 9 rebounds, and 7 assists. Guarding James that day for Mater Dei was DJ Strawberry, son of baseball star Darryl Strawberry. In the following weeks, James would have games of 52 and 50 points. Six days before the Fiesta Bowl, St. Vincent-St. Mary—on its way to a state championship, naturally—had played in the Schottenstein Center on Ohio State's campus, and won in overtime, naturally, over Columbus Brookhaven, which was, naturally, a defending state champion. The game went into overtime helped by good fortune for the winning team; Brookhaven missed two free throws in the final seconds of regulation. A little over twenty years later, James would become the all-time scoring leader in the NBA.

Fittingly, the celebration to honor the Buckeyes took place in Ohio Stadium on January 18, 2003, exactly two years after Coach Tressel's hiring and his "310 days" speech.

WHAT IF?

Listing some of the "what-ifs" … if any of these had gone otherwise, the outcome could have been different, and would we have called this one of the best games of all time?

- What if the Buckeyes had kicked a field goal instead of running on a fake in the second quarter?

- What if the 57-yard pass to Gamble had not been underthrown?

- What if video review had been in effect, and Gamble's 57-yard catch had been reviewed to confirm that he had not fumbled? Dan Fouts was comfortable that Gamble was down before the ball popped out, but what if a review had ruled otherwise, or the delay of a review had affected the Buckeyes' momentum and strategy?

- What if the Buckeyes had not passed on first down for their two interceptions?

- What if on the pass intercepted by Sean Taylor in the end zone, Krenzel had thrown to Branden Joe, wide open outside the hash marks, instead of throwing to Ben Hartsock, who was inside the hash marks?

- What if Taylor, intercepting about five yards deep in the end zone, had not decided to bring it out? When he caught the ball, his momentum was toward the center of the field, though he quickly pivoted to the left sideline.

- What if Taylor had carried the ball in his outside arm following his interception?

- What if video review had been in effect, to confirm whether Clarett truly had possession before the play was dead?

- What if Nugent had made his 42-yard field goal? He had only one other miss in the season between 40 and 49 yards, out of 11 attempts. With a six-point lead, it would have been highly unlikely that the game would have gone to overtime.

- What if Sievers had made his 54-yard field goal attempt, which was nine yards shorter than one that he had made in high school?

- What if a block in the back had been called on Parrish's punt return?

- What if, on the coin toss to decide possession for overtime, the referee, Randy Christal, had let the coin fall to the turf, Miami won the toss, and the Buckeyes had to go on offense first?

- What if a penalty on the obvious grab of Gamble's jersey had been called, or if his catch along the sideline had been ruled a completion? What if video review had been in effect?

- What if the trajectory of Sievers's field goal kick on the last play of regulation had been a tad lower?

- What if Miami had not blitzed on the pass play to Gamble that drew the pass interference penalty?

- Miami had used the shotgun formation a few times in the game. If they had had Ken Dorsey in the shotgun instead of under center on the last play, would Cie Grant have blitzed, or if he did, would Dorsey have reacted better? Miami had both of their touchdown passes with the Buckeyes blitzing.

- What if Gamble had not interfered on the pass in the second overtime, and Miami had scored?

- What if Miami had scored on fourth down? Would they have gone for two points and the win, knowing that they were without their leading rusher and had a banged-up Ken Dorsey? Would they have been involved in a second monumental "go for two in the national championship game", as they had on January 2, 1984, when Nebraska failed and Bernie Kosar was the winning quarterback?

- What if the game had gone to a third overtime, where two-point conversion attempts were required after touchdowns? Would that have favored one team more than the other?

- What if Miami had called a different play than a screen pass on third-and-ten, which resulted in McGahee being injured? The Buckeyes defense knew that a screen pass was coming.

- McGahee and Dorsey were involved in 349 of the Hurricanes' 369 total yards.

  - What if McGahee had not been injured? He had shown his speed on his nine-yard touchdown run in the third quarter and had 42 yards on eight carries in the second half, compared to 25 yards on 12 carries in the first half.

  - What if Dorsey had not been shaken up in the second overtime? His pass on the second-and-goal play was way off the mark, as Dan Fouts pointed out.

  - What if running back Clinton Portis, tight end Jeremy Shockey, and defensive back Phillip Buchanon of Miami had not turned pro after the 2001 season? What if the Buckeyes had faced Portis instead of McGahee, or both? What if they had faced Shockey instead of Winslow, or both? In his book, "Haven't They Suffered Enough?: An Unbelievable Career in Sports, PR and Television", Beano Cook wrote that the most talented college football teams that he had seen, in terms of NFL stars, were the 2001 Miami and the 1972 USC teams; USC trounced Ohio State, 42-17, in the Rose Bowl of the 1972 season.

  - Ohio State, conversely, had fifth-year seniors Donnie Nickey, Cie Grant, and Kenny Peterson (Grant and Peterson are second cousins). What if they had not redshirted in 1998, so that they would have not played in 2002?

  - What if Frank Gore of Miami had not spent the season recovering from knee surgery? As a freshman the year before, he rushed for 562 yards on 62 carries, a 9.1 average.

- What if defensive tackle Cornelius Green and wide receiver Kevin Beard of Miami had not had his season ended by an injury in the tenth game of the season?

OHIO STATE MISSTEPS

The Buckeyes did not seem to have many missteps in the first 13 games. However, in the Miami game:

- It was the only game of the season where OSU fell behind after having a lead of at least 10 points.

- Krenzel threw two interceptions; he had only five before the game. Both of his interceptions came on first down plays, but Miami did not score after either one.

- The Buckeyes averaged five penalties per game in the regular season, but had a season-high nine penalties against Miami. The penalties included one on the first play of the game for having 12 men on the field and one for delay of game. In Tressel's book, "The Winners Manual: For the Game of Life", co-authored by Chris Fabry, he wrote that the cause of the penalty on the first play was that Gamble thought that he was supposed to be on offense, when in fact Coach Tressel was trying not to use him on every play. The Buckeyes actually had five penalties in regulation and four in the overtime periods, plus another in overtime that was declined.

- The Buckeyes' longest drive of 66 yards netted no points, though it led to the Clarett strip fumble that resulted in a field goal.

- The Buckeyes' longest drive in time of possession and number of plays ended in a missed field goal. If Nugent had made the field goal, he would have tied Billy Bennett of Georgia for the most successful field goals in the season.

- Coach Tressel stressed the kicking game—including saying that the punt most is the most important play in football—and Andy Groom was fourth in punting in college football with a 45.0 yard average, but:

  - Groom was not able to steer his last punt away from Roscoe Parrish, whose 50-yard return set up Miami's tying field goal to force overtime. His five previous punts had only one return for six yards, and his last two had gone out of bounds.

  - Groom had a 30-yard punt that led to Miami's touchdown that made the score 17-14..

  - The combined kickoff and punt return yards were 95 for Miami, 16 for Ohio State.

  - The fake field goal play, which was unsuccessful, was very un-Tressel-like.

SIMILARITIES TO THE 1986 NEW YORK METS, THE WORLD SERIES WINNER

- In game 6 of the World Series, the Mets were on the brink of losing the Series to the Boston Red Sox, down to their last out in the ninth inning and down by two runs with no runners on base, in a home game in Shea Stadium. OSU faced 4th down twice on offense when trailing in the first overtime, and the game in the Fiesta Bowl stadium was virtually a home game.

- The fielding miscue by Bill Buckner in game 6 only evened the series; the Red Sox still had an opportunity to win the World Series. The touchdown following the pass interference call only evened the game; the Hurricanes still had an opportunity to win.

- The Shea Stadium scoreboard accidentally displayed "Congratulations Boston Red Sox, 1986 World Champions" for a brief moment, and the Sun Devil Stadium staff launched premature celebratory fireworks for Miami when it appeared that they had won, following the pass interference call in the first overtime.

- One team (Red Sox/Buckeyes) wore red/scarlet, and the other (Mets/Hurricanes) had orange as one of its colors.

- The losing manager, John McNamara, was in his second season with the Red Sox, similar to Larry Coker.

FUN FACTS

- The score was 31-24, and in their previous two bowl games, the Buckeyes had given up 31 and 24 points, both to South Carolina.

- The Buckeyes had outgained South Carolina in the Outback Bowl by 388 to 347 yards, but lost, and were outgained by Miami by 369 to 267 yards, but won.

- The Hurricanes came in on a streak of having increased their scoring in the last three games, from 26 to 28 to 49 to 56, but the Buckeyes defense held them to 17 in regulation.

- Miami had averaged 9.3 and 8.2 yards per play in its last two regular season games and at least 5.7 in every game, but averaged only 4.8 against the Buckeyes.

- Miami averaged 474 yards per game in the regular season, but was held 145 below that in regulation by the Buckeyes.

- Thanks to the overtimes, Miami gave up its two highest scores on defense in its last two games. Even without the overtimes, the 62 points given up in the last two games represented the most in consecutive games, topping the previous high of 50.

- This was the only game of the season where the Buckeyes scored only three points in the second half.

- This was the second game of the season where the Buckeyes were shut out in the fourth quarter. The other game was against Penn State; the Penn State and Miami games had the two biggest margins of victory in the seven games decided by seven points or less.

- In the 15 years of the BCS championship game, this was the only overtime game, with only one other game decided by less than seven points in regulation.

- The last time that the Buckeyes had beaten the #1 team was against Iowa in 1985, Tressel's last season as an assistant. In that game, the defense forced five turnovers.

- Miami's regular season schedule had three teams who had won a national championship since 1996—Tennessee, Florida, and Florida State—and a runner-up, Virginia Tech. Ohio State's schedule had one, Michigan.

- In the regular season, Ohio State played three teams in the top 16 of the final Associated Press poll—#9 Michigan, #10 Washington State, and #16 Penn State. The highest ranked opponent for Miami was #18 Virginia Tech.

- Krenzel had been sacked 30 times in the regular season, but only once by Miami, and that came in the first overtime.

Dorsey had been sacked eight times in the regular season and only once in the 2001 season, but the Buckeyes sacked him four times.

- The Buckeye defense had 11 tackles for a loss, compared to five by Miami's defense.

- The five turnovers recorded by the Buckeyes were a season high.

- After this game, the combined score in regulation in the three games between these two teams was 40 for Miami, 39 for Ohio State.

- Miami won its six regular season games on the road by an average of 26 points, with the closest game decided by 17 points.

- The Hurricanes had averaged 40 points in games away from home coming into the game, with a low of 26.

- Both teams had survived in a regular season game where their rival had the last play in regulation with one second remaining—Ohio State had the interception against Michigan, and Miami had the missed field goal attempt by Florida State.

- The Buckeyes faced five of the top ten players in the voting for the 2002 Heisman Trophy—McGahee, Dorsey, Larry Johnson, Jason Gesser, and Kliff Kingsbury. Miami faced none.

- Both defensive coordinators would become head coaches in 2007—Dantonio at Michigan State, and Randy Shannon at Miami.

- Larry Coker faced three former Ohio State assistant coaches in the season—Jim Tressel, Ron Zook of Florida, and Walt Harris of Pitt—and a future one, Greg Schiano of Rutgers. Tressel faced two—Coker and Glen Mason of Minnesota.

- Former Ohio State assistant Jim Tressel broke the 34-game winning streak of Miami, coached by former Ohio State assistant Larry Coker. Other notable winning streaks in college football history were—note that Bruce (1968), Holtz (1968), and Dantonio (2002) had been assistants on an Ohio State national championship team, and that Dantonio had also been an assistant for Tressel at Youngstown State:

  - Former Ohio State assistant Earle Bruce broke the previous longest streak when his Tampa team, in his first game as its coach, stopped Toledo's 35-game streak in 1972.

  - Former Ohio State assistant Lou Holtz of Notre Dame broke Miami's 36-game regular season streak in 1988.

  - Former Ohio State assistant Bo Schembechler of Michigan broke Ohio State's 22-game streak in 1969.

  - Former Ohio State assistant coach Pete Carroll saw his 34-game winning streak snapped in the BCS Championship game of the 2005 season, when Texas beat his USC team. His streak started after a triple-overtime defeat to California in 2003.

  - Former Ohio State assistant coach Ron Zook of Illinois snapped Ohio State's 28-game regular season streak in 2007.

  - Former Ohio State assistant Mark Dantonio of Michigan State broke Ohio State's 24-game streak in the Big Ten championship game of 2013, beating former Ohio State graduate assistant Urban Meyer.

  - Dantonio broke Ohio State's 23-game streak in 2015 with a 17-14 win, beating Urban Meyer with a field goal on the last play of the game.

- Florida's Urban Meyer broke Ohio State's 19-game streak in the 2006 season, beating former Ohio State assistant Jim Tressel.

- Both Tressel and Coker had been the quarterbacks coach at their current university. Coker had also been an assistant coach at Tulsa (1979-1982) under John Cooper.

- None of the 11 Ohio State starters on offense were seniors.

- On the first three of the Buckeyes' four touchdown drives, they were helped by Miami penalties, but for a total of only ten yards. The most significant one was the pass interference in the end zone.

- In regulation, the Buckeyes had four possessions in Miami territory following a Miami turnover and one possession in Ohio State territory following a Miami turnover. In their eight other possessions, their average starting position was their own 20-yard line.

- In regulation, the Buckeyes' two touchdown drives averaged 15.5 yards, and the Hurricanes' two touchdown drives averaged 53.5 yards.

- The teams combined for one successful field goal in three attempts in the fourth quarter, after a combined one attempt in the first three quarters—Nugent's successful kick in the third quarter. Factor in the unsuccessful fake field goal, and the field goal units had a rocky game.

- Of the seven touchdowns, two were scored by a true freshman (Clarett), one by a second-year freshman (Parrish), one by a second-year sophomore (McGahee), one by a true sophomore (Winslow), and two by a fourth-year junior (Krenzel).

- The Buckeyes never had consecutive plays of at least 10 yards, and Miami achieved it once.

- The Buckeyes had only one possession in regulation in which they had multiple first downs, and that was the fourth quarter possession where Nugent missed the field goal. In the overtimes, both of their possessions had multiple first downs.

- Krenzel completed one-third of his pass attempts in the first half and one-third of his pass attempts after halftime. His completion percentage of 33% was his lowest of the season.

- Jenkins had 28 receiving yards in regulation, a season low for him.

- Some of the big plays were by Clarett, Doss, and Peterson, all of whom had Thom McDaniels as their coach in high school—Clarett at Warren Harding High, and Doss and Peterson at Canton McKinley.

- Clarett had only one touchdown in 68 carries in his previous four games before scoring twice against Miami. Krenzel had only one rushing touchdown in his 106 carries in the season before scoring twice against Miami, and that came against Cincinnati in the fourth game.

- Miami set a school record with 527 points scored in the 2002 season, but scored its fewest points against Ohio State. Their last regular season game had their highest output against their Division I-A opponents, but the Buckeyes held them in regulation to nine points lower than their previous low of the season and their lowest since 1999. Miami's 17 points in regulation would continue to be its lowest until November 1, 2003, when they lost to Virginia Tech, 31-7.

- Dorsey's 28 completions were a career high, and his 25 completions in regulation were a season high. His 65% completion rate in the game was his second highest of the season and his highest in three months.

- Dorsey's one touchdown pass in regulation tied his season low for a game.

- Dorsey's four sacks count as rushing attempts and gave him 23 for the season. Krenzel had 19 in the game and 125 in the season.

- The Buckeyes held Miami to its lowest rushing output of the season.

- Miami's longest possession was its first one; it lasted 5:05 and 11 plays, and ended with a punt. Their second-longest possession lasted 3:24 and nine plays, and ended with a missed field goal. Their third-longest, eight plays, was their last one to end the game.

- Willis McGahee's average of 3.4 yards per rush was a season low. His average of 1.7 yards per reception was also a season low.

- In the 2001 season, the Buckeyes were +10 on the turnover advantage. Going into the Miami game, they were +10, and they finished the season +13.

- In 1948, Bennie Oosterbaan of Michigan won the national championship in his first season as its coach. The next time that happened was in 2001 for Larry Coker. When Oosterbaan faced Ohio State the following season in 1949, the score at the end of regulation was tied at 7-7. When Coker faced Ohio State the following season in 2002, the score at the end of regulation was tied at 17-17.

- In 2001, the season before the Buckeyes' national championship, the Phoenix area had also seen a dramatic conclusion in a championship game, in the World Series, when the Diamondbacks beat the defending champions and a dynasty team, the Yankees, scoring in their last at-bat. The series had four one-run games, with two in overtime (extra innings). The losing team, the Yankees, had its superstar pitcher, Mariano Rivera, fail to close out the game. Just as the Buckeyes scored the last two touchdowns, the Diamondbacks scored the last two runs in the deciding game and won the last two games in a home environment. Like the Hurricanes, the Yankees had the edge in talent, with three future Hall of Famers—Rivera, Derek Jeter, and Mike Mussina. In that year, it was the first season leading his team for both Jim Tressel and Diamondbacks manager Bob Brenly, both of whom are from Ohio—Brenly is from Coshocton.

- For the seven players who scored in the game, their NFL stats are: Winslow, McGahee, and Parrish combined to score 97 touchdowns. Krenzel and Clarett (no NFL career) had none. Nugent scored 1,180 points; Sievers did not have an NFL career.

- Future teammates:
  - Glenn Sharpe and Michael Jenkins on the Atlanta Falcons.
  - Will Allen, Mike Nugent, and Kellen Winslow on the Tampa Bay Buccaneers.
  - Dustin Fox and Willis McGahee on the Buffalo Bills.
  - Nugent and Jonathan Vilma on the New York Jets.
  - Andy Groom and Sean Taylor on the Washington Redskins.
  - Groom and Dorsey on the San Francisco 49ers.

CHAPTER 5

Recapping the Improbable Season

JIM TRESSEL WAS WRONG about one thing. Building on the saying that "Nothing good ever happens after midnight," which Bo Schembechler espoused, Tressel often told his players that, "Nothing good happens past 10 p.m." Given the outcome of the Fiesta Bowl, he may have revised his thinking.

A story in *Sports Illustrated* had related that Fred Martinelli, who had coached at Ashland University for 35 seasons and would be inducted to the College Football Hall of Fame in 2002, had predicted that the 2001 Michigan game would come down to a fourth-and-one play. Not only was he right then, as Jonathan Wells scored on a 46-yard run on fourth-and-one, but it would carry over to some of the biggest plays of the 2002 season—the Holy Buckeye play, Krenzel's sneak against Michigan, his sneak for the first touchdown against Miami, and Cie Grant's pressure on the last play of the season.

The season was a reward for the players who had experienced the 6-6 season of 1999, the program's worst record since the 1988 season, and for the seniors who had been redshirted—Cie Grant, Donnie Nickey, Kenny Peterson, and Scott Kuhnhein—and had watched the

Buckeyes go 11-1 in 1998 and ranked Number 1 until the upset by Michigan State.

Buckeye football fans were beginning to wish that every month could be January (other than November wins over Michigan, of course):

January 2001: The Hiring and The Speech

January 2002: The Return

January 2003: Mission Accomplished

If you were to make a movie about the season, what would you call it? It should include the word "Improbable", and I would break it up into two chapters, with the second one called "The Magnificent Seven", assuming that there is no copyright law issue. If I were to create a Hollywood ending, I would have Cie Grant convincing Coach Dantonio that he would make the decisive play if Dantonio would approve, as Jimmy Chitwood did with Norman Dale in the movie "Hoosiers". The perfect person to mastermind this project would be Maurice Hall, who has directed, produced, and starred in multiple movies.

THE SEVEN GAMES DECIDED BY SEVEN POINTS OR LESS

- The Buckeyes outscored the opponents in the fourth quarter by a combined score of 32-9, with Illinois and Miami kicking a field goal on the last play of regulation. All nine points, including the field goal at Purdue, were scored in games away from Columbus.

- The Buckeyes had the last score in each game.

- The Buckeyes were outgained by an average of 65 yards per game. Ironically, the game of the seven where they had the biggest advantage—outgaining Penn State by 74 yards—was the only game where they did not have an offensive touchdown.

In the seven "breather" games, they had an average advantage of 187 yards per game.

- The Buckeyes had an average of four fewer first downs per game than the opponent.

- In the five non-overtime games, after the Buckeyes took the lead, the defense shut out the opponents for a combined length of 48:21. Add in the overtime against Illinois and the last overtime against Miami, that's the equivalent of practically one full game of shutting out the opponent.

- In the first quarter, the Buckeyes were outscored 36-23, managing a total of two touchdowns, and were shut out in four of the games.

- The Buckeyes trailed at halftime in four of the games and were tied at halftime in another.

- The Buckeyes trailed in the fourth quarter in four of the games, with three of those games on the road.

- The Buckeyes finished the first four games of the seven by running out the clock on offense and the last three games by denying a score on defense.

- These seven games had a total of 14 lead changes. The other seven games had a total of four lead changes.

- The Buckeyes' turnover advantage was a combined 19 to 10.

- Of the 14 games, the lowest average gain per play by the Buckeyes was 3.7 yards, against both Miami and Penn State.

- Groom had twice as many punts (40) in these seven games as he did (20) in the other seven.

- Groom had 11 of his 15 punts on the season that put the opponents inside their 20-yard line in these seven games.

- The Buckeyes had their two highest number of penalties (nine and eight) in the season against Miami and Cincinnati, but also had their two fewest (three each) against Penn State and Purdue.

- In five of the games, other than the Penn State and Illinois games, the Buckeyes forced a turnover in the fourth quarter.

- Due to injuries, Clarett had only 91 carries and three touchdowns in the seven games, missing two of them, and had 131 carries and 15 touchdowns in the other seven, missing one.

- All of Krenzel's seven interceptions occurred in the Cincinnati, Penn State, Purdue, and Miami games.

- Mike Doss had his only fumble recovery of the season against Wisconsin, Will Smith had his only fumble recovery of the season against Michigan, David Thompson had his only fumble recovery of the season against Cincinnati (where it was his only stat of the game), Tim Anderson had his only fumble recovery of the season against Illinois, and Will Allen had his only fumble recovery of the season against Miami.

- Seven players had an interception—Gamble (four), Fox (two), Allen (two), and Hawk, Smith, Wilhelm, and Doss had one each. Twelve of the team's 18 interceptions came in these games. The Illinois game was the only one without an interception.

- Four different players led the team in rushing in the games: Clarett (three times), Ross (twice), Hall (once), and Krenzel (once). In the last three games, it was three different players— Hall, Clarett, and Krenzel.

- Six different players had the winning touchdown:
  - Cincinnati: Krenzel, with 3:44 remaining

- Wisconsin: Hartsock, with 9:59 remaining
- Penn State: Gamble, in the third quarter
- Purdue: Jenkins, with 1:36 remaining
- Illinois: Hall, in overtime
- Michigan: Hall, with 4:55 remaining
- Miami: Clarett, in the second overtime

Could the Buckeyes execute key plays in close games in 2002? Except for the Penn State game, they came on offense and defense.

- Cincinnati: Krenzel's touchdown scramble with 3:44 remaining and Will Allen's interception in the end zone with 26 seconds remaining.
- Wisconsin: Krenzel's touchdown pass to Hartsock with 9:59 remaining and Chris Gamble's interception with 7:09 remaining.
- Penn State: Gamble's interception for a touchdown and his tackle when Penn State returned Krenzel's fumble.
- Purdue: Nugent's field goal at the end of the first half, Wilhelm's sack that limited Purdue to a field goal, Krenzel's Holy Buckeye touchdown pass with 1:36 remaining, and Gamble's interception with 45 seconds remaining.
- Illinois: Maurice Hall's touchdown and Tim Anderson's pass breakup in overtime.
- Michigan: Hall's touchdown with 4:55 remaining and Will Allen's interception on the last play of the game.
- Miami: Krenzel's pass to Jenkins on 4th-and-14 in the first overtime and Cie Grant's blitz on the last play of the game.

In the regular season, the Buckeyes' six wins by seven points or less were the most in Division I-A. It was fitting that the most desperate of the seven games was the last one, with the most at stake. It was the only game where the Buckeyes trailed by at least seven points after halftime and the only one where they lost a 10-point lead; and, they needed to prolong the game when facing fourth down, twice. Ranking the other six nail-biters, in order of drama:

- Purdue: Going into the wind on fourth-and-one, passing into the end zone was a huge risk, as were running for the first down and a 54-yard field goal attempt.
- Cincinnati: When Krenzel ran for the winning touchdown, the Buckeyes were in range for a field goal, which would have produced the lead. Cincinnati had four shots from the 15-yard line, and a touchdown would win it.
- Michigan: The Wolverines had two shots from the 24-yard line, and a touchdown would win it.
- Illinois: The Buckeyes were not trailing when they made the winning score, and an Illinois touchdown would have only tied the score.
- Wisconsin: The deepest advance for the Badgers after losing the lead was the Ohio State 29-yard line.
- Penn State: The deepest advance for the Nittany Lions after losing the lead was the Ohio State 36-yard line.

None of the seven games were decided by less than four points, which meant that the defense had a smaller stress level, knowing that the opponent needed a touchdown in its last possession. Of course, Illinois and Miami in regulation needed only a field goal to extend the game into overtime.

THE LAST FOUR GAMES—PURDUE, ILLINOIS, MICHIGAN, AND MIAMI

- After 10 games, the Buckeyes were +5 in turnovers. In the last four games, decided by a total of nine points in regulation, they forced 11 turnovers and turned it over only three times.

- Three of the games—Purdue, Illinois, and Miami—had a field goal on the last play of a half.

- The offense was successful a combined four times in five fourth down plays, all in touchdown drives. In addition to the three mentioned above, they had the 17-yard completion on fourth-and-14 against Miami. The only unsuccessful one was the fake field goal attempt against Miami. They had no fourth-down plays against Illinois.

- Jenkins had a reception in the fourth quarter of each game, and touchdowns in two of the games.

- The opponents had 83 first downs to 56 for the Buckeyes.

- The opponents had 39, 46, 48, and 44 passes for 285, 305, 247, and 304 yards.

- The Buckeyes' total offense yards were 267, 321, 264, and 267. The opponents' total offense yards were 341, 358, 368, and 369. Total: 1,119 for the Buckeyes and 1,436 for the opponents; the Buckeyes were outgained by an average of 79 yards total and 137 yards passing per game.

- If not for the overtime of the Illinois game, the Buckeyes would have had less than 300 yards of total offense in each of the last four games.

- The Buckeyes had an average of seven fewer first downs per game.

- The Buckeyes converted on only 29% of their third down plays, compared to 39% in the other ten games.

- The Buckeyes' total offense numbers against Michigan and Miami were almost identical:

  - Against Michigan: 140 yards rushing and 124 passing

  - Against Miami: 145 yards rushing and 122 passing

JIM TRESSEL'S HISTORY

The season must have felt very familiar to Coach Tressel for his playing days. The book, "… And We Must Excel", by Bill Nichols, details his 1974 season as a senior playing quarterback for his father at Baldwin Wallace. The Yellow Jackets opened their season at home against defending NCAA Division III Champion Wittenberg with a 10-3 victory (a low score). They ended a 12-game winning streak by the visiting Tigers on a 13-yard down-and-out pass on third-and-nine (Krenzel to Jenkins, anyone?) from Tressel to Doug Shook in the third quarter for the only touchdown of the game. Like Craig Krenzel, Tressel moved into the starting quarterback job late in his career; for Tressel, it was in his senior season.

The book has this excerpt on the Wittenberg game: "Mark Summers made two game-saving plays, including a pass interception on Wittenberg's 27-yard line to set up a six-pointer. In the fourth quarter, Summers also recovered a Tiger fumble at the BW 10-yard line to stop a scoring threat. The Jackets defense was under the proverbial gun the entire fourth period."

Jim and Lee Tressel are the only father and son combination to coach college teams to national championships, with Lee winning at Baldwin Wallace in 1978. Similar to the 2002 Buckeyes, the 12-game season with an 11-0-1 record had the most games in Baldwin Wallace history. The tie was a 17-17 game against Wittenberg, matching the score of the end of regulation in the Fiesta Bowl. In a re-match, Baldwin Wallace beat

Wittenberg in the championship game, 24-10. Baldwin Wallace won its three playoff games by a combined score of 126-17, a trait that Jim did not inherit from his father.

Tressel continued the pattern of every Ohio State coach who won a national championship also having a connection to Miami University in Ohio. Paul Brown, like Tressel at Baldwin Wallace, was a starting quarterback; in his last two years, Miami won 13 of 17 games. Brown was the ultra-successful coach at Massillon Washington High School—even topping Lee Tressel with a 35-game winning streak—before taking the Ohio State job. He had recruited Lee Tressel to come to Ohio State in the 1940s. Woody Hayes was the head coach at Miami University before coming to Ohio State, and Tressel was an assistant coach at Miami in 1979 and 1980. All three coaches grew up in the northeast quadrant of Ohio.

When Tressel was the offensive backs coach at Akron in 1976, the Zips had their most wins (10) in school history and played in the Division II national championship game, losing to Number 1 Montana State. In the previous game, Akron hosted the semifinal playoff game, where it defeated a team from the state up north, Northern Michigan, the defending 1975 National Champions, 29-26, in the first overtime game in NCAA football playoff history. Akron's kicker made a field goal with one second remaining to tie the contest at 23-23.

In his first year as the quarterbacks coach at Syracuse, Tressel's quarterback ran for 418 yards and seven touchdowns. That team had Joe Morris, who ran for 1,194 yards and would be a star for the New York Giants.

Tressel was making it a habit of beating the defending national champion. In 1993, his Youngstown State team beat the defending Division I-AA national champion, Marshall, for his second national championship.

In his first year at Youngstown State, the team lost six games by seven points or less. In his second year, the team won six games by seven points or less, including an overtime game. At Ohio State, those corresponding numbers were four and seven. He won two of his four national championships at Youngstown State in the fourth quarter of the game. In his 1997 championship year, the team entered the season ranked as the 11th best team in the nation.

He spent three years as an assistant at Ohio State under another coach who had had huge success as the coach at Massillon Washington High School; Earle Bruce had a 20-0 record as the head of the Tigers. In those three years, the team won a total of six games by seven points or less. The one in 1983 was in the Fiesta Bowl, on a 39-yard pass from Mike Tomczak to Thad Jemison down the left sideline into the south end zone with 39 seconds remaining. In 1984, they had consecutive nail-biters; they survived a missed 43-yard field goal attempt by Michigan State with three seconds remaining that would have tied the game, and beat Illinois, 45-38, on Keith Byars's fifth touchdown of the game with 36 seconds remaining.

In 1985, they had bookend 10-7 wins; the first was over Pittsburgh with the winning two-yard touchdown pass from Jim Karsatos to Cris Carter on fourth down with 4:19 remaining. In another game, they had a 23-19 win over Lou Holtz's Minnesota team, where they scored two touchdowns in the fourth quarter and stopped the Golden Gophers on downs at the Ohio State 12-yard line with 48 seconds remaining.

The second 10-7 win was over Brigham Young—which was the national champion with a 13-0 record the season before—in the Citrus Bowl, with the only touchdown on an interception return by defensive lineman Larry Kolic and Terry White intercepting a pass in the end zone with three seconds remaining. White's interception was the sixth turnover recorded by the Buckeye defense; the Buckeyes turned the ball over twice. On the possession preceding Terry White's pick, William White had an interception in the end zone. In the first half, Brigham Young fumbled at the Ohio State 16-yard line and fumbled into the end zone in another possession. The 47-yard field goal was by Rich Spangler, the Buckeyes' last non-soccer style kicker. On Brigham Young's touchdown reception with

52 seconds remaining in the first half, it appeared that the receiver had stepped out of bounds at the one-yard line before scoring. If the ball had been placed at the one, could the Buckeye defense have made a goal line stand? We will never know. Besides, a 10-7 win is much more enjoyable than a 10-0 or a 10-3 win, right? The Side Judge who signaled the touchdown was Jerry McGee, the same Jerry McGee who was the Field Judge who signaled the touchdown for Arizona State in the 1997 Rose Bowl on the catch that appeared not to be controlled by the receiver. In the book, "Sidelines and Bloodlines: A Father, His Sons, and Our Life in College Football", Jerry lists those two calls as two out of three in his 404-game career where he later questioned himself. His co-author and son, Ryan McGee of ESPN, says that he got both calls right.

Buckeye fans were denied the opportunity to watch the last three seconds of the game, as NBC cut to the New York Jets vs. the New England Patriots playoff game. On this occasion, the decision did not backfire on NBC. In 1968, they had cut away from a Jets-Raiders regular season game with the Jets ahead, 32-29, and 1:05 remaining in the game, to show the movie "Heidi", thereby denying their viewers the opportunity to see the Raiders score two touchdowns in nine seconds for a 43-32 win. The Jets would go on to win Super Bowl III, with former OSU running back Matt Snell running for 121 yards and the Jets' lone touchdown.

Like Krenzel, Karsatos (wearing jersey #16) was from out of state (California), became the starter as a junior, and was the winning quarterback in the bowl games of his junior and senior seasons.

That bowl game against BYU was Tressel's last game before taking the Youngstown State job, and the message was probably something like, "This going-away present is the gift that keeps on giving, Coach Tressel, you'll be experiencing several similar games when you are back at Ohio State in the 2002 season."

Conversely, eight of the nine Buckeye losses in his three seasons— including the Rose Bowl of the 1984 season—were by six points or less, with the ninth one a 27-17 loss at Michigan in 1985. In other words, in 1983 and 1984, making one more play in six games could have produced undefeated seasons.

In his last season of 2000 at Youngstown State, Tressel's last win came on the day that Ohio State lost to Michigan in John Cooper's last home game. It was a typical Tressel season in many ways. The Penguins won five games by seven points or less, including four straight, starting with a 26-20 (the same score as the 2001 Ohio State win over Michigan) win at Division I-A Kent State, and later had a two-overtime win over Hofstra, ranked Number 8. On Hofstra's final possession, Youngstown State linebacker Tim Johnson intercepted the final pass in the end zone to end the game. The Youngstown State website reported that the Penguins "took advantage of [a] Hofstra holding penalty on a would-be interception that would have ended the game." The Penguins scored twice in the last eight minutes of regulation, and trailed by a touchdown in the first overtime. Their season ended in the first round of the NCAA Division I-AA Playoffs with a 10-3 loss to Richmond. They led 3-0 after the third quarter, but the Spiders kicked a 24-yard field goal and had a 44-yard interception return in a span of 1:25.

THE BIG TEN CHAMPIONSHIP CONUNDRUM

The Buckeyes won the national championship without winning the Big Ten outright. Between 1981 and 2002, they tied for first place in the Big Ten three times, not winning outright due to another team making a significant improvement over the previous year. The Buckeyes did not have Iowa on the schedule in 1981 or 2002, for a chance to win the conference outright.

- 1981: Iowa improved from 4-7 (4-4 in the Big Ten) in 1980 to 8-4 and 6-2. Michigan, whom Ohio State beat, finished higher in both polls than the Buckeyes.

- 1993: Wisconsin improved from 5-6 (3-5 in the Big Ten) in 1992 to 10-1-1 and 6-1-1. Wisconsin, whom Ohio State tied, and Penn State, whom Ohio State beat, finished higher in both polls than the Buckeyes.

- 2002: Iowa improved from 7-5 (4-4 in the Big Ten) in 2001 to 11-2 and 8-0. The 2002 season was the first one since 1943 that two Big Ten teams went undefeated in league play, when Michigan and Purdue were 6-0.

The Buckeyes actually had a pattern of better fortune when they tied for the Big Ten championship than when they won it outright.

- Between 1970 and 2007, they won it outright six times—in 1970, 1975, 1979, 1984, 2006, and 2007—and lost their bowl game each time. Tressel was on the staff for the last three of these.

- Between 1981 and 2005, they tied for the championship seven times—in 1981, 1986, 1993, 1996, 1998, 2002, and 2005—and won their bowl game each time. The 1981 season was significant for having Earle Bruce's first bowl win in his third season and the Buckeyes' first bowl win since the 1976 season. The 1993 season was significant for having John Cooper's first bowl win in his sixth season and the Buckeyes' first bowl win since the 1986 season.

THE LUCKY NUMBER 13

- The Fiesta Bowl took place on January 3 (1/3).

- Miami was facing a ranked opponent for the 13th time since their 34-game winning streak began.

- The Buckeyes had won the 13th Fiesta Bowl in dramatic fashion in the 1983 season.

- The last play of the game was Miami's 13th in the two overtimes.

- The Fiesta Bowl was Miami's 13th bowl loss.

- Miami had scored in 13 consecutive quarters before being blanked in the second quarter by the Buckeyes.

- Miami finished 13 victories shy of the all-time mark of 47 consecutive wins set by Oklahoma in 1953 through 1957.

- The field goal by Sievers was his 13th of the season.

- It was the first time that the program had 13 regular season games.

- The opening game against Texas Tech was the 13th Pigskin Classic.

- The game against Cincinnati was the 13th meeting between the two teams.

- The Michigan win was Tressel's 13th Big Ten win.

- The team was ranked #13 in the Associated Press and ESPN/ USA Today preseason polls.

- The team had 13 seniors.

- Clarett wore #13.

- The jersey numbers of Cie Grant (#6) and Chris Gamble (#7), two players who took on different roles after the 2001 season and were involved in two of the biggest plays against Miami, sum to 13.

- The Buckeyes scored 13 against Penn State.

- The Buckeyes had 13 first downs against Michigan, who had 13 more first downs than the Buckeyes,

- Krenzel's 13th completion against Purdue was the Holy Buckeye play.

- Krenzel passed or ran for 13 touchdowns in the 13-game regular season.

- After the 2002 season, Krenzel had 13 career touchdown passes.

- The defense gave up 13 points per game.

- The Buckeyes had a +13 advantage in turnovers.

- The defense played 13 straight quarters without giving up a touchdown.

- A. J. Hawk had 13 solo and 13 assisted tackles.

- Simon Fraser had 13 solo tackles, and his last one was a sack of Dorsey on the Hurricanes' last possession in regulation.

- Chris Vance had 13 receptions, and his last one picked up a first down on the Buckeyes' drive for their first touchdown against Miami.

- San Jose State had 13 rushing plays, the lowest ever by an OSU opponent.

- Dr. Karen Holbrook, the president during the season, was Ohio State's 13th president.

THE MAGIC NUMBER 14

- The 14 wins were a Division I-A record.

- The Buckeyes returned 14 players who had started the Outback Bowl the season before.

- The 2002 season was Tressel's 14th with a winning record as a head coach.

- Tressel's 1994 Youngstown State team won its last 14 games for a 14-0-1 record. The tie in the first game against Stephen F. Austin came when the Penguins kicked a field goal on the game's final play.

- The Buckeyes and the opponents had 14 passing touchdowns, even though the opponents threw 166 more passes and had 142 more completions.

- The Buckeyes averaged 14 yards per reception.

- Fourteen players had a reception.

- Clarett had 14 rushing touchdowns in the regular season and 14 total touchdowns in Ohio Stadium.

- Clarett's 230-yard game came on the 14th of September.

- Krenzel had 14 incompletions against Miami.

- Krenzel had 14 yards rushing in the two overtimes of the Miami game.

- The Buckeyes had 14 first downs in the Miami game.

- Michigan and Miami had 14 passing first downs.

- The Buckeyes scored 14 against Michigan.

- The Buckeyes scored 14 points in overtime against Miami.

- The Buckeyes had 14 points off turnovers in the second quarter against Miami.

- The pass to Jenkins in the first overtime against Miami came on a 4th-and-14 play.

- The four rushing touchdowns against Miami covered a total of 14 yards.

- Miami had 14 possessions in regulation.

- Miami's Jonathan Vilma led all defenders with 14 tackles in the championship game.

- Krenzel had a 14-yard scramble on third-and-ten in overtime against Illinois to set up Maurice Hall's game-winning score.

- Krenzel's highest number of completions in a game was 14, which came in the Cincinnati game.

- Krenzel's most frequent number of pass attempts in a game was 14, which occurred four times. That included the Michigan game.

- The Buckeyes' second touchdown against Miami came on a 14-yard drive.

- The Buckeyes' last possession against Miami in regulation covered 14 yards, though replays showed Kelly Jennings grabbing Gamble's jersey on the third-down pass play before the punt and showed that Gamble may have caught the ball inbounds anyway.

- The two players who started the Miami game and have 14 letters in their name were Maurice Clarett and Michael Jenkins.

- Dustin Fox had 14 pass break-ups to lead the team, with the 14th (and the 13th) coming in the Michigan game.

- Ohio State had 14 yards in penalties in the two overtimes of the Fiesta Bowl.

- 14 years earlier, in 1988, the Buckeyes had their worst record since 1959, a record of 4-6-1.

- Ohio State would lose 14 Big Ten games in Tressel's ten-year tenure.

- The Big Ten championship was the Buckeyes' 14th shared title.

- Mike Doss and Kenny Peterson played on a Canton McKinley team that won a state championship with a 14-0 record.

- Clarett was tied for 14th place in rushing touchdowns in Division I-A college football.

- Krenzel ranked 14th nationally in passing efficiency in Division I-A college football with a 140.90 statistic.

- Fourteen years later, in 2016, the Buckeyes had a similar two-overtime win, 30-27 over Michigan, a game that also had a controversial call on fourth down in overtime go in their favor. In both 2002 and 2016, the starting quarterback (J.T. Barrett in 2016) wore #16, and no starting quarterback between Krenzel and Barrett wore #16.

THE MAGIC NUMBER 34

- The win over Miami broke the Hurricanes' 34-game winning streak, and it was the Buckeyes' first national championship won on the field in 34 years.

- Miami's 34-game streak, which was the sixth-longest in Division I-A history, had started after giving up 34 points in their loss to Washington in 2000.

- The Fiesta Bowl game had the 34th meeting between the Number 1 and Number 2 teams in the Associated Press media poll.

- The Fiesta Bowl was the Buckeyes' 34th bowl game.

- The Fiesta Bowl had 34 points in regulation.

- The last play with positive yardage for the Hurricanes was by Payton, wearing jersey #34.

- The win over Purdue was the Buckeyes' 34th all-time in the series against the Boilermakers.

- A. J. Hawk's only interception return for a touchdown in his career was a 34-yard return against Kent State.

- The last comfortable win, against Minnesota, had a 34-point scoring run by the Buckeyes, which stopped the next week when Purdue kicked a field goal for the first points of that game.

- Three years later in the 2005 season, Texas would end Southern Cal's 34-game winning streak in the national championship game. The losing coach for Miami (Larry Coker) and Southern Cal (Pete Carroll) had been an Ohio State assistant coach.

- Tressel's father, Lee, had a 34-game winning streak while coaching at Mentor High School.

- Krenzel's high school coach at Henry Ford II, Terry Copacia, whom Krenzel credits for his development as a quarterback, was inducted into the Michigan High School Football Coaches Hall Of Fame in 2020, after coaching at high schools in Michigan for 34 years.

- The game in Cincinnati was the first game against an Ohio team on the road in Ohio since '34—when they played at Western Reserve—which was 34 years prior to the national championship in 1968. In that 1934 season, the defense gave up 34 points in total, and the team scored 34 against Michigan.

CHRIS GAMBLE

- He had the Buckeyes' longest reception (57 yards), longest kickoff return (56 yards), and longest punt return (27 yards) of the year, and the most interceptions (four).

- His 1,134 all-purpose yards—499 receiving, 49 rushing, 293 on punt returns, 253 on kickoff returns, and 40 on interception returns—trailed only the 1,341 of Clarett.

- He had the team's longest punt return for the second straight year.

- Three of his four interceptions ended up in an end zone—two in the opponent's end zone and one on a return against Penn State. The fourth was at Ohio State's 11-yard line at Purdue.

- He had all four of his interceptions in games decided by six points or less, and all four were in the second half. Three of them were in the fourth quarter.

- His 40-yard interception for a touchdown against Penn State came in the same game where he had his best performance returning punts—five for 64 yards.

- Gamble, wearing #7 in 2002 and 2003, would finish his Ohio State career with seven interceptions. All four of his interceptions in the 2002 season came while the team was defending the north goal, and all three of his interceptions in the 2003 season would come while the team was defending the south goal. His 40-yard interception for a touchdown would turn out to be his only one of his seven with any return yards.

- He had his three longest receptions in away games —57 yards against Miami, 48 at Wisconsin, and 48 at Northwestern. These were three of the team's six longest receptions.

- His longest reception of 57 yards and longest run of 43 yards add up to 100.

- He had all of his 24 tackles in the last seven games of the season. If he had played on defense the entire season and maintained his average number of tackles, he would have finished with the sixth-highest number of solo tackles and the eighth-highest number of total tackles on the team.

- His only tackle for a loss came in the Michigan game.

MAURICE CLARETT

- He ran for 1,237 yards and had 16 rushing touchdowns, following the season that Jonathan Wells had—1,294 yards and 16 rushing touchdowns.

- He ran for at least 100 yards in seven of his 11 games. In the other four games, his highest was 66 yards, which was in the lopsided win over Kent State. His other three games were the Miami game and the two where he exited with an injury—Penn State and Purdue.

- In the regular season, he scored as many touchdowns (16) as the opponents, despite missing three games.

- He scored more touchdowns than the opponent in four games, and the same number of touchdowns as the opponent in two games.

- He set team records for the most 100-yard games by a freshman (7), most points by a freshman (108), and most touchdowns by a freshman (18).

- He had 222 carries for 1,237 yards and a 5.6 average per carry in his only year with the Buckeyes. The 222 carries matched the number that Keith Byars had in his first year of significant action (1983) with the Buckeyes, when he had 1,199 yards and a 5.4 average. Each had two touchdowns in the bowl game that year, in the same stadium, against a team currently in the Atlantic Coast Conference.

155

- In two of the three games that he missed, the Buckeyes won by four points at Cincinnati and were even in regulation at Illinois. In the Penn State game, when he exited after four carries, the Buckeyes won by six points and did not score an offensive touchdown.

- In the two lowest scoring games of the season—Penn State and Purdue—he had a total of 18 carries, and the team had a total of one offensive touchdown.

- What if he had been healthy for the Cincinnati and Illinois games, and for all of the Penn State and Purdue games? The Buckeyes averaged 121 rushing yards per game in those games and 220 yards per game in the other ten. Assuming that the Buckeyes would have won those games more decisively, the season would have been less magical with only three tight games, and what would critics have said in place of, "The Buckeyes were lucky to have won seven games by seven points or less"?

THE OFFENSE

- The edge in rushing touchdowns was 31-5. Despite this, and despite outgaining the opponents in rushing—2,678 yards to 1,088—the Buckeyes won four Big Ten games without scoring a rushing touchdown in regulation. Those four games were against Wisconsin, Penn State, Purdue, and Illinois, and in a span of five games. Those four games were decided by a total of 22 points (15 in regulation).

- Clarett (16) and Lydell Ross (six) had more rushing touchdowns than the opponents had in total.

- In nine games, the Buckeyes had at least one player with more rushing yards than the opponent had as a team.

- Chris Gamble and Scott McMullen had a combined seven rushes and two touchdowns.

- Home, Sweet Home: Krenzel completed 69% of his passes in home games and 51% of his passes in games away from home.

- Four of the last five games away from Columbus had a Buckeyes pass play of at least 48 yards. The exception was at Purdue, which had the 37-yard Holy Buckeye play.

- Six of the nine longest Buckeye pass plays were in games away from Columbus, with only two of the six for touchdowns.

- The Buckeyes had exactly 3,000 yards on rushing plays before losses were factored in.

- The total offense per game actually decreased from 370.6 yards per game in 2001 to 364.5 in 2002.

- The average gain per reception by Buckeye receivers decreased from 15.5 in 2001 to 14.0 in 2002.

- The Buckeyes had only two more first downs than the opponents on the season. The 2001 team, with a record of 7-5, had 14 more first downs than the opponents.

- In the last seven games, the Buckeyes averaged 18.6 points per game on offense in regulation, scoring at least 22 points in two of the games. In the last seven games of the 2001 season, they averaged 28 points per game on offense, scoring at least 22 points in each game.

- The Buckeyes averaged 38 points per game in the first seven games (no overtime games) and 18 points per game in regulation in the last seven games.

- The Buckeyes averaged 432 yards per game in the first seven games and 297 yards per game in the last seven games.

- The five highest games for rushing yards came in the first seven games.

- The opponents averaged 70 more passing yards per game, but in nine of the 14 games, the Buckeyes had the longest completion of the game.

- Ben Hartsock had his two touchdown receptions against Cincinnati and Wisconsin, road games decided by four and five points.

- Six different players had the longest reception in a game: Jenkins (7 times), Gamble (3), and Drew Carter, Clarett, Hartsock, and Ross once each.

- Krenzel and Clarett combined for 3,715 yards of total offense and 73% of the team's total offense. The year before, they had combined for 278 yards—all by Krenzel, with Clarett being in high school—and 6% of the team's total offense.

THE DEFENSE

- The five rushing touchdowns allowed by the defense marked an improvement of nine over the 14 allowed by the 2001 team, which had two fewer games.

- The five rushing touchdowns allowed led the nation.

- The defense gave up an average of 1.4 touchdowns per game, compared to 2.5 in the 2001 season.

- No opponent had multiple rushing touchdowns, and the Buckeye defense gave up a rushing touchdown in consecutive games only once—to Wisconsin and Penn State.

- In the last five regular season games, the defense gave up a total of two touchdowns, one each to Penn State and Illinois. The average score for those five opponents was eight points per game.

- In the last five games, the longest rush for an opponent was 11, seven, 10, 12, and 10 yards.

- The defense gave up only one rushing touchdown at home, and it was in the game when they scored no offensive touchdowns, the Penn State game.

- The defense gave up nine passing touchdowns in the first five games and five passing touchdowns in the last nine games.

- In the last eight regular season games, the defense gave up a total of three passing touchdowns.

- In the fourth quarter of the last seven games, the defense gave up no touchdowns and a total of three field goals, two of those on the last play of regulation.

- In the last three games of the regular season, the Buckeyes outscored the opponents in the fourth quarter by a combined score of 17-6. The difference at the end of regulation of those three games was four, zero, and five points.

- The defense allowed 112 points in the first half and 64 in the second half.

- The defense gave up less than 10 points in six games, the best performance since the 1979 team that accomplished it seven times, under first-year coach Earle Bruce. That 1979 team had an 11-0 record in the regular season.

- The defense gave up its most points in the first and last games of the season.

- The defense ranked as the second best in college football for points allowed, behind Kansas State, whom they would face a year later in the bowl game in the same stadium and also beat by seven points.

- Against the same eight Big Ten opponents that the Buckeyes had faced in 2001, the defense gave up an average of 10 fewer points in the 2002 game than in the 2001 game. Only Indiana (by three points) scored more in 2002 than in 2001.

- In the game preceding the Ohio State game, all 13 opponents scored more points than in the Ohio State game, by an average of 24 points. The most dramatic declines in scoring were 42 points by Washington State and Penn State, and 39 in regulation by Miami.

- In the game following the Ohio State game, all 13 opponents scored more points than in the Ohio State game, by an average of 21 points.

- The defense held six of the last eight opponents—San Jose State, Penn State, Minnesota, Purdue, Michigan, and Miami—to its lowest scoring output of its season.

- The defense held Kent State to 17 points, the Golden Flashes' average for the season, and held their other opponents to these points under their season average:

Texas Tech	17	Washington State	26
Cincinnati	5	Indiana	5
Northwestern	7	San Jose State	22
Wisconsin	13	Penn State	27
Minnesota	26	Purdue	24
Illinois	13	Michigan	19
Miami	17		

- Opponents averaged only 77.7 rushing yards and five rushing first downs per game. The defense ranked as the third best in college football in rushing yards allowed. In home games, the average was 66.3. The opponents averaged 2.6 yards per carry; in home games, it was 2.3.

- Against top running backs:

  - Willis McGahee of Miami had 1,753 yards in the season with a 6.2 average gain; 67 yards and a 3.3 average, his lowest in a game in the season, against Ohio State.

  - Chris Perry of Michigan had 1,110 yards in the season with a 4.2 average gain; 76 yards and a 2.7 average against Ohio State.

  - Larry Johnson of Penn State had 2,087 yards in the season with a 7.7 average gain; 66 yards and a 4.1 average against Ohio State. Like McGahee, he broke the team record for most yards in a season.

  - Antoineo Harris of Illinois had 1,330 yards in the season with a 4.8 average gain; 62 yards and a 3.0 average against Ohio State. Like McGahee, he broke the team record for most yards in a season.

- The three games with the highest number of pass breakups were decided by four, five, and seven (tied at the end of regulation) points. The defense had nine against Cincinnati, eight against Illinois, and seven against Michigan.

- In 2001, the opponents were successful 46% of the time on third down. In 2002, the Buckeyes defense improved that statistic to 36%.

- A painful loss in recent seasons was the 28-24 loss to Michigan State in 1998, when the Buckeyes had four plays at the Spartan 15-yard line on their last possession. That was their only loss in a bid for the national championship. In four games this season, the opponent had a first down inside the Buckeyes' 16-yard line late in the game and came away with a total of three points:

- Cincinnati had a first-and-ten from the Ohio State 15-yard line with under a minute to go.

- Purdue had a first-and-ten from the Ohio State 11-yard line and had to settle for a field goal with 7:50 remaining.

- Illinois had a first-and-ten from the Ohio State 11-yard line in the second overtime.

- Miami had a first-and-goal from the Ohio State two-yard line in the second overtime.

Bend but don't break—on the last possession in regulation (total: 165 yards, three points):

- Cincinnati gained 65 yards; the possession started with 3:39 remaining and ended in an interception.

- Illinois gained 44 yards; the possession started with 1:04 remaining and ended in a field goal.

- Michigan gained 56 yards; the possession started with :58 remaining and ended in an interception.

The last set of downs by the opponent in the seven tight games (total: 25 plays, 14 total yards, five carries for minus-six yards, three completions for 20 yards and three interceptions in 20 passes):

- Cincinnati: 4 plays, zero yards, interception
- Wisconsin: 3 plays, 1 yard
- Penn State: 4 plays, 4 yards
- Purdue: 3 plays, 6 yards, interception
- Illinois: 4 plays, 2 yards
- Michigan: 3 plays, zero yards, interception
- Miami: 4 plays, 1 yard

THE INTERCEPTIONS

- The Buckeyes' edge in interceptions was 18-7. They actually had two more interceptions in 2001 than in 2002, in two fewer games.

- Eight of the team's 18 interceptions ended in an end zone, either producing a score with a return or preventing a score. Chris Gamble had three (with one touchdown), Dustin Fox had two, Mike Doss had one (a touchdown), A. J. Hawk had one (a touchdown), and Will Allen had one. In addition, Allen intercepted at the three-yard line to end the Michigan game, with the Wolverines' Braylon Edwards in the end zone waiting on the pass. In addition, Tyler Everett intercepted a Washington State pass at the four-yard line in the fourth quarter.

- The last four of Doss's eight career interceptions (including the two in the 2001 Michigan game) had a total return yardage of 151, and all four were returned to the opponent's 17-yard line or deeper—to the four, to the nine, for a touchdown, and to the 17.

- In the two games (Penn State and Purdue) where the defense had the most interceptions (3), the offense scored a total of one offensive touchdown, and that came with 1:36 remaining.

- Oddly, in the four games where the defense had no interceptions, the average winning margin was 27 points. In the ten games where the defense had an interception, the average winning margin was 12 points.

- Dustin Fox's 12-yard interception return against Miami was the only one of his three in his sophomore season that had any return yards, and was the first of his career with any return yardage, as his only one as a freshman ended the game in Ann Arbor in 2001. It would turn out to be the longest return of his seven career interceptions.

- Will Allen had two interceptions with no return yards—in a 4-point win over Cincinnati and a 5-point win over Michigan—but he would have the opposite extreme in 2003 with a 100-yard return for a touchdown in a three-point win over San Diego State.

- Matt Wilhelm was positioned inside the 5-yard line for each of Allen's two interceptions, deflecting the pass in the Cincinnati game.

- In a battle of Wills: Will Allen, Will Smith, and Matt Wilhelm combined for five interceptions for zero yards returned.

- For the second straight year, the leaders in interceptions—Derek Ross in 2001 and Chris Gamble in 2002—wore #7 and had an interception return for a touchdown.

- Fourth quarter interceptions in games decided by five points or less, with three of them on the road:

- Cincinnati—Chris Gamble with 11:01 remaining, and Will Allen with 26 seconds remaining, both in the end zone

- Wisconsin—Gamble with 7:09 remaining, in the end zone

- Purdue—Gamble with 45 seconds remaining

- Michigan—Allen on the final play of the game

In addition, Cie Grant had a fourth quarter interception with 3:33 remaining in the 11-point road game at Northwestern.

THE KICKING GAME

- Andy Groom, a former walk-on who had tried out for the team in 1998, averaged 44.95 yards per punt, after averaging 44.98 yards in 2001.

- In each of the seven games decided by seven points or less, Groom had a punt of at least 52 yards.

- Mike Nugent

  - He was successful on 25 of 28 field goal attempts (89%). In the 2001 season, the team was successful on 10 of 24 field goal attempts (42%).

  - In the first six games, he was successful on eight field goals of at least 40 yards. In the next five games, he had no attempts of at least 40 yards. He doubled his total attempts from 14 in 2001 ro 28 in 2002.

  - He was successful on one field goal of at least 40 yards in 2001 and on ten field goals of at least 40 yards in 2002.

  - He increased his scoring from 48 points in 2001 to 120 points in 2002.

THE TWO OVERTIME GAMES—ILLINOIS AND MIAMI

- The Buckeyes, who had never had an overtime game since the rule started in 1996, had two in the span of three games.

- These were the only two games where the opponent outscored the Buckeyes in the second half.

- In each game, the winning touchdown possession took five plays, with a player named Maurice scoring the winning touchdown.

- In their last set of downs, Illinois had four plays and gained two yards, and Miami had four plays and gained one yard. The combined totals were three carries for three yards and no completions in five attempts.

- Miami had a first down on the two-yard line and couldn't score, ending the game. Ohio State had a first down on the one-yard line against Illinois and had to settle for a field goal.

- The defense gave up a total of 118 rushing yards on 67 carries in the two games, for an average of 1.8 yards per carry,

- The defense had a combined 10 of their 40 sacks in the two games.

- In each game, the disruption on defense on the last play of the game was by an Ohio native—Tim Anderson and Cie Grant.

- Cie Grant had an assist on the last two tackles recorded by the Buckeyes against Illinois and had the last two tackles (one solo and one assist) and the pressure on Dorsey on the last play against Miami.

- Gamble's longest reception of 57 yards of the season (Miami) and Jenkins's longest of 50 yards (Illinois) came in these two games. For a team not known for its passing, these two completions were longer than the opponent's longest in the game. No other Buckeye had a reception longer than 37 yards in the season.

- Conversely, these two games had the lowest first-half passing yards—20 against Miami and 37 against Illinois.

- The opponents' two longest punt returns of the season were in these two games, and each led to a score on a three-play possession in the second half. Each return was toward the north end zone, and the opponent's score gave them a 10-0 run.

  - In the Illinois game, the punt was returned 52 yards from the opponent's 25-yard line to the Buckeyes' 23-yard line. The Illini scored on a touchdown.

  - In the Miami game, the punt was returned 50 yards from the opponent's 24-yard line to the Buckeyes' 26-yard line. The Hurricanes scored on a field goal.

- Nugent was successful on four of seven field goals in overtime games and on all 21 attempts in non-overtime games. He missed attempts in the fourth quarter of 41 yards (Miami) and 42 yards (Illinois), and had made longer field goals in each game. After making his 24th straight in 2002, he was within reach of the single-season record of 25, which Washington's Chuck Nelson set in 1982.

- Nugent missed a field goal after a 12-play drive against Illinois and after an 11-play drive against Miami. They were the drives with the most plays in each game.

- The opponent kicked a field goal as time expired in regulation to force overtime in each game. They also missed a field goal in the fourth quarter. Their misses were from 59 (Illinois) and 54 (Miami) yards.

- In each game, Krenzel had 21 pass attempts and completed less than half of them—a combined 17 of 42.

- The Buckeyes were in their white road uniforms against a team whose colors include orange.

- The two orange-colored end zones in the south end were good for the Buckeyes, as that is where they scored both touchdowns against Illinois and three of the four against Miami.

THE SCHEDULE

- In the last six games, five opponents—Penn State, Minnesota, Illinois, Michigan, and Miami—had been named a national champion in its history, according to www.ncaa.com. None of the first eight opponents had this distinction.

- A tougher schedule: In 2001, the Buckeyes had played four teams with a winning record and one with a .500 record. In 2002, they played eight teams with a winning record and one with a .500 record.

- The eight home opponents finished with a collective 56% winning percentage, while the five road opponents finished with a 46% mark. All of the top five opponents with the best record—Texas Tech, Washington State, Penn State, Minnesota, and Michigan—were visitors to Ohio Stadium.

What if Ohio State had played Iowa?

- As in 1981, Ohio State and Iowa tied for first place in the

Big Ten without playing each other. In 2002, each had an 8-0 conference record, and each had a 7-5 overall record in 2001. In 1981, Ohio State and Iowa were the only two Big Ten teams to play eight conference games instead of nine, and they finished with a 6-2 record. Michigan, Illinois, and Wisconsin each had a 6-3 record.

- Against their seven common opponents, Iowa outscored them 258-114, and OSU outscored them 162-72. Iowa beat Michigan, Wisconsin, and Northwestern more decisively than the Buckeyes did, while Ohio State beat Indiana and Minnesota more decisively. The Buckeyes beat Penn State by six points and Purdue by four; Iowa beat Penn State by seven (in overtime) and Purdue by three.

- Iowa had the highest scoring offense in the Big Ten, and was third in scoring defense.

- Iowa was fifth in the nation in rushing defense, with the Buckeyes at third.

- If they had played, the Buckeyes would have faced the runner-up in the Heisman Trophy voting, quarterback Brad Banks.

- Ironically, Iowa also had a tight game in 2002 against Miami, except that it was against the Miami RedHawks of Ohio, a 29-24 win that was played in Oxford. Like the Buckeyes, they had a tight game against an in-state opponent, losing to Iowa State, 36-31. Like the Buckeyes, they played two teams from Ohio, also playing Akron.

- Both Jim Tressel and Kirk Ferentz of Iowa won multiple Coach of the Year awards in 2002. Ferentz had masterminded a huge improvement himself, increasing Iowa's wins from one to three to seven to eleven in his first four seasons.

What if Ohio State had played Michigan State?

- The Spartans had only a 4-8 record in 2002, but they had a combined record of 18-14-2 in 1972, 1974, and 1998 when they gave the Buckeyes their only regular season loss.

- Michigan State was 7-5 in 2001 and won the Silicon Valley Bowl over Fresno State, and would have an 8-4 record in 2003, losing the Alamo Bowl to Nebraska.

- Their 2002 team had Charles Rogers, who would catch 135 passes for 2,821 yards and 27 touchdowns in his two seasons. He set an NCAA record with a TD reception in 13 consecutive games.

What if the Big Ten had the practice of having Penn State as a road game for Ohio State in the season where Michigan is a home game? The separation started in 2011.

The Buckeyes played against these award winners:

- Brett Romberg of Miami won the Dave Rimington Trophy.

- Larry Johnson of Penn State won the Doak Walker, Maxwell, and Walter Camp Player of the Year Awards.

- Rien Long of Washington State won the John Outland Trophy.

- Kliff Kingsbury of Texas Tech won the Sammy Baugh Trophy.

By not playing Iowa or Michigan State, they avoided these award winners:

- Brad Banks of Iowa won the AP Player of the Year and Davey O'Brien Awards.

- Dallas Clark of Iowa won the John Mackey Award.

- Nate Kaeding of Iowa won the Lou Groza Award.

- Kirk Ferentz of Iowa won the Associated Press Coach of the Year Award and the Walter Camp Coach of the Year Award.

- Charles Rogers of Michigan State won the Fred Biletnikoff Award.

THE BUCKEYES DID BENEFIT FROM A NUMBER OF BREAKS IN THE SEASON:

- Cincinnati had the dropped pass in the end zone on their last possession.

- Northwestern missed field goal attempts of 18 and 39 yards in the second half, and settled for a field goal after the pass into the end zone that was ruled incomplete. That's 10 lost points that could have changed the strategy in an 11-point game.

- Purdue missed a 36-yard field goal attempt. The score could have been 9-3 when the Buckeyes prepared for the Holy Buckeye play, and could have been 10-9 in favor of the Buckeyes when the Boilermakers had the ball on the next possession, needing only a field goal to win.

- Illinois's receiver juggled the ball while falling out of bounds in overtime.

SIMILARITIES TO THE 1969 SEASON OF THE NEW YORK MIRACLE METS

- Both teams made a dramatic improvement over the year before. The Mets had a 73-89 record in 1968.

- The Buckeyes played the national champions of the previous year, and the Mets played the team (Baltimore) that would win the World Series the next year. Both the Hurricanes and the Orioles have orange as one of their colors.

- Jim Tressel and Gil Hodges (same number of syllables) were in the second year of leading his team.

- Both teams made huge defensive plays in the championship game/series.

- Both teams won with offenses in unconventional ways. The Buckeyes won with their quarterback using his legs. The Mets won both games of a doubleheader in the regular season by 1-0 scores where the pitcher drove in the only run.

SIMILARITIES TO THE 1983 NORTH CAROLINA STATE BASKETBALL CHAMPIONSHIP TEAM

Twenty years previously, the 1983 North Carolina State basketball team had a similar set of dramatic wins on its way to the national championship, beating Houston in the championship game.

Another Coach Jim, Valvano, was in his third year as coach of the Wolfpack, and Tressel was in his second in 2002. Valvano had come from a smaller college, Iona, and Tressel had come from a smaller college, Youngstown State. Both coached at the state university in the capital city for ten seasons. Valvano started at NC State at age 34. NC State was ranked 16th in the Associated Press preseason poll, and the 2002 Ohio State football team was ranked 13th. When Valvano gave his memorable speech on March 4, 1993, at the first ESPY Awards at Madison Square Garden, Lou Holtz was in attendance.

In each case, the state university team beat a team named for a city. Ohio State played a team that played for the national championship in consecutive seasons, as did NC State; Houston also lost to Georgetown in the 1984 title game. The OSU final game was played in Arizona; the NC State game was played in New Mexico. In the ESPN 30 For 30 documentary: "Survive And Advance", it relates that Valvano told his team on the day of his hiring, "I know I'm going to win a national championship", a statement somewhat stronger than "In 310 days …". It also shows him coaching a game wearing a vest as part of his suit. One of Tressel's favorite adjectives is "extraordinary"; the documentary shows Valvano quoting the Olympic decathlete Bob Richards with, "Every day, ordinary people do extraordinary things."

In each national championship game, the winning team came from behind and scored the winning points with no time on the clock (In Ohio State's case, the clock was turned off in overtime). While Ohio State's good fortune was helped by opponents dropping passes in the end zone during the season, NC State was helped by opponents missing free throws in the post-season games. The Wolfpack also benefited from the fact that the double bonus rule, starting with the tenth foul in the half, was not yet in effect.

Ohio State broke Miami's 34-game winning streak, and NC State broke Houston's 26-game winning streak in Houston's 34th game of the season. While Ohio State won seven games by seven points or less, in NC State's two post-season tournaments, they won seven games where the margin at the end of regulation was three points or less .

In the ACC Tournament, NC State beat Wake Forest, 71-70, thanks to a late steal and Lorenzo Charles making the second of two free throws.

They beat top-seed and defending NCAA champion North Carolina, led by Michael Jordan, in the semifinals in overtime, after trailing 75-62 with a little more than three minutes remaining. The game went to overtime when a Sam Perkins shot rattled out at buzzer. In overtime, they were down by six points with 2:13 remaining; Ohio State trailed Miami in overtime by seven points. Jordan fouled out of that game, leaving the Tar Heels without a prime player, as was the case with Miami and Willis McGahee. The Wolfpack were helped by the Tar Heels failing to make key free throws. They then knocked off second-ranked Virginia, which had three-time National Player of the Year Ralph Sampson, by three points in the championship game.

In the NCAA Tournament, the Wolfpack needed double overtime to get past Pepperdine, 69-67. They were down by six points with less than a minute remaining in the first overtime, and again were helped by missed free throws; an 84% foul shooter missed the front end of a one-and-one twice. In the second overtime, they made 10 free throws, but had no field goals. They defeated the University of Nevada, Las Vegas, whose record was 28-2 heading into the game, by another 71-70 score, a game in which they were down 12 points with less than 12 minutes remaining and by three points with 40 seconds remaining. They were helped by a missed free throw on the front-end of a one-and-one by UNLV with 32 seconds remaining. They won on a rebound basket with four seconds remaining off a miss by Dereck Whittenburg, a scenario that would repeat itself in a week. They survived again by one point by defeating top-seed Virginia in the Elite Eight; Lorenzo Charles made two free throws with 23 seconds remaining for the win.

They defeated Georgia in the Final Four to set up a meeting in the National Championship game with the Houston Cougars. NC State led by eight at halftime; the Buckeyes led Miami by seven at halftime. NC State fell behind by seven points, just as Ohio State would against Miami. Houston made only 10 of 19 free throws in the game. The Wolfpack completed their improbable run by knocking off the heavily favored Cougars, 54-52, on a Lorenzo Charles dunk off a Dereck Whittenburg air ball right before the final buzzer. Charles was shooting 63% in the NCAA Tournament, but was only 1-for-7 before his winning dunk. Whittenburg, the Wolfpack's second leading scorer, had missed a significant part of the season with a foot injury. Clarett, who was the Buckeyes' second leader in total offense, had missed three games in the 2002 season.

The NC State team was invited to the White House, where George H. W. Bush was the Vice President, and the Ohio State team was invited to the White House, where George W. Bush was the President.

FUN FACTS:

- Tressel improved his regular season wins by six in his second season, just as he had at Youngstown State.

- Tressel's team tied for first place in the conference, as he had done in his second season at Youngstown State.

- The Buckeyes doubled their wins from the previous year, which was not unusual for Coach Tressel, who had four seasons at Youngstown State with at least twice as many wins as the season before. The coach whom Tressel replaced, John Cooper, had also doubled his wins from year one to year two—from four in 1988 to eight in 1989.

- The Buckeyes made a seven-win improvement over the 2001 season. The last time that the Buckeyes made a six-win improvement over the previous season was in another perfect-record season—from 3-6 in 1943 to 9-0 in 1944, under first-year coach Carroll Widdoes.

- The average score at home was 35-11, and the average score away from home was 22-16 (19-15 in regulation).

- The two closest games, won by four points each, came in the two locations closest to Columbus—Cincinnati and West Lafayette.

- The Buckeyes trailed in all six games that were not played in Columbus, and trailed in each of the last seven games.

- The Buckeyes trailed or were tied at halftime in six games, trailed in the second half of seven games, and trailed or were tied in the fourth quarter of six games.

- Neither Krenzel nor any of the opposing starting quarterbacks were Ohio natives, despite playing Cincinnati and Kent State.

- The only opponents to score exactly seven points were "State" universities—Washington State, San Jose State, and Penn State.

- The Buckeyes, who would set a college football record in 2022 by scoring at least 20 points in their 70th consecutive game, scored less than 20 four times in the 2002 season and had a fifth (Miami) where they scored less than 20 in regulation.

- Winning four games where they scored less than 20 points occurred for the first time since the 1963 season.

- The Buckeyes did not score multiple touchdowns in the fourth quarter of any game.

- The average winning margin was 23 points in the first seven games, and was seven points per game (inflated by a 31-point win over Minnesota) in regulation in the last seven games.

- If pass interference had not been called, and the Fiesta Bowl had ended in a 24-17 loss, it would have matched the score of the last game of the seniors' freshman season (1999, Michigan). The Buckeyes had a 14-7 lead at halftime of that game, too.

- Texas Tech, Kent State, Cincinnati, and Indiana, which had a combined record of 22-30, each scored as many points or more in regulation against the Buckeyes than Miami did.

- The Buckeyes scored at least 50 points against Division I-A teams (they played all 14 games against Division I-A teams) twice, and Miami accomplished it only once, which occurred in its last regular season game.

- The 25-7 score (Washington State), the 51-17 score (Kent State), the 45-17 score (Indiana), and the 23-16 score (Illinois) have never been duplicated in Ohio State history, through the 2022 season.

- The 16-16 score at the end of regulation in the Illinois game has never been duplicated in Ohio State history, through the 2022 season.

- The 17-17 score at the end of regulation in the Miami game marked the first time that it had occurred in Ohio State history, with the next one being the 30-27 double-overtime win over Michigan in 2016.

- The 23-19 score of the Cincinnati game was only the second game in OSU history with that score. The other one occurred in 1985 against Minnesota, also a road game. Tressel was an OSU assistant in that game, and the Minnesota coach was former OSU assistant Lou Holtz, who, like Tressel in 2002, was in his second season leading a Big Ten team. The Buckeyes trailed by nine points in each game and scored the last touchdown of each game.

- The 13-7 win over Penn State was the first win without scoring an offensive touchdown since the 10-7 Citrus Bowl win over Brigham Young in the 1985 season, which also had an interception return for a touchdown. However, they would accomplish this twice in 2003 at home, in the 16-13 win over San Diego State (interception return) and the 19-10 win over Iowa (punt return and blocked punt return).

- The 13-7 win over Penn State was the first win with scoring 13 points or less at home since 1986, when they beat Colorado, 13-10.

- The 10-6 win over Purdue was the first win with scoring 10 points or less in the last 15 years, matching the 10-6 win over Illinois in 1987, which was also a Big Ten game on the road. That was also the last time that the Buckeyes had a game with a combined 16 points or less. The Buckeyes also had a win where they scored 10 points in 1977, over Miami.

- The leaders in kickoff returns and punt returns—Hall and Gamble—had a different jersey number in 2001.

- Krenzel had six touchdown passes in home games and six touchdown passes away from home.

- Ohio State quarterbacks had 369 yards rushing (368 by Krenzel), and opposing quarterbacks had a total of negative-four.

- The Buckeyes had at least 20 first downs in four of the first seven games and in none of the last seven games.

- The Buckeyes had their two highest games for rushing touchdowns in their first game (six) and their last game (four, tied with the Indiana game).

- The Buckeyes did not have more pass attempts than the opponent in any game. In the Wisconsin game, both teams had 19.

- In the last three games, Jenkins had his longest reception of the season (50 yards, against Illinois), Clarett had his longest (26 yards, against Michigan), and Gamble had his longest (57 yards, against Miami).

- Jenkins's first three touchdown receptions came in Ohio Stadium, and his last three touchdown receptions came in the last three road games, against Wisconsin, Purdue, and Illinois. The total difference in regulation of those three road games was nine points.

- In his book, "One and Done: How My Life Started When My Football Career Ended", Clarett wrote that the night before the Michigan game, Coach Tressel had Clarett and Cie Grant room together for the first time. They were the players who made the last big play on offense and on defense against Miami.

- In two matchups between premier running backs, Clarett and McGahee combined for 114 yards (McGahee was injured in the fourth quarter), and Clarett and Larry Johnson combined for 105 yards (Clarett was injured on the first possession of the game).

- The Buckeyes lost no fumbles in the last 19 quarters of the season, and had no turnovers in the last 11 quarters of the regular season.

- Non-seniors had:
  - All 31 rushing touchdowns.
  - 44 of the 48 touchdowns (92%).
  - 42 of the 45 touchdowns (93%) on offense.
  - 386 of the 410 points (94%).

- 2,666 of the 2,678 rushing yards (99.6%). The other 12 yards were by special-team players.

- 2,247 of the 2,425 receiving yards (93%).

- 160 of the 173 receptions (92%).

- All of the 173 receptions were by players from Ohio or Florida.

- The Buckeyes averaged one touchdown for every 20 plays, and the opponents averaged one touchdown for every 51 plays.

- The Buckeyes averaged one rushing touchdown for every 20 attempts, and the opponents averaged one rushing touchdown for every 84 attempts.

- The Buckeyes averaged 27.8 points per game in regulation, compared to 26 in 2001, but improved their defense by averaging 12.6 points per game on defense in regulation, compared to 20.3 in 2001.

- The 2001 team scored at least 26 points in nine of their 12 games. The 2002 team scored at least 26 points in seven of their 14 games, with one of those seven (Miami) requiring overtime.

- The defense faced four of the top 15 leaders in passing yards and three of the top nine leaders in passing touchdowns.

- In the last five games, the opponents had 10 of their 17 field goals.

- To validate Tressel's belief that the punt is the most important play in football, there was almost a one-to-one relation between the opponent's punt return success and the closeness of the score. In the eight closest games (11 points or less), seven opponents had a punt return between 18 and 52 yards; Penn State was the exception. In the other six games, the longest punt return was 15 yards, with two teams having no return yardage.

- The attendance of 77,502 at the national championship game was exactly 1,000 more than in the Buckeyes' last bowl win, in the Sugar Bowl of the 1998 season.

- Ten years later, in Ohio State's next undefeated season of 2012, they would also win half their games by seven points or less, and also finish the last two games of the regular season with a seven-point overtime win on the road (Wisconsin)—in which they scored first in overtime and made a stop on defense—and a five-point home win over Michigan.

- Coach Tressel won his national championship in his second season at Ohio State, improving from a 7-5 record to 14-0. Fred Taylor, a native of Zanesville, won his basketball national championship in 1960—his second season at Ohio State—improving his record by 14 wins, from a 11-11 record to 25-3. Like Tressel, Taylor beat the defending champion, the California Golden Bears.

- The Columbus Touchdown Club has an annual event where "athletes from all sports are recognized each year", as its website states. In both 2001 and 2002, it awarded the Chic Harley Award for the College Football Player of the Year and the Archie Griffin Award for the College Football Most Valuable Player to Ken Dorsey. In 2002, it awarded the Sammy Baugh Award for the Top College Passer to Kliff Kingsbury of Texas Tech.

- The Buckeyes played nine teams who appeared in bowl games, and five of them won. Miami played six teams who appeared in bowl games, and three of them won.

- Ohio State opponents followed the Buckeyes' lead in the bowl games by playing in three of the four closest bowl games—Wisconsin (three point win), Penn State (four point loss), and Cincinnati (five point loss).

- The next four teams in the final Associated Press poll, following Ohio State and Miami, also had coaches who were in their fifth year or less, or had an Ohio connection, or both. In addition, Iowa was #8, with Kirk Ferentz in his fourth year.

   #3 Georgia, 13-1   Mark Richt, second year
   #4 USC, 11-2   Pete Carroll, second year,
                       former OSU assistant
   #5 Oklahoma, 12-2   Bob Stoops, fourth year,
                       born in Youngstown
   #6 Texas, 11-2   Mack Brown, fifth year

CHAPTER 6

The 1968 and 2002
National Championships
Deja Vu All Over Again

OHIO STATE'S 2002 AND 1968 National Championship seasons had many similarities.

- Neither team was ranked in the Top 10 of the Associated Press preseason poll; the 1968 team was ranked #11, and the 2002 team was ranked #13.

- The 2002 team was three years removed from a 6-6 season, and the 1968 team was two years removed from a 4-5 season. Those two down years had two of the three worst records for Ohio State between 1960 and 1999.

- The calendar was the same, so that both teams played on each Saturday from September 28 through the Michigan game on November 23.

- The 2002 team outscored the opponents by 17.5 points per game, and the 1968 team outscored the opponents by 17.3 points per game.

- Each team had a player on defense named Tim Anderson.

- The 1968 team had Jim Otis at fullback, and the 2002 team had his son, Jim Otis, a backup quarterback.

- The 1968 team had Mark Stier and Dick Kuhn, and the 2002 team had their nephew, Dustin Fox.

- Each team had a player from New York City. The 1968 team had John Brockington from Brooklyn, and the 2002 team had Will Smith, who was born in Queens.

- In each season, the leading rusher was from Ohio; in 1968, it was Otis.

- Both Clarett and Otis had 16 touchdowns in the regular season.

- In each season, the leading receiver was from out of state; in 1968, it was Bruce Jankowski, from New Jersey. Similar to the 2002 team having several key players from out of state, Woody had made a conscious effort to add out-of-state players to his team, such as Jan White from Pennsylvania, John Brockington from New York, Tim Anderson from West Virginia, and Jack Tatum from New Jersey.

- Each team averaged one passing touchdown per game.

- In each season, the opponent in the bowl game had at least one regular season game after the Buckeyes' season had ended.

- Each team played a team ranked Number 1 at the time— Miami in the 2002 season and Purdue in the 1968 season.

- Each team beat Illinois by seven points in Champaign, scoring the last touchdown on a run to break a tie.

- Each team had seven wins by more than seven points.

- The Buckeyes shut out Michigan in the second half in each season.

- The 2002 team did not play Iowa, and the 1968 team did not play two teams in the top half of the Big Ten—Minnesota (6-4, 5-2 in the Big Ten) and Indiana (6-4, 4-3), two of the three teams that tied for first place in 1967.

- The first game in each case was against a team from the second-most populous state, Texas—Southern Methodist in 1968 and Texas Tech in 2002. The last game in the 1968 season was against a team from the most populous state (California), and the last game in the 2002 season was against a team from the third-most populous state (Florida).

- The first game of each season did not have a sellout crowd.

- In 2002, the first three games were at home, followed by a close game on the road against Cincinnati, where the Buckeyes took the lead with 3:44 remaining. In 1968, the first four games were at home, followed by a close game on the road against Illinois, where the Buckeyes took the lead with 1:30 remaining. The week after each game, the Buckeyes had a five-point win at home over a team from Michigan; the 1968 team beat Michigan State, 25-20.

- Each team had an October game in Columbus where they scored 13 points and had an interception for a touchdown against a team that started with the letter P—13-0 over Purdue in 1968 with Ted Provost's interception and 13-7 over Penn State in 2002 with Chris Gamble's.

  - In each case, it was against a team that they had lost to the year before.

  - In each case, the Buckeyes scored six points on offense.

  - Purdue in 1968 was averaging 41.3 points entering the game, and Penn State in 2002 was averaging 36.9.

- Each interception play started with the opponent having the ball on the far right hash mark, each interception was returned down the right sideline and was scored in the south end zone, and each interception was on the opponent's first possession of the third quarter.

- Both Provost and Gamble had four interceptions that year, and the interception for the score was his only one with any return yards.

- The Buckeyes added another score after the interception return.

- In each case, the opposing quarterback's last name ended with the letter S—Phipps and Mills.

- In each game, the Buckeyes had another interception by a lineman—Jim Stillwagon in 1968 and Will Smith in 2002—with no return yards, and it was his only interception of the year.

- Each team played a regular season game against a team from the conference now known as the Pacific-12—Oregon in 1968 and Washington State in 2002.

- Each team had played its opponent in the National Championship game within the previous four years. The 1968 team had played USC in the 1964 and 1963 seasons, and the 2002 team had played Miami in the 1999 season.

- Each team had a 27-16 and 31-24 win away from Columbus, a 45-21 win at home, and wins at home where they scored 13, 25, and 50 points.

- Before the 2002 season, the 31-24 and the 45-21 scores had occurred only in the 1968 season.

- The 31-24 game of each season was tied in the fourth quarter, and the Buckeyes scored the last touchdown on a run.

- In the Michigan game the year before, the Buckeyes had all three touchdowns on runs, had a 21-0 lead, and kicked a field goal in the fourth quarter.

- In 1968, Ohio State had no players in the top ten of the Heisman Trophy voting, but faced three of the top six—O. J. Simpson of USC, Leroy Keyes of Purdue, and Ron Johnson of Michigan. In 2002, Ohio State had no players in the top ten of the Heisman Trophy voting, but faced five of the top nine—Larry Johnson of Penn State, Willis McGahee and Ken Dorsey of Miami, Jason Gesser of Washington State, and Kliff Kingsbury of Texas Tech.

- In 1968, the Buckeyes faced college football's leader in rushing yards and rushing touchdowns (O. J. Simpson). In 2002, the Buckeyes faced college football's leader in rushing yards (Larry Johnson) and rushing touchdowns (Willis McGahee). Both Simpson and McGahee ran for one touchdown in the championship game against the Buckeyes.

- The 1968 team's defense also put the clamps on high profile ground gainers—Leroy Keyes of Purdue (seven carries for 19 yards), Ron Johnson of Michigan (21 carries for 99 yards, but 39 on one carry), O. J. Simpson of USC (28 carries for 171 yards, but 80 on one carry), and Ed Podolak of Iowa (45 yards on 15 carries).

- In 1968, the Buckeyes faced five of college football's top 20 leaders in rushing yards—Simpson, Ron Johnson of Michigan, Mike Richardson of SMU, Leroy Keyes, and Rich Johnson of Illinois. In 2002, they faced four of the top 20—Larry Johnson, Willis McGahee, Anthony Davis, and Demarco McCleskey.

- The 1968 team also had some offense-to-defense switches. The *Ohio State University 1968 Football Information* publication mentions that Jack Tatum was an all-New Jersey as a fullback, and that safety Mike Sensibaugh was an all-Ohio quarterback in high school; he still holds the Ohio State season and career records for interceptions. Jan White had been a wide receiver in high school but was moved to tight end at Ohio State.

- In the book, "What It Means to Be a Buckeye: Jim Tressel and Ohio State's Greatest Players", Cie Grant mentions a position switch for him—he was a quarterback in high school—and that an assistant coach for his high school team was Jim Roman, who was a center and also led the team in kick-scoring in 1968. The OSU media guide reported that Grant spent the first two years at Ohio State as a strong safety, 2000 as a linebacker, 2001 as a cornerback, and 2002 back to linebacker.

- In '68, a key defensive player (Jim Stillwagon) wore jersey #68. In '02, a key defensive player (Mike Doss) wore #2.

Craig Krenzel and Rex Kern

- The letters in "Kern" appear in "Krenzel".

- Tressel has said that as a kid, Rex Kern was his idol.

- Kern as a sophomore had no playing time before the season due to freshmen being ineligible, and Krenzel had two starts but only one full game before the 2002 season—the Michigan game and the bowl game, where he had a combined six rushes and passes.

- Kern's teams had a 27-2 record, and Krenzel's had a 25-2 record in his two full years.

- The two losses for Kern's teams were by a combined 22 points, and the two losses for Krenzel's teams in his two full years were by a combined 21 points.

- Each had a 2-1 record against Michigan, with a loss at Michigan and a win as a sophomore.

- Krenzel was the offensive Most Valuable Player of the Fiesta Bowl, his first bowl playing the entire game, and Kern was the Most Valuable Player of the Rose Bowl, his first bowl.

- Each accounted for 15 touchdowns in the national championship season. Kern had eight rushing and seven passing, and Krenzel had 12 passing and three rushing.

- Each accounted for two touchdowns in the national championship game; Kern had two touchdown passes.

- The Buckeyes never lost at home in Kern's three years or in Krenzel's two full years.

- Krenzel replaced the incumbent senior quarterback (Steve Bellisari) in 2001, out of necessity, and Kern replaced the incumbent senior quarterback (Bill Long) in 1968.

- After the 2002 season, Krenzel's 2,453 career passing yards placed him 10th on OSU's all time list, just ahead of Rex Kern (2,444 yards).

The games for the National Championship—the January 1, 1969 Rose Bowl and the BCS Championship—had the similarities:

- The game matched the #1 and #2 ranked teams.

- The Buckeyes were outgained on offense.

- The defense recorded two interceptions and recovered three fumbles.

- The Buckeyes wore their road white uniforms and beat the defending champions.

- The opposing team had 19 first downs.

- The Buckeyes' leading receiver—Ray Gillian in the Rose Bowl and Jenkins—was from out of state and had four receptions.

- The opposing team scored first and had only one touchdown in the first half.

- Each game had a pass intercepted in the end zone; in the Rose Bowl, the Buckeyes intercepted a pass by O. J. Simpson.

- The Buckeyes were scoreless in the first quarter.

- The Buckeyes scored twice in the second quarter and once (on a field goal) in the third quarter.

- The Buckeyes had the momentum at the end of the first half; scoring the last 10 points in the Rose Bowl and the last 14 points of the Fiesta Bowl.

- The Buckeyes led by three points at the end of the third quarter.

- The opposing team scored a rushing touchdown, a passing touchdown, and a field goal in regulation.

- In the Rose Bowl, all three Buckeye touchdowns were in the south end zone. In the BCS Championship game, both Buckeye touchdowns in regulation and the third one in overtime were in the south end zone.

- In the Rose Bowl, USC scored a touchdown in the north end zone with 45 seconds remaining, and the disputed catch was barely inbounds. In the BCS Championship game, Miami kicked a field goal that was barely good with no time remaining in regulation, in the north end zone.

- The opposing quarterback—Steve Sogge and Ken Dorsey— was a senior from California.

- The Buckeyes had the more mobile quarterback. Kern ran for 534 yards in the season and 35 in the Rose Bowl. Sogge ran for 49 yards in the season and minus-19 in the Rose Bowl.

- The opposing star running back was in his last year at his university.

Unlike the 2002 team, the 1968 team struggled with its kick-scoring all season, although they made two field goals in the Rose Bowl, from 32 and 33 yards. They made only five of 14 attempts on the season and had four—yes, four!—different kickers with attempts. The four were Larry Zelina, a wingback, who missed an attempt in the Rose Bowl; Jim Oppermann, an offensive lineman; Dick Merryman, who transferred from Ohio University a week before the season began; and Jim Roman, a center who made the two in the Rose Bowl.

Jim Tressel and Woody Hayes

- The names of Jim Tressel and Woody Hayes contain 10 letters. Even replacing "Wayne" for "Woody" retains the pattern.

- Each was born in Ohio, the son of an educator. Tressel was the first Ohio State coach born in Ohio since Woody, and was born 13 days after Woody's first win over Michigan.

- Tressel's father, Lee, was a navy lieutenant, and Woody was a navy Lieutenant Commander, and both served in the Pacific during World War II.

- Tressel's first team won seven games, the first time that the Buckeyes had won seven games since Woody's last season

THE IMPROBABLE NATIONAL CHAMPIONSHIP

of 1978. In each season following the seven-win season, the team won all of its regular season games.

- Tressel's first year (2001) was exactly 50 years after Woody's.

- The February 19, 1951 *Columbus Dispatch* reported Woody's hiring, and the men's basketball team won at Michigan that day, 68-66. On January 18, 2001, Tressel was introduced to OSU fans at halftime of the men's basketball game against Michigan, which the Buckeyes won, 78-61.

- The headline on the front page had "Hayes to Coach OSU; Miami U Mentor Wins Five-Year Agreement". That same story reported, "... his contract would be for one year 'according to university regulations.' Later, it was learned that Hayes has been given a 'gentleman's agreement' for five years." When Tressel was hired, the *Dispatch* reported that he was given a five-year contract.

- The *Columbus Dispatch* on that same date in 1951 had some Woody Hayes facts with a familiar ring: "His first venture wasn't a complete success [2-6], but Denison did manage to win its final game from Wittenberg that season. In the next two years, Denison was undefeated ..."

- Woody's last game at Miami was the Salad Bowl, played in Phoenix at Montgomery Stadium, which was demolished in 1987, the year of his death. His team beat Arizona State, 34-21, with the 55 combined points matching the 55 of the Buckeyes' Fiesta Bowl win. Arizona State, like the Hurricanes, lost three fumbles in the game. The *Miami Student* newspaper reported that Arizona State's Wilford White was leading the nation in rushing; the 2002 Buckeyes faced the leading rusher, Larry Johnson. On the same day, Bear Bryant's Kentucky team beat Number 1 Oklahoma, 13-7 in the Sugar

Bowl, breaking the Sooners' 31-game winning streak. Four weeks before the Salad Bowl game, the Miami basketball team had upset Michigan in Ann Arbor, 44-36.

- Each faced a Pennsylvania team in the seventh game in his first year—Pitt in 1951 and Penn State in 2001.

- Each had a non-conference game embedded in the schedule in his first year—Pitt in the seventh game of 1951 and San Diego State in the sixth game of 2001.

- Each was left-handed.

- Each graduated from a private university in Ohio—Hayes at Denison in 1935 and Tressel at Baldwin Wallace, 40 years later.

- Each received a master's degree from a four-year public university in Ohio—Hayes at Ohio State and Tressel at the University of Akron.

- The job previous to Ohio State for each was at another four-year public university in Ohio—Miami for Hayes and Youngstown State for Tressel.

- Each had been a head coach at colleges in Ohio—Woody at Denison and Miami, Tressel at Youngstown State. Also, Tressel was an assistant coach at Miami.

- Each had a worse record in his first year than his predecessor. Woody's was 4-3-2, compared to Wes Fessler's 6-3, and Tressel's was 7-5, following Cooper's 8-4.

- Each won a national championship within four years.

- Each holds the Big Ten record with six straight conference championships.

- In his second season, each had a freshman on his squad who was a native Ohioan and who would eventually win the

Heisman Trophy. Hayes had Howard Cassady, who played as a freshman in 1952, and Tressel had Troy Smith, who was redshirted in 2002.

- Tressel said that the punt was the most important play in football. In the book "Buckeye Madness: The Glorious, Tumultuous, Behind-the-Scenes Story of Ohio State Football" by Joe Menzer, it quotes Woody as saying that a blocked punt was one of the five big mistakes in football.

- Tressel used a line almost verbatim to one that Woody had used. In a story by Ivan Maisel on www.espn.com, Syracuse coach Dick MacPherson talked about a game against Illinois where Tressel called for the sprint draw play for Joe Morris ten times in a row, and MacPherson asked him whether they had any other play. "He said, 'Yes we do, Coach. As soon as they stop this one, I'll call it.' "

- Hayes in 1968 and Tressel in 2002 received multiple Coach of the Year awards. Tressel won the Division I Coach of the Year award by the American Football Coaches Association (AFCA), the Bear Bryant Award, the Eddie Robinson Award, and the *Sporting News* Award. He also won the AFCA award three times while at Youngstown State, becoming the first person in the history of the AFCA to be Coach of the Year at two different schools.

Assistant coaches who would become head coaches:

- The 1968 team had Earle Bruce (who would coach at Tampa, Iowa State, Ohio State, Northern Iowa, and Colorado State), George Chaump (Marshall and Navy), Lou Holtz (William and Mary, North Carolina State, Arkansas, Minnesota, Notre

Dame, and South Carolina), Rudy Hubbard (Florida A&M), and Bill Mallory (Miami of Ohio, Colorado, Northern Illinois, and Indiana). The staff also had Lou McCullough, who became the Athletic Director at Iowa State and hired Earle Bruce.

- The 2002 team had Mark Dantonio (Cincinnati and Michigan State), Mel Tucker (Colorado and Michigan State), Mark Snyder (Marshall), and Luke Fickell (Ohio State, Cincinnati, and Wisconsin).

CHAPTER

7

A Bit of College Football History, with Ohio Connections

MANY OF THE MEMORABLE, controversial games in college football history, with improbable endings, that took place between 1966 and 1982 had a connection to Ohio State or Ohioans. And, Ohio State and Notre Dame have many parallels in their history.

THE 1988 AND 2002 NATIONAL CHAMPIONSHIPS

Ohio State's 2002 National Championship and Notre Dame's 1988 National Championship had many similarities. The two championships came 14 years apart, with the number 14 being a common theme in the Buckeyes' 2002 championship. Each team recorded the most wins in program history.

Thirty-four years before Ohio State's 2002 national championship, Ohio State had won a national championship (in 1968), and thirty-four years before Notre Dame's 1988 national championship (in 1954), Ohio State had also won a national championship.

Ohio State's and Notre Dame's bowl game of each year both took place in Tempe in the Fiesta Bowl. In each case, the two teams were undefeated, the combined score was 55 points (Notre Dame beat West Virginia, 34-21), and the losing team scored three touchdowns. In those games, Notre Dame's quarterback Tony Rice had a career high in passing yards, and Krenzel had a career high in rushing yards. Both Rice and Krenzel threw seven interceptions during his championship season. Both completed seven passes in his bowl game. Rice had been ineligible as a freshman, and Krenzel had only 14 plays for 46 yards as a freshman. In the book, "The 100-Yard War: Inside the 100-Year-Old Michigan-Ohio State Football Rivalry", author Greg Emmanuel wrote that Krenzel was actually a Notre Dame fan as a kid, wearing Tim Brown and Tony Rice jerseys.

The losing coaches in the bowl game had been assistants at an Ohio college—Larry Coker of Miami at Ohio State, and Don Nehlen of West Virginia at Cincinnati and Bowling Green (before becoming its head coach).

Notre Dame gave up 13 points per game (12.3 in the regular season) in the 1988 season, and Ohio State gave up 13.1 points per game (12.2 in the regular season) in the 2002 season.

In 1988, Notre Dame faced four of the top six vote-getters for the Heisman Trophy: Rodney Peete of USC (#2), Steve Walsh of Miami (#4), Major Harris of West Virginia (#5), and Tony Mandarich of Michigan State (#6). In 2002, Ohio State faced five of the top nine vote-getters for the Heisman Trophy: Larry Johnson of Penn State (#3), Willis McGahee of Miami (#4), Ken Dorsey of Miami (#5), Jason Gesser of Washington State (#7), and Kliff Kingsbury of Texas Tech (#9).

For Notre Dame, three and eleven were the magical numbers; they won national championships eleven years apart, in 1966 (Coach Ara Parseghian), 1977 (Dan Devine), and 1988 (Lou Holtz). In each case, the coach was in his third year, as was Frank Leahy, when he won a national championship in 1943, the year following Ohio State's first one.

Notre Dame's 1988 team was recognized at the White House when George H. W. Bush was the Vice President, and Ohio State's 2002 team was recognized at the White House when George W. Bush was the President.

OSU VS. MIAMI IN THE 2002 SEASON AND NOTRE DAME VS. MIAMI IN THE 1988 SEASON

For both Ohio State and Notre Dame, the biggest game of its championship season was against Miami, with the Notre Dame vs. Miami game taking place in the regular season. For Notre Dame, it was a home game; for Ohio State, it was a virtual home game, based on its dominant fan attendance. Miami was the defending national champion in each case.

Miami had a 36-game regular season winning streak snapped by Notre Dame in the 1988 game, giving up 31 points and losing to a former OSU assistant, Lou Holtz. Miami had a 34-game winning streak snapped by OSU in the 2002 season, giving up 31 points and losing to a former OSU assistant, Jim Tressel. Note: In 1988, Ohio State scored 31 points against its arch-rival, Michigan; Ohio State has not scored at least 31 points in a losing home game since then.

The winning quarterback (Krenzel and Rice) was a junior, and the losing Miami quarterback (Ken Dorsey and Steve Walsh) was in his last year. None of the four quarterbacks played for a team located in his home state; Krenzel is from Michigan, Rice is from South Carolina, Dorsey is from California, and Walsh is from Minnesota. Krenzel had 19 carries in the Fiesta Bowl, and Rice had 22 carries in the 1988 game.

In the 1988 season, Walsh had 390 pass attempts, 29 touchdowns, and 12 interceptions. In the 2002 season, Dorsey had 393 attempts, 28 touchdowns, and 12 interceptions. The loss to Ohio State for Dorsey and to Notre Dame for Walsh was the only one for each in his last two seasons at Miami.

Kellen Winslow had 11 receptions in the Fiesta Bowl, and Miami's running back Cleveland Gary had 11 receptions in the 1988 game. The

Hurricanes outgained the Buckeyes in the Fiesta Bowl by 102 yards, and outgained the Irish in 1988, 481 yards to 331. Rob Chudzinski, who played in high school at Toledo St. John's, was the Hurricanes' offensive coordinator in the Fiesta Bowl and was a Hurricanes tight end in the 1988 game.

The Notre Dame vs. Miami game—dubbed "Catholics vs. Convicts", generated by Notre Dame students and referring to Miami's reputation of legal issues—had a fake punt by Miami that failed, and the Ohio State vs. Miami game had a fake field goal by the Buckeyes that failed.

In each game, Miami trailed by 10 points in the third quarter, and the winning team was scoreless in the fourth quarter.

The Notre Dame vs. Miami game had a 57-yard catch by the Irish's Raghib Ismail, and the Ohio State vs. Miami game had a 57-yard catch by Chris Gamble. The Hurricanes had seven turnovers against Notre Dame and five against the Buckeyes. The Hurricanes had 73 yards rushing with a 2.6 average against Notre Dame and 65 yards rushing with a 2.0 average against the Buckeyes.

Defensive backs Chris Gamble of Ohio State and Pat Terrell of Notre Dame were from Florida, and both had switched from offense to defense that season, though Gamble continued to play on offense. D'Juan Francisco of Notre Dame—who played high school in Cincinnati, Ohio—had switched from offense to defense after the 1986 season. Both Terrell—with a pick-six—and Francisco had interceptions against Miami.

Another prominent Ohioan for Notre Dame was linebacker Frank Stams, from Akron, who wreaked havoc on Walsh and the Hurricanes all game long, causing two fumbles and recovering another. In the book "Unbeatable: Notre Dame's 1988 Championship and the Last Great College Football Season", the author Jerry Barca quoted Walsh as saying, "We had no answer for Frank Stams." In a www.espn.com story, Walsh said that Notre Dame "... had a much better pass rush than I was expecting. They put a lot of pressure on me ... We couldn't run it very well ... we were a little out of our element ... It kept us from winning the national championship."

Miami's coach in 1988 was Jimmy Johnson, who had been the head coach at Oklahoma State, and its coach in 2002 was Larry Coker, who had been an assistant coach at Oklahoma State under Jimmy Johnson in 1983.

CONTROVERSIAL CALLS

- Against Notre Dame in the fourth quarter, Miami fans thought that they were robbed on a play when it was ruled that Cleveland Gary had fumbled near the goal line, which gave the Irish the ball on their own one-yard line, but they had a huge break with 45 seconds remaining when their last touchdown came as the receiver appeared not to have control of the ball. The score before that touchdown was 31-24, the same as Ohio State's winning score.

- Against OSU in overtime, Miami fans thought that they were robbed on a play that was ruled pass interference, but they had a huge break in the fourth quarter when they were not called for an obvious hold on a pass to Chris Gamble, and Gamble may have caught the ball inbounds anyway.

- The bobbled catch by Miami in 1988 and the pass interference call in the Fiesta Bowl were in similar locations of the south end zone.

- Pat Terrell's break-up of Miami's pass attempt for a two-point conversion following the last touchdown—with Miami trailing 31-30—and the pass interference call in the Fiesta Bowl were also in that same similar location of the south end zone.

JIM TRESSEL AND LOU HOLTZ

- Holtz won his national championship in his third year, and Tressel won his national championship in his second year.

- Tressel in 2002 and Holtz in 1988 won the College Football Coach of the Year award by *Sporting News*.

- Both would coach another eight years at his college, as would Parseghian after his 1966 national championship.

- Both grew up in Ohio.

- Both were assistants on an Ohio State team that played Southern California in a Rose Bowl—Holtz in the 1968 season and Tressel in the 1984 season. Southern California scored two touchdowns in each of those Rose Bowls.

- Both left a coaching job in the Big Ten at the end of 1985 to be a head coach for non-Big Ten teams that are located in adjacent states—Holtz from Minnesota to Notre Dame and Tressel from Ohio State to Youngstown State.

- Both had finished his first regular season with a road upset over an arch-rival—Ohio State over Michigan in 2001 and Notre Dame over USC in 1986.

- The year before his national championship, each had beaten his arch-rival by scoring 26 points. For Holtz, it was USC in 1987.

- The year before his national championship, each had lost his bowl game.

- Tressel had a 9-1 record against arch-rival Michigan, and Holtz had a 9-1-1 record against arch-rival USC. The Notre Dame vs. USC tie came in 1994 with a score of 17-17, the same score at the end of regulation as the OSU vs. Miami game in the 2002 season.

- Tressel had his brother, Dick, on his coaching staff at Ohio State, and Holtz would have his son, Skip, on his coaching staff at Notre Dame.

- They faced each other in the Outback Bowl of the 2001 season, where Holtz's South Carolina team scored 31 points, matching the 31 that OSU scored against Miami in the BCS Championship game and the 31 that Notre Dame scored against Miami in 1988. Holtz had an eight-win improvement from his first to his second season at South Carolina, and Tressel had a seven-win improvement from his first to his second season at Ohio State.

- Tressel's first bowl game at Ohio State was against Holtz, and his last one was a win over Arkansas, a team that Holtz had coached.

- Tressel's win over Arkansas and Holtz's last bowl game at Notre Dame (a loss to Florida State in the Orange Bowl) both had a score of 31-26 and came in the coach's tenth year as the coach.

- Tressel had four bowl losses at Ohio State, and Holtz had four bowl losses at Notre Dame.

- In the year before Notre Dame's national championship, Holtz coached a Heisman Trophy winner, Tim Brown. In 2002, Tressel had a future Heisman Trophy winner who was being redshirted, Troy Smith.

- In the three seasons before Notre Dame's national championship, Holtz's teams (including one at Minnesota) lost a combined 15 games. In the three seasons before Ohio State's national championship, the Buckeyes lost a combined 15 games.

- In Notre Dame's championship year of 1988, Tressel lost seven games at Youngstown State, and in Ohio State's championship year of 2002, Holtz lost seven games at South Carolina.

- Purdue's coach against Holtz in 1988 was Fred Akers, and Purdue's coach against Tressel in 2002 was Joe Tiller. Both Akers and Tiller had been the head coach at Wyoming.

FIVE YEARS AFTER THE
1988 AND 2002
NATIONAL CHAMPIONSHIPS

- In 1993, five years after Notre Dame's national championship, a game matching the top two teams took place between #1 Florida State and #2 Notre Dame. It was another home regular season game victory for Notre Dame against a team from Florida, and they scored 31 points again in the 31-24 win.

- In 2007, five years after Ohio State's national championship, a game matching the top two teams took place between #1 Ohio State and #2 LSU. As in the 2002 season, it was another BCS Championship game where the losing team scored 24 points, a 38-24 win for LSU. Whereas the Buckeyes' 2002 national championship game was played in front of a virtual home crowd, LSU's win came in front of a virtual home crowd in the Superdome.

THE MONUMENTAL TIE GAMES IN THE
1966 AND 1973 SEASONS

In the span of seven years, both Ohio State and Notre Dame played in a famous 10-10 tie game, with national championship implications, in the state of Michigan in November.

- In 1966, Notre Dame played to a 10-10 tie at Michigan State. In 1973, Ohio State played to a 10-10 tie at Michigan.

- Notre Dame was ranked #1 going into its 1966 game against #2 Michigan State, and Ohio State was ranked #1 going into its 1973 game. Ten was number of the day in 1966; it was the 10th time that the #1 and #2 teams in the Associated Press poll had met since the poll started in 1936.

- In each case, it was the Michigan's team's last game of the year, although in the Wolverines' case, it was due to a majority of the Big Ten athletic directors voting to send Ohio State to the Rose Bowl. Michigan State had no bowl game in 1966 due to the Big Ten's policy at the time that prevented consecutive Rose Bowl appearances by the same team. In 1975, the Big Ten would change its rule and allow more than one team to play in a bowl.

- In each case, the home Michigan team came out on the short end, once the season was over.

- Each game had one team leading 10-0—Michigan State in 1966 and Ohio State in 1973.

- Each game had one team—Michigan State and Ohio State—scoring all its points in the second quarter, with the other tying the score in the fourth quarter.

- In each game, the home team had more yards and first downs.

- Notre Dame's Joe Azzaro missed a 41-yard field goal with 4:39 remaining in its game, and Michigan missed on two field goal attempts in the last 1:06 of its game. In each case, the kicks were into the north end of the stadium. ABC's Chris Schenkel said that Azzaro was three-for-three on field goals before the miss.

- In its game, Notre Dame had the ball last, and its coach Ara Parseghian chose to play the series conservatively, due to his team's injuries. In its game, Ohio State had the ball last; the Buckeyes did not throw a pass until its last four plays. Backup quarterback Greg Hare's first pass on its next-to-last possession was intercepted, and Woody had Hare pass on the last three plays in order to try for a win. In the 1972 and 1973 Michigan games combined, the Buckeyes threw more interceptions (two) than completed passes (one).

- Each game featured a notable player who served in the Vietnam War. Michigan's kicker Mike Lantry had served in the war before his playing days, and Notre Dame's Rocky Bleier would serve after his college football career.

- The Notre Dame-Michigan State game had several prominent Ohioans.

  - Notre Dame had Tom Schoen, who had two interceptions in the fourth quarter, from Villa Angela-St. Joseph High School in Cleveland. He fumbled the last punt but was able to recover the ball. He had switched from quarterback to defensive back in 1966—Chris Gamble, anyone?

  - Notre Dame's Alan Page, a future member of the Pro Football Hall of Fame, was from Canton Central Catholic High School.

- Bob Gladieux, a first-team all-Ohio fullback from Louisville, scored Notre Dame's only touchdown. The Associated Press's account of Gladieux's all-Ohio selection in 1964 had, "Bob, who does everything from his fullback spot, scored 196 points; rushed for 1481 yards to outgain by 38 yards the pass-run efforts of 10 beaten foes; completed 10 of 19 passes for 178 yards and three touchdowns; intercepted six passes; punted for a 35-plus yard average; and returned two punts and one kickoff for touchdowns."

- The *Columbus Dispatch* reported that Columbus native Tom O'Leary led the Irish with seven solo tackles and four assists, and broke up five passes intended for Gene Washington in the fourth quarter.

- Michigan State had running back Clinton Jones, from Cathedral Latin School in Cleveland, who would be inducted into the College Football Hall of Fame in 2015, along with Jim Tressel.

- Notre Dame's coach Ara Parseghian, Woody Hayes, and Michigan's coach Bo Schembechler were born in Ohio. Parseghian had followed Hayes as the head coach at Miami University in Ohio, and Schembechler followed Parseghian. Like Hayes, Parseghian had served in the navy during World War II. Schembechler played for Hayes at Miami, was an assistant under Hayes at Ohio State, and was the Miami coach from 1963 through 1968.

- Parseghian, Daugherty, Hayes, and Schembechler would all win the College Football Coach of the Year award from *Sporting News* at some point of their career. Parseghian was the odd man out in one respect; he did not have a nickname.

- Injuries were significant in both games:

  - Notre Dame was without halfback Nick Eddy, who aggravated his shoulder injury during a mishap exiting the train at Michigan State. In the book, "The Biggest Game of Them All: Notre Dame, Michigan State and the Fall of 1966", Mike Celizic wrote that Eddy had reinjured his shoulder in practice the Wednesday before, and that, ironically, it was the last time that Notre Dame would travel by train. The Irish's quarterback, Terry Hanratty, separated his right shoulder on a tackle by Bubba Smith and was replaced by Coley O'Brien. Notre Dame's center, George Goeddeke, also would not return to the game after an injury. Gladieux would also exit the game with an injury.

  - Michigan's quarterback Dennis Franklin, who scored Michigan's only touchdown, suffered a fractured collarbone on a tackle by Van DeCree in the fourth quarter, which may have been a factor when some of the athletic directors voted in favor of Ohio State going to the Rose Bowl. For Ohio State, quarterback Cornelius Greene played with an injured right thumb, which prevented him from throwing any passes. Tom Skladany, who handled the kickoffs and was the Buckeyes' punter, had his season ended with a broken leg and a dislocated ankle on a kickoff.

- Both Hanratty and Greene were sophomores who traveled west to play their college ball—Hanratty from Pennsylvania and Greene from Washington, D.C. Quarterbacks Jimmy Raye of MSU and Franklin, another sophomore, had come from North Carolina and Ohio, respectively. Backup quarterbacks who saw action in their games were Greg Hare of Ohio State, from Maryland; Larry Cipa of Michigan, who attended

Archbishop McNicholas High School in Cincinnati, Ohio; and Coley O'Brien of Notre Dame, from Virginia.

- The ABC broadcast of the Ohio State vs. Michigan game had as its color commentator someone familiar with a 10-10 game—Duffy Daugherty, the Michigan State coach in 1966.

- On the same day as the Notre Dame vs. Michigan State game in 1966, Ohio State and Michigan also combined for 20 points, but it was a lopsided 17-3 win for Michigan. It would take another ten years for Michigan to win in Columbus. That Ohio State vs. Michigan game in 1966 had a clipping penalty that nullified a long run for the Buckeyes, and Woody was quoted in the *Columbus Dispatch* as saying about the call, "I'm bitter about it, sure I'm bitter." Bo Schembechler would use practically those same words after the vote by the Big Ten athletic directors denied his team the Rose Bowl bid in 1973.

- Notre Dame gave up 38 points in its 10-game regular season (no bowl game) of 1966, and Ohio State gave up 43 points in its 10-game regular season of 1973.

- Both Notre Dame and Ohio State played USC in the Los Angeles area in its next game following the tie and won easily; Notre Dame won a regular-season game, 51-0, and Ohio State won, 42-21, in the Rose Bowl.

- Each Rose Bowl had a controversial representative. In 1966, the Pac-8 Conference sent USC instead of UCLA, despite the fact that UCLA had beaten USC and had a better record than the Trojans. The voting by the Big Ten athletic directors to send Ohio State to the Rose Bowl in 1973 surprised the football world and embittered Bo Schembechler. The *Columbus Dispatch* in 1966 had a headline in anticipation: "Bruins Trip Trojans, Head for Rose Bowl". After the 1973 game,

Columbus Dispatch sports journalist Dick Otte wrote: "The odds look like a zillion to one the vote will favor Michigan."

- In 1966, Alabama was the only team with a perfect record, but they finished third in the Associated Press poll. In 1973, Penn State had a perfect record along with Notre Dame, but finished fifth in the Associated Press poll, and Miami of Ohio had a perfect 11-0 record and finished 15th.

- Notre Dame claimed a national championship in 1966 in the Associated Press poll, and Ohio State would fall just short in 1973.

THE 1973 SEASON

Going into the Michigan game, OSU was ranked #1, Oklahoma #2 (but on probation), Notre Dame #3, and Michigan #4.

Two coaches must have been psychic. In his book, "Ara's Knights", Frank Pomarico—an Irish offensive lineman and tri-captain on that team—writes that on the day that the Buckeyes and the Wolverines were to play, Ara said "Let's hope that Michigan and Ohio State tie. That's what we need." His wish came true. And, on that day, Notre Dame beat Miami, of all teams, 44-0. Indiana coach Lee Corso got in on the action, too. In the book, "War as They Knew It: Woody Hayes, Bo Schembechler and America in a Time of Unrest", author Michael Rosenberg mentions that Corso pronounced, "I predict that it will be decided in the fourth quarter on the kicking game."

Noted author James Michener had spoken to Michigan's athletic director Don Canham before the game and learned about the pressure on Michigan to match Ohio State's national exposure; the Buckeyes had played in the Rose Bowl the season before. In Michener's book, "Sports in America", Canham said, "That's why the game tomorrow is so crucial.

We've got to win. We've simply got to win. To keep our image before the national audience."

Coach Schembechler elected to attempt the last field goal in the 10-10 tie game on third down with 28 seconds remaining, instead of trying a running play to get closer and run more time off the clock. In an immortalized game in 1982, a similar decision would backfire more dramatically for the kicking team.

Incredibly, Ohio State had no penalties in the game, though they may have gotten away with one on the two Michigan field goal attempts, where Randy Gradishar climbed the back of lineman Arnie Jones to try to block the kicks. Michigan fans point out that the Wolverines had 303 yards to 234 for Ohio State, and that the Buckeyes had no passing yards, but the average gain per play reflected the closeness of the score—4.46 for Michigan, 4.41 for Ohio State. The attendance of 105,223 set an NCAA record and was more than 17,000 larger than the next highest figure at Michigan Stadium that season.

The voting by the Big Ten athletic directors to send Ohio State to the Rose Bowl led to the documentary "Tiebreaker". Of the vote, Bo Schembechler said, "I am bitterly resentful of the way this thing was handled." Jack Harbaugh, a first-year assistant coach for the Wolverines, appears in the documentary. In 2016, his son, Jim, would be the Michigan coach when the Buckeyes and Wolverines tied at the end of regulation again, 17-17, and the Buckeyes won in double overtime, 30-27. Jim Harbaugh, almost echoing the coach whom he played for, said that he was "bitterly disappointed with the officiating", referring to a favorable spot for the Buckeyes on a fourth-down play in the second overtime.

A few days after the game, a lawsuit filed on behalf of a student at Michigan questioned the legitimacy of the vote and asked the Big Ten to overturn their decision regarding their Rose Bowl pick. *The New York Times* reported, "The lawyer said that he was as concerned about the way in which the Rose Bowl decision was made as about the decision itself.

The secret vote, he charged, violated a Michigan statute requiring governmental agencies to make public their decisions."

The "Ten Year War" between Woody and Bo ended with Michigan winning five and Ohio State winning four, but the one tie actually must have felt like a loss to the Wolverines.

The next time that Ohio State and MIchigan would tie would also be the last time; in 1992, they tied 13-13, with the home team, Ohio State in this case, again being the team to score the last 10 points in the fourth quarter. The last time before 1973 that Ohio State had a tie against a Big Ten team was a 20-20 home game against Illinois in 1963. The Buckeyes would not have another Big Ten tie game until 1988, so this was a rarity in the span of 25 years.

Notre Dame owns a national championship in 1973—voted by the Associated Press, the Football Writers Association of America, and the National Football Foundation—with an 11-0 record. However, their 24-23 win over Alabama in the Sugar Bowl—in what was called "The Game of the Century"—had the help of a missed extra point by the Crimson Tide. It was the first-ever meeting between the Irish and the Crimson Tide. Like Krenzel against Miami, the Irish quarterback Tom Clements, also a junior, completed seven passes in this game. A key play in the final minutes was Clements throwing a pass out of his end zone on 3rd-and-eight to Robin Weber, who caught it for a 35-yard gain on only his second reception of the season and his first reception from Clements. Now, that's a real *Holy Something* play. Ara Parseghian had played the last possession of the 1966 tie game with Michigan State conservatively, but gambled on this occasion.

That Notre Dame vs. Alabama game could have finished in a tie in regulation, just as the Ohio State vs. Miami game did; if it had, Ohio State, Alabama, Notre Dame, Michigan (no bowl game due to the Big Ten rule of only one team playing in a bowl), and Oklahoma (no bowl game due to being on probation) would have had a only a tie on their record, while

Penn State had a 12-0 record. If it had ended in a tie, perhaps Ohio State, which finished second in the Associated Press poll, could have earned a national championship, based on its convincing 42-21 win over USC in the Rose Bowl, which was played the day after Alabama's Sugar Bowl win. Ohio State finished third in the United Press International poll. Alabama was named the national champion by the United Press International; Ohio State had the better record than the Crimson Tide (11-1), and had the better defense—six points per game, compared to Alabama's nine points per game. Alabama finished third in scoring, two points per game better than Ohio State, which was fourth. Like Ohio State, Notre Dame played only a ten-game regular season schedule, while most teams added an 11th game.

Miami University in Ohio finished with an 11-0 record, joining three other teams—Ohio State, Notre Dame, and Michigan—that had a former Miami coach and an undefeated record. Miami, "The Cradle of Coaches", would also figure prominently in Rose Bowl games; it had a former coach—John Pont at Indiana, Woody Hayes, and Bo Schembechler—in the Rose Bowl in 12 straight seasons, from 1967 through 1978. John Pont had played for Woody Hayes—scoring a touchdown in the Salad Bowl—and Parseghian at Miami. Furthermore, it was a great season for Ohio and its border states of Michigan, Indiana, and Pennsylvania.

Ohio State and Notre Dame had three common opponents. The Buckeyes defeated USC, Northwestern, and Michigan State by the scores of 42-21 (in California), 60-0, and 35-0, while Notre Dame won with scores of 23-14 (at home), 44-0, and 14-10.

Unfortunately for Ohio State, Notre Dame chose 1973 as their first season with a perfect record since 1949. In that 1949 season, Ohio State also had a tie with Michigan in Ann Arbor and also had a Rose Bowl win, its first-ever. Notre Dame benefitted from both its tie game in 1966 against Michigan State and the Ohio State vs. Michigan tie game in 1973, winning a national championship in both seasons.

Prominent Ohioans for Notre Dame included Ross Browner from Warren Western Reserve High School, Steve Niehaus from Archbishop Moeller in Cincinnati, Art Best from Columbus Bishop Hartley, and Mike Townsend and Willie Townsend from Hamilton Garfield.

Coach Parseghian was another coach who had a deep Ohio background and who had broken a defending champion's lengthy winning streak; his 1970 team had ended the 30-game streak of Texas in the Cotton Bowl. Notre Dame improved by seven wins in his first season; Ohio State improved by seven wins in Tressel's second season.

Nineteen days after the Sugar Bowl, Notre Dame athletics would experience another monumental one-point win, as the men's basketball team broke UCLA's 88-game winning streak. Whereas Robin Weber had one reception in his game, the basketball Irish's Dwight Clay was slightly more productive; his second field goal of the game was the game-winner. UCLA was on an unlucky 13-game winning streak that season before the game. Like Miami in the Fiesta Bowl, UCLA had a star player, Bill Walton, who was not 100% physically. Like Miami, UCLA had multiple shots, literally, on their last possession, as they misfired on three in the last six seconds. On Walton's last shot, he was contested by John Shumate, wearing jersey #34.

MIRACLE ENDINGS

The third infamous—and most improbable—tie game, sandwiched between the 10-10 ties in 1966 and 1973, and featuring another pair of undefeated teams, was the 1968 Harvard-Yale game on November 23.

Other monumental rivalry games on that day to decide the Rose Bowl participants were Ohio State vs. Michigan, won by the Buckeyes, 50-14, and USC vs. UCLA, won by the Trojans, 28-16. Both of those games paled by comparison to the drama of the Harvard-Yale game. Harvard, trailing 22-0 at one point, scored 16 points in the last 42 seconds to make the final score 29-29 and prompted the headline in the *Harvard Crimson*, the student newspaper: "HARVARD BEATS YALE, 29-29". A documentary produced in 2008 is titled with that headline wording, and Harvard grad George Howe Colt wrote the book detailing the game, "The Game: Harvard, Yale, and America in 1968". After scoring with 42 seconds remaining to make the score 29-21, Harvard executed an onside kick and scored a touchdown and a second two-point conversion with no time remaining. Harvard's backup quarterback, Frank Champi, came off the bench in the second quarter and engineered the comeback.

The headlines on the front page of the *New York Times* sports section the following day had the Harvard-Yale game first, with the Ohio State win over Michigan below it.

Until 1982, the Ivy League at the time was considered on a par with the other major conferences. Yale was ranked 18th before the game against Harvard. Ed Marinaro of Cornell finished second to quarterback Pat Sullivan of Auburn in the 1971 Heisman Trophy voting and held the record for career rushing yards before it was broken by Archie Griffin. Yale had played Connecticut and Rutgers in the seasons of the Bulldogs' star quarterback of the late 1960s, Brian Dowling.

Just as Woody Hayes opened up his offense in 1968, so did Harvard. The *Harvard Crimson* newspaper borrowed Woody's phrase for his previous offense in this excerpt from www.thecrimson.com: "The implementation of a passing offense allowed the Harvard squad to escape its previous 'three yards and a cloud of dust' billing and set the stage for Champi's heroics to come." The second quarter of the game would illustrate just how effective the passing game would be. Ironically, Harvard was known for its stingy defense that season.

Both Harvard and Yale finished with an 8-0-1 record. Yale entered the game with college football's longest winning streak at 16. Ohio State extended its streak to 13 on the same day with the win over Michigan. Ohio State, Penn State, USC, Ohio University, Georgia, Harvard, and

Yale all finished the regular season with no losses. The three teams in the adjacent states of Ohio and Pennsylvania had no tie games, while the other four teams had at least one tie. Georgia had an 8-0-2 record but lost in the Sugar Bowl to Arkansas. Ohio University lost its bowl game, which left only Ohio State and Penn State with perfect records.

Yale had never trailed the entire season, outscoring their opponents 288-118 entering the game. Yale had converted a two-point conversion, contrary to conventional wisdom, to make the score 22-0, and Harvard had faltered on the extra point snap after their first touchdown, making the score 22-6. These were just two what-ifs that may have made the drama, the documentary, and the book merely figments of our imagination. In a theme that would be repeated, Harvard's touchdown came with 39 seconds remaining in the first half.

Yale turned the ball over once on an interception and six times on fumbles to tie a school record—including three inside the Harvard 20-yard line and three in the third quarter—with the last one on the Harvard 14-yard line and 3:34 remaining, and with the 29-13 lead. At that point, the Harvard team must have been thinking, "All we gotta do is go 86 yards for a touchdown, make a two-point conversion on a second try, recover an onside kick, advance a desperation lateral 26 yards, run a draw play on third-and-ten, pass for a touchdown to an injured player with no time on the clock, and make another two-point conversion. We're future businessmen and engineers from Harvard. How hard can it be?"

The game had several individuals with Ohio connections—Brian Dowling, Calvin Hill, Del Marting, Carmen Cozza, Pat Madden, Rich Pont, Gus Crim, Fritz Reed, and Ken Coleman.

For Harvard, the 1968 roster on www.gocrimson.com shows Ohio and Illinois as the only two states other than Massachusetts, its bordering states, and New Jersey to have at least five representatives.

Yale had quarterback Brian Dowling, who was the Class AA second team Associated Press all-Ohio quarterback in 1964 for Cleveland St.

Ignatius High School and had passed up offers from Ohio State and Notre Dame. In Colt's book, he writes that Jack Nicklaus and Ohio Governor James Rhodes tried to make a sales pitch. In an article on the game by Steve Cady, Special to the *New York Times*, he may have been exaggerating a bit when he wrote that "Dowling would have been playing for Ohio State today against Michigan if he had not decided to go to Yale ..." He had not lost a game since the seventh grade and had a 15-0 record as the Bulldogs' quarterback entering the game. In a 2013 article in *The Dayton Daily News*, Doug Harris wrote that Dowling was the number one quarterback prospect in Ohio for his class, and the second prospect was Bill Long, who started for the 1966 and 1967 seasons at Ohio State before giving way to Rex Kern in 1968. Interestingly, Dowling returned a punt in the game and was one of the deep backs for other punt returns. A multi-sport athlete, Dowling had scored on a touchdown catch in the season.

Del Marting was a native of Gates Mills, Ohio, led Yale in receptions, tied with Hill for touchdown receptions on the season, and caught a touchdown pass in the game. Pat Madden was a defensive end from Mingo Junction, Ohio, and played at Steubenville Central Catholic High School. Like Dowling, he had a nickname; the *Yale Daily News* reported that he went by "The Pope", as he had wanted to be a priest. His high school coach was Rich Pont—the brother of John Pont—who was born in Canton, played at Bowling Green, and was in his first season as an assistant at Yale.

Calvin Hill would play for the Cleveland Browns and serve as a consultant for the Browns. He was Yale's leading rusher, tied for the lead in touchdown receptions, and broke the Yale career scoring record in the game.

The Yale coach was Carmen Cozza, who was born in Parma, Ohio, played for Woody Hayes and Ara Parseghian at Miami, and was an assistant coach at Miami. He was elected into the College Football Hall of Fame in 2002, ironically along with former Ohio State head coach Earle

Bruce and Kellen Winslow, Sr. He was a minor league outfielder in the Cleveland Indians and Chicago White Sox systems in 1952 and 1953.

Harvard had fullback Gus Crim from Upper Arlington, who scored an earlier touchdown and a two-point conversion (after a pass interference call in the end zone gave Harvard a second chance, sound familiar?) to make the score 29-21 with 42 seconds remaining. He had a key 14-yard gain on a draw play on third-and-10 play in the last possession. Crim had also passed up on an offer from Ohio State.

Fritz Reed, a Harvard offensive lineman, was from Lancaster, Ohio, where he was teammates with Rex Kern in multiple sports. On a third-and-18 play, Reed picked up a lateral by Champi and ran it for 26 yards to set up their touchdown that trimmed the deficit to 29-21 with 42 seconds remaining. Reed's agility was no accident; he had been an offensive end the year before. Thanks to that play, Reed had Harvard's longest run of the game, which made him the third-leading ground gainer for his team in the game.

Ohioans were involved in five of the eight touchdowns—Crim's touchdown and Dowling's two touchdown runs and two touchdown passes, one of them to Del Marting.

Harvard benefited from a rule that existed at the time but would eventually be modified. With the ball on the Harvard 29-yard line and less than three minutes remaining, Yale was penalized for defensive holding. With the rule of marking off the penalty yards from the spot of the foul, the ball was placed at the Yale 47-yard line.

Harvard had scored two touchdowns and two two-point conversions for their last 16 points. In the same season, Ohio State saw Illinois score 24 consecutive points on three touchdowns and three two-point conversions to tie the game on their home field. In that game, it was Ohio State that used a backup quarterback; Ron Maciejowski led the winning drive when Rex Kern was injured. Harvard's two-point conversion pass for the final points was caught by Pete Varney; he would be named a baseball

All-American and lead Harvard into the 1971 College World Series, spend parts of four seasons with the Chicago White Sox and Atlanta Braves, and collect one of his 47 career hits against Cleveland in a 1975 game. After Varney's catch, the referee raced to the center of the field, only to be swallowed up by hundreds of Harvard fans.

This was in the day when some quarterbacks wore jersey numbers such as 27; that was Champi's number. Dowling wore the more conventional number 10, and his scrambling ability mimicked that of two other contemporary number 10's—Ohio State's Rex Kern and Fran Tarkenton of the NFL. In the Ohio State vs. Michigan game that day, Michigan's quarterback Don Moorhead also wore #27.

For Harvard, Bruce Freeman had his only two touchdown receptions of the season. Vic Gatto, a running back who had left the game with an injury, had the last touchdown reception of the game, his only one of the season, on a play where Champi did his best Dowling-scrambling impersonation. Ohio State fans can compare Champi's dance steps to Braxton Miller's against Purdue in November of 2011, where he connected with Jordan Hall to produce a tie with 55 seconds remaining; unfortunately, Purdue blocked the extra point attempt and won in overtime. A photo from the Yale Athletic Department in Colt's book shows dozens of fans infringing on the end zone and an official standing in the middle of the end zone mere feet away from Gatto and the Yale defender, signaling the touchdown. Prophetically, the cover of the souvenir program for the game had a photo of the two team captains—Gatto and Dowling. Colt wrote that Gatto consoled Dowling in Yale's locker room after The Game, with Dowling saying, "What a way to go out." The Nils V. "Swede" Nelson Award is the fourth oldest award in college football, presented by the Gridiron Club of Boston. Dowling won the award in 1967, and Gatto won it in 1968.

Champi had thrown only 12 passes before the game, but threw three of his four touchdown passes of the season in the game. As a team,

Harvard had four touchdown passes in the season entering the game, compared to 24 for Yale. In less than three quarters, Champi matched the three touchdown passes that starter George Lalich had in the entire season. He entered the game with five completions in the season and added six more in the game. In fact, before the game, Calvin Hill, a running back, had completed two more than Champi did. The book "The Only Game That Matters: The Harvard/Yale Rivalry" by Bernard M. Corbett and Paul Simpson mentions that Champi did not have enough minutes during the season to qualify for a varsity H letter, but the Harvard Athletic Association issued a waiver to grant him the letter. The book also mentions that the junior varsity game between the two teams the day before ended in a 7-7 tie, foreshadowing the varsity contest. And, it mentions that a reporter asked Cozza in the week leading up to the game if he'd be satisfied with a scoreless tie and a share of the Ivy League crown, and he replied, "Why, that's like kissing your sister."

Crim and Reed have extensive commentary in the documentary, along with other players, including the actor Tommy Lee Jones, a Harvard offensive lineman. Both Crim and Calvin Hill wore jersey #30.

Dowling and future NFL star Calvin Hill begged Coach Cozza to put them in on defense for Harvard's last drive—Chris Gamble, anyone?—but Cozza declined, out of respect for the players who had battled all season. The Ohio High School Athletic Association website shows that Dowling still holds the state record for career interceptions with 33 and is tied for the second-most in a season with 16. Hill had played linebacker on the freshman team.

Broadcasting the game on WHDH radio was Ken Coleman, who would also call games for the Cleveland Browns, the Cleveland Indians, the Cincinnati Reds, and Ohio State football.

A story on www.yalealumnimagazine.org quotes former New York governor George Pataki, a Yale grad, "I take some solace in the knowledge that Harvard considers a tie with Yale to be its greatest 'victory'." Ohio

State's president E. Gordon Gee used similar wording when the Buckeyes and Wolverines tied 13-13 in 1992; the Buckeyes had lost the four previous games in the rivalry under coach John Cooper. Dr. Gee would later become the president of Brown University, so he may have felt some influence from the Ivy League. The 1992 tie game was the last home tie game for the Buckeyes; the previous home tie game occurred, naturally, 14 years earlier in 1978.

The same story has "A few days after the game, the Harvard team invited their Yale counterparts to a joint Ivy League championship banquet. The Yale players voted, overwhelmingly, to decline the offer." Four years later, a similar scenario took place when the members of the men's Olympic basketball team refused to accept their silver medals due to the disputed ending of the game against Russia, another case where the final play started with three seconds on the clock.

Like the 1966 Michigan State vs. Notre Dame and the 1973 OSU vs. Michigan games, this game had at least one Vietnam War veteran; Don Conway of Harvard had served in Vietnam that year. He forced a fumble in the second quarter, after which Champi entered, and later forced another.

In other non-football news, the year 1968 was a landmark year for Yale admitting women, and, in 1973, the Ohio State marching band included women for the first time. George W. Bush, who would welcome the 2002 Ohio State football team to the White House, had graduated from Yale earlier in 1968.

The Harvard coach was John Yovicsin, who would have a 14-year tenure there. His last game was a 14-12 win over Yale on the same day in 1970 that Woody beat Bo, 20-9.

Another game that day had no such drama; Houston beat Tulsa, 100-6. On the following weekend, USC and Notre Dame met and tied, 21-21, in a rare game between two powerhouses that, unlike the other three, no one seems to be talking about decades later.

In 1982, 14 years later, the NCAA demoted the Ivy League from Division I-A to Division I-AA. In that year, another famous game with a chaotic ending on the opposite coast, the California-Stanford game that California won on a kickoff return that had five laterals as time expired—a sequence called The Play—took place. The California kick return team had to hustle to get eleven players onto the field for the return, and their disadvantage grew significantly when the majority of the 144-member Stanford band and several Stanford players from the bench took the field, thinking that the game was over when it appeared that Dwight Garner was tackled after receiving one of the laterals. Kevin Moen threw the first lateral and took the final lateral in for the winning score, flattening trombone player Gary Tyrrell in the process. Moen's overhand lateral was to Richard Rodgers on the left sideline, where several defenders were closing in. Why? A method to the madness?

The Associated Press story included that Moen "weaved his way through literally hundreds of people", and was "fighting his way through Stanford band members and fans." For Moen, a defensive back, it was the only touchdown of his career at California. Ironically, the Stanford band, thinking that the play had been stopped, was performing their customary "All Right Now" number at the time. The Play was helped by the fact that both Moen and Richard Rodgers had been option quarterbacks in high school.

The laterals from Moen to Rodgers to Garner to Rodgers to Ford to Moen read more like a baseball rundown sequence. Stanford was the second-highest scoring team in the Pac-10 that season, but was held seven points below its season average by Cal.

Prior to the final kickoff with four seconds remaining, Joe Starkey, the Cal radio broadcaster, said, "Only a miracle can save the Bears." A few hundred miles to the south, Al Michaels's ears must have been burning. The Golden Bear team must have been thinking, "All we gotta do is scramble to set up our kick return team, hope that the officials don't notice that we aren't set up properly, lateral the ball five times, and run through additional Stanford players and dozens of band members on the field to the end zone before we get tackled or fumble the ball. Compared to what Harvard faced 14 years ago, this is a piece of cake. We're free-thinkers from Cal Berkeley. How hard can it be?"

The story on www.si.com/college/cal/news/the-play-as-told-by-those-involved quotes game referee Charles Moffett (who was working his last game and passed away in 2002): "Three rule changes resulted from that play, including one that does not allow a band onto the field until the game is over." That the rule change was necessary in the first place was highly ... improbable.

Forty years after this game, the book "Five Laterals and a Trombone: Cal, Stanford, and the Wildest Ending in College Football History" by Tyler Bridges does a deep-dive into the game and the events before and after. Ironically, Bridges was a former trombone player in the Stanford band, a 2011-12 Nieman Fellow at Harvard, and a Shorenstein Center Fellow at Harvard in the fall of 2017. And, Tyrrell had visited Yale as a possible college destination. Richard Rodgers, naturally, would become an assistant coach at the College of the Holy Cross in Worcester, Massachusetts, some 40 miles from the Harvard campus in Cambridge.

A photo by Art Ray on www.paloaltoonline.com shows Moen and Elway shaking hands after the game. Moen had the middle and ring fingers on his right hand taped together, which obviously did not affect his lateral or his ability to carry the ball.

The previous week, Southern Methodist had beaten Texas Tech, 34-27, on a 91-yard kickoff return by Bobby Leach in the final seconds; it featured only one lateral, and like the Cal-Stanford game, it followed a field goal by the opponent. On the same day as the Cal-Stanford game, SMU finished its regular season with, naturally, a 17-17 tie against Arkansas. Tie games would cease to exist when overtime rules began, naturally, 14 years later in 1996. After beating Pitt in the Cotton Bowl, SMU finished with an 11-0-1 record.

If the chaotic, five-lateral touchdown had not occurred, the 20-19 score would have matched that of another rivalry game taking place on the same day down the road, as UCLA topped USC, 20-19. In that game, USC scored on the last play on fourth down, but was stopped on their two-point conversion try for the win. UCLA blitzed the quarterback, who could not get a pass off. Cie Grant, anyone? With Al Michaels calling the game for ABC, there would be no Miracle in this game. Michaels said that the touchdown catch by USC's Mark Boyer was his first the year. Robin Weber, anyone? In other rivalry games in the conference that season, Oregon beat Oregon State, 7-6, and Washington State beat Washington 24-20.

This Cal-Stanford game had a few connections to Ohio. Someone who had a birds-eye view of the game was the Stanford athletic director, Andy Geiger, who tried his best to get the outcome overturned. Geiger would become the Ohio State athletic director—during the time of a Heisman Trophy winner, Eddie George, and an eventual winner, Troy Smith—and nearly was associated with a third in John Elway. Garin Veris, from Chillicothe, was a linebacker for Stanford, played for the New England Patriots and San Francisco 49ers, and was elected to the Stanford Athletics Hall of Fame in 2006. Stanford's coach, Paul Wiggin, who was born in '34, had played for the Cleveland Browns. Stanford had beaten Ohio State 23-20 in 1982, when Elway threw for 407 yards, with 284 in the second half, and led the team to the winning score with 34 seconds remaining. All 80 yards of the drive were through the air. It would not be the last time that Elway would break hearts in Ohio. In the 1986 AFC title game, Elway engineered a 98-yard come-from-behind touchdown drive to tie the Cleveland Browns and send the game into overtime. The Broncos went on to win 23-20, the same score as Stanford's win over Ohio State in 1982.

The OSU-Stanford game, played in front of the largest crowd in Ohio Stadium history at the time, also featured a touchdown with a lateral by a player who had played quarterback in high school. Wide receiver Gary Williams "took a long lateral left from Tomczak", as the OSU official play-by-play shows, and threw a 63-yard pass to Cedric Anderson to set up the Buckeyes' last touchdown for a 20-13 lead. Veris had 11 tackles, including a sack, in the game.

In Tyler Bridges's book, he writes that Ron Rivera, Cal's linebacker who would be a consensus All-America in 1983 and an eventual NFL coach, had turned down Notre Dame, Ohio State, and Michigan all on the same day during his recruiting process. In twenty-two years, Rivera would connect with a certain Ohio State legend. Both Veris and Rivera wore jersey #80.

Cal's coach, Joe Kapp, had been a quarterback for the Minnesota Vikings, where a teammate was Gene Washington, who played for Michigan State in the 10-10 tie game against Notre Dame in 1966. Like Jim Tressel, Kapp won seven games in his first year, beating his rival while giving up 20 points. This season would be the only one of his five at Cal with a winning record. Both Kapp and Wiggin were coaching his alma mater. Wiggin would later become the defensive line coach and an administrator for the Vikings. Both are members of the National Football Foundation Hall of Fame. Kapp was inducted in 2004, just ahead of Wiggin, naturally, who was inducted in 2005.

This game was in 1982, a year containing the same digits as the year in which the rivalry started, 1892. In 1928, the only other year containing the same digits, the two teams played to, naturally, a 13-13 tie.

It was Stanford's sixth game of the season that was decided by five points or less. The loss may have cost Elway the Heisman Trophy, which running back Herschel Walker (wearing jersey #34) of Georgia won. Two years later, a quarterback may have secured the Heisman Trophy instead of a running back, when Boston College's Doug Flutie's miracle touchdown pass against Miami—whose quarterback was Bernie Kosar, born in Youngstown and a future Cleveland Brown—may have swung the vote from Ohio State's Keith Byars. That game was on the same date as the Harvard-Yale 29-29 game, 16 years previously.

A *Sports Illustrated* story had, "More than a month later, as he prepared to play in the East-West Shrine Game, Elway told *Oakland Tribune* reporter Ron Bergman, 'I still feel the same way about it now as I did in the locker room after the game. Maybe in time it'll wear off, but I'm still bitter. Very bitter.'" Elway was echoing Woody Hayes from 1966 and Bo Schembechler from 1973 in his use of the word "bitter".

Penalties and kickoffs were instrumental (no pun intended) in both the Harvard-Yale and the Cal-Stanford games. Harvard benefitted from a face-mask penalty, a penalty that gave Harvard another chance at their first two-point conversion, and a defensive holding penalty that resulted in a 38-yard swing. The winning kickoff return for Cal was shortened by 15 yards when Stanford had to kick off from their 25-yard line, due to a penalty when some bench players came on the field after they kicked the go-ahead field goal that appeared to have won the game.

The play for the last touchdown for Harvard started with three seconds on the clock, and the play for the last touchdown for California started with four seconds on the clock. Both touchdowns were scored in the south end zone, unseen by hundreds of Cal and Harvard fans who had left their respective games early. Cal was prepared for its chaotic kick return, as they had a rugby-like drill every Sunday for fun, while Yale was not prepared for an onside kick, by virtue of not having any close games.

Both games had an ill-advised timeout called by the team that would suffer. Yale called a timeout with 1:13 remaining and Harvard facing a 3rd-and-18 on the Yale 38-yard line. Fritz Reed's 26-yard advance of Champi's lateral was the next play after the timeout. Stanford called a timeout with eight seconds remaining to set up their go-ahead field goal—kicked, naturally by Mark Harmon, wearing #8—leaving four seconds on the clock for California's kick return.

In Colt's book, he writes, regarding the Fritz Reed advance of the lateral, "The Yale players seemed momentarily paralyzed; some of them thought they'd heard a whistle." In the Cal-Stanford game, several Stanford players stopped when they were convinced that Dwight Garner had been tackled after one of the laterals.

The visiting quarterbacks: Elway was considered by many the best college quarterback of all time, while Dowling had even higher esteem; Yale fans called him "God". Both were extremely mobile. While Dowling was called "God", Ohio State fans in 1968 were more than content with their mobile quarterback, Rex—which means "King"—Kern. Elway was quoted as saying that the outcome "ruined my last game as a college football player", while Dowling was less dramatic, saying that the tie was a "blemish on my career at Yale." Dowling had to watch helplessly for the last 3:34 of the game; Elway thought that he had done enough with four seconds remaining.

The media would provide memorable moments in both the Harvard vs. Yale and California vs. Stanford games. After Harvard's last touchdown and before the two-point conversion for the win—er, tie—Ken Coleman's call on the radio had "People are all over this field!", while Joe Starkey had the iconic call during the kickoff return, "Oh, the band is out on the field!" Starkey also had the famous call after the referee signaled the winning touchdown, "Oh, my God! The most amazing, sensational, dramatic, heartrending, exciting, thrilling finish in the history of college football!"

The Yale cheerleaders fired off a small cannon along the sideline as victory seemed imminent, and the California supporters fired a cannon shot from the California Victory Cannon, positioned on Tightwad Hill outside the stadium, at the beginning of each home football game, after each score, and after each victory by the Golden Bears. The last cannon shot of 1982 came as a huge and confusing surprise to those Cal fans who had left the game prematurely.

The *Harvard Crimson* student newspaper had the headline "HARVARD BEATS YALE, 29-29", and reporters for *The Stanford Daily* published a bogus "extra" edition of the University of California's student newspaper, the *Daily Californian*, with the headline "NCAA AWARDS BIG GAME TO STANFORD" and the lead story, which began "The National Collegiate Athletic Association (NCAA) has awarded last Saturday's Big Game to Stanford, the *Daily Californian* was told late last night," and a box containing a phony NCAA rule by which an "injustice" may be corrected. Seven thousand copies of the bogus issue were planted in newsstands on the Berkeley campus. Tom Mulvoy, a deputy managing editor of the *Boston Globe*—who may have had some Harvard influence—was attending Stanford on a journalism fellowship and encouraged the *Stanford Daily* staff to proceed with their prank. A bogus quote in the publication attributed to Cal's Mariet Ford was years ahead of its time, foreseeing the NFL's video review process: "What really burns me up is that … a group of people back in New York who weren't even there, have the authority to call this game. It just isn't fair."

The Harvard vs. Yale game had the iconic photo by Frank O'Brien in the *Boston Globe* of Pete Varney catching the final two-point conversion pass and holding the ball over his head in his right hand, while bear-hugged by a Yale defender from behind. Crim and Reed also appear in the photo, in celebration mode. The California vs. Stanford game had the iconic photo by Robert Stinnett in the *Oakland Tribune* of Kevin Moen celebrating in the end zone, airborne, holding the football over his head.

In a www.espn.com story, Adam Rittenberg reported that Starkey's color commentator Jan Hutchins had been a young sports reporter in Pittsburgh on the sideline ten years earlier at Three Rivers Stadium as Steelers fullback Franco Harris made the "Immaculate Reception"—named by NFL Films as the most controversial play in league history—on a fourth-down play and ran right by him. That deflected pass was the result of a hard hit by the Oakland Raiders' defensive back Jack Tatum, who was, naturally, a former Ohio State star. The controversy was whether the Steelers' Frenchy Fuqua was the last to touch the ball on the deflection. The September 2007 edition of *Referee* magazine also cited this determination among the 18 best calls in officiating history.

Like Cal, the Steelers trailed by one point at the time. As in the Cal-Stanford game, the officials conferred to ensure that the touchdown stood. Unlike the Cal-Stanford game, the touchdown occurred with five seconds remaining; the Raiders had no such miracle return on the ensuing kickoff. Similar to thirty years later in the 2002 season, that 1972 season involved a team from Miami with a perfect record late in the season, though the Miami Dolphins would complete their season with a perfect 17-0 record. That Dolphins team featured Pro Football Hall of Fame members—former Ohio State star Paul Warfield, Larry Csonka from Stow, Ohio, and Coach Don Shula, who was born in Ohio, had degrees from John Carroll University and Western Reserve University, and played professionally for the Cleveland Browns.

Other members of that Steelers team were Terry Hanratty and Rocky Bleier from Notre Dame, and George Webster from Michigan State, all of whom had played in the 10-10 tie game in 1966. Also on the team was offensive lineman Larry Little, who attended Bethune-Cookman in the state of Florida and would coach the Ohio Glory—a team in the NFL-sponsored World League of American Football—in Columbus twenty years later. The quarterback on that team was Greg Frey from Ohio State.

Jan Hutchins, naturally, grew up in Ohio in the city of Wooster and graduated from Yale, having attended the 1968 Yale-Harvard game as a student.

Jan Hutchins: *On "The Play", I was just screaming so much they had to remove my mic track from the broadcast. As I waited for the officials to decide if Franco's catch was legal, I felt the powerful Pittsburgh crowd energy and moved near the players' exit to the locker room to be ready to run from what I imagined would be a riot if the play was called back. I imagine being involved with all three miracles as just extra dramatic parts of a magical life."*

At the Harvard-Yale game, Yale fans waved white handkerchiefs at the Harvard fans when they thought that they had the game won; the Terrible Towels would arrive in Three Rivers Stadium three years after the Immaculate Reception.

Gary M. Pomerantz wrote about the Steelers-Raiders game in his book, "Their Life's Work: The Brotherhood of the 1970s Pittsburgh Steelers, Then and Now". Pomerantz, naturally, has been a visiting lecturer in the Department of Communication at Stanford University.

In his book "Fighting Back", Bleier is extremely complimentary of Rex Kern, the quarterback on Ohio State's 1968 national championship team, who played defensive back in the NFL; in the matchup against Buffalo in the 1974 playoffs, Bleier called Kern the best player on the field and praised his toughness.

The game with a chaotic ending that Ohio State fans can relate to most closely would be the 16-13 loss at Michigan State in 1974, when the Spartans scored the last 13 points of the game in the fourth quarter, and confusion reigned on the last two plays as the Buckeyes tried to score from the one-yard line.

That was the agony of defeat for Ohio State fans. A thrill of victory would come in 2016, naturally, 34 years after the Cal-Stanford game and 14 years after the Ohio State-Miami game. The 30-27 walk-off win in the second overtime over Michigan was another game with great controversy; the Buckeyes' quarterback J.T. Barrett was ruled to have gained the yard needed for a first down one play before the winning touchdown run by Curtis Samuel. Channeling Bo Schembechler and others, Michigan's coach Jim Harbaugh said, "I was bitterly disappointed with the officiating."

What is it about college games in November?

The three tie games had a total of seven players who finished in the top ten of the Heisman Trophy voting that year. In 1966, Nick Eddy was third, Clinton Jones was sixth, and Terry Hanratty was eighth. In 1968, Brian Dowling was ninth, and in 1973, three Buckeyes finished high— John Hicks was second, Archie Griffin was fifth, and Randy Gradishar was sixth.

RECAP

Both the Ohio State vs. Michigan and the Harvard vs. Yale rivalry games bear the nickname "The Game", while the California-Stanford rivalry game has the tag of "The Big Game". These three games had various versions of red vs. blue—Harvard's crimson against the Yale blue, Ohio State's scarlet against Michigan's blue, and Stanford's cardinal against California's blue.

The Michigan State vs. Notre Dame game in 1966 had the only tie game in its series, while the Harvard vs. Yale game in 1968 had the eighth and last tie in its series.

The Harvard vs. Yale and California vs. Stanford games had chaotic endings, while the 1973 OSU vs. Michigan game had a chaotic scene before the game—the Buckeye players tried to tear down Michigan's M Club banner. The ending of the 1966 Notre Dame vs. Michigan State game is described as being one of the quietest ever, as the Spartan fans had nothing to cheer about.

In the two 10-10 games, the visiting team played a remarkably clean game, penalty-wise. Notre Dame had five yards in penalties to 32 for Michigan State, and the Buckeyes had none, compared to four for 37 yards for Michigan.

Oftentimes, huge games like these will have at most one disputed touchdown. Stanford fans dispute all three by California—a catch by

Mariet Ford that appeared to have bounced on the turf, another catch along the sideline by Wes Howell, and the intensely disputed winning kickoff return. The other three games had no disputed touchdowns; in his book "Born to Referee", Jerry Markbreit writes,"We didn't have one controversial call or a single complaint from anyone.", regarding his role as the back judge in the 10-10 tie game between Notre Dame and Michigan State in 1966. Markbreit would not be as fortunate in the 1971 Ohio State-Michigan game, when he caught an earful from Woody Hayes, who protested that pass interference should have been called on a late interception by Michigan.

The four backup quarterbacks in three tie games combined to complete only 13 of 39 passes, though Champi was the most effective and the most satisfying to his fans; half of his six completions in his 15 attempts went for touchdowns. O'Brien also had a touchdown pass for Notre Dame, to Ohio native Bob Gladieux.

Of these eight teams, it was the last game of the season for six of them. Notre Dame was an exception, playing a regular season game against USC the following week, but the only team to play in a bowl was Ohio State, for a variety of reasons:

- Notre Dame's school policy prohibited bowl games at the time.

- Michigan State was denied due to the Big Ten's no-repeat rule.

- The Ivy League prohibited bowl games, denying Harvard and Yale.

- Michigan was denied by the Big Ten athletic directors' vote and by the Big Ten's rule at the time that allowed only one team to play in a bowl game.

- Stanford finished with a 5-6 record, losing its last three games. If they had beaten California, they would have been invited to the Hall of Fame Bowl with a 6-5 record, due to Elway's potential appeal as the Heisman Trophy winner. The game against California turned out to be Elway's last college game, and Stanford did not play in a bowl game in his four seasons. A Heisman Trophy winner on a losing team? It had occurred in 1956, when Paul Hornung of Notre Dame won the trophy despite the Irish's 2-8 record.

- California finished with a 7-4 record—better than Stanford's best-case scenario record of 6-5, had they won—but was not selected for a bowl game. The Hall of Fame Bowl chose Air Force after Stanford lost. Air Force beat Vanderbilt, 36-28, scoring the second-most points in the 16 bowl games that existed at the time, behind Ohio State's total in its 47-17 win over Brigham Young in the Holiday Bowl.

CHAPTER 8

Craig Krenzel's Legacy

IF YOU WERE TO CONSTRUCT an ideal college football quarter-back, based on stats alone, it would probably not produce Craig Krenzel. Several noted quarterbacks, including Heisman Trophy winners, have had more than double his 2,110 passing yards and more than twice as many as his 368 rushing yards of the 2002 season. His three rushing touchdowns? A drop in the bucket, compared to several other quarterbacks.

However, at 6' 4" and 215 pounds, Krenzel was able to absorb hard hits multiple times in the Fiesta Bowl. In a *Sports Illustrated* online story, Miami linebacker Rocky McIntosh, referring to Krenzel's first touchdown sneak, said, "I hit him solid but he spun and his momentum took him in ... He was a big guy and he was able to withstand all the hits we put on him."

Ohio State played in a combined 27 games in 2002 and 2003, and Krenzel threw 27 touchdown passes in those two years. If the North Carolina State game in 2003 had not gone into three overtimes, he would have had 12 touchdown passes and three rushing touchdowns in each season.

In his first three overtime games, including the North Carolina State game of 2003, he accounted for eight of the team's 12 touchdowns, rushing or passing. Three of his six career rushing touchdowns came in overtime games. He had five of his six career rushing touchdowns in the span of four games. Two were in the Miami game, two were in the Washington game in 2003, and one was in the game against North Carolina State in 2003. In the 2002 season, his three rushing touchdowns covered one, one, and six yards; in 2003, they covered 23, 11, and six yards.

His two one-yard touchdown runs against Miami may have sounded familiar to his coach; when Tressel was a senior quarterback at Baldwin Wallace, he scored a touchdown on a "1-yard dive", and he "dived in from the 1", quoting from the book, "...And We Must Excel." That book also mentions that Coach Lee Tressel "loved the passing game," which Coach Jim Tressel may have learned to love in his later years at Ohio State.

Coach Tressel had a third captain join captains Nickey and Doss on a rotating basis in the 2002 season. Krenzel, a junior, was the choice on four occasions, the Texas Tech, Penn State, Michigan, and Miami games.

Krenzel was the MVP of both of the 2002 and 2003 bowl games, despite completing less than half of his passes in each game. Using another baseball analogy, there is the saying that being successful three out of ten times will get you into the Hall of Fame. Krenzel knew how to pick his spots. In the Fiesta Bowl of the 2003 season against Kansas State, two of his eight carries picked up a first down. In his three games against Michigan, his combined stats were 41 of 65 (63%, higher than his career percentage of 56%) for 463 yards with two touchdown passes and one interception, which came in his first matchup and did not hurt the team. In his three bowl games, which included one-for-two for four passing yards against South Carolina, he had two wins; he completed 19 of 47 for 315 yards. In the bowl games, he had a higher average gain per completion than he did in Michigan games—16.6 compared to 11.3. In the bowl games, he accounted for six of the eight offensive touchdowns.

In his senior year of high school, he had a game with 418 passing yards and tied the Michigan high school state record with seven touchdown passes, a record that has since been broken.

As a freshman in 2000, he gave glimpses of what was to come. In the spring game, played in Crew Stadium while Ohio Stadium was under reconstruction, the *Columbus Dispatch* reported, "McMullen looked terrific in the first half when he was playing with the first team, completing 7 of 12 passes for 120 yards and a touchdown. Meanwhile, Krenzel struggled, throwing two interceptions for the Gray. But when they switched sides in the second half it was Krenzel who shined." He led the Scarlet to two field goals, ran four times for 19 yards, and was a combined 11-for-21 passing for 107 yards.

In the 2000 regular season, his first carry in his first game was a one-yard fourth-down sneak for a first down against Fresno State. His first completion in the same game was a 16-yard pass on third-and-goal from the 17-yard line, and his second completion was to fellow freshman Ben Hartsock for 11 yards and a first down. In the Outback Bowl, the 24-7 loss to South Carolina, he played in only the last series, completing two of three passes—including one to fellow Michigan native Ricky Bryant—for one first down. His last pass was intercepted on a throw of 35-plus yards.

After the spring game in 2001, played again at Crew Stadium, Matt Wilhelm showed that he was a good judge of character, as he was quoted in the *Columbus Dispatch* with, "The thing that sticks in my mind quarterback-wise is Craig Krenzel ... leading us in from the 30-yard line, running three or four quarterback draws, and he's taking massive hits from a defense that's trying to swarm on the ball and stop him from getting to the goal line, and he scores to give us the win." Krenzel ran 11 times for 42 yards and said, "I'm not one of the most athletic guys, but I just do what I can to get it in the end zone." The *Dispatch* reported that "Krenzel put a spin move on linebacker Cie Grant at the 2-yard line and dived for the stripe to complete a 4-yard scoring run with 1:05 left, giving the Scarlet a

22-21 victory over the Gray." Was he preparing for the Cincinnati game, about 17 months later?

In the Outback Bowl of the 2001 season, which he started, he had only four carries, but his first one for seven yards, scrambling to his right out of a designed pass play on third-and-four, produced the Buckeyes' first first down of the game.

In the 2002 season:

- He had more than twice as many rushes in the last seven games (85) as he did in the first seven (40), but his yardage difference was much closer—198 to 170. His three highest average per carry games came in his first six games.

- His 81 yards rushing against Miami were more than what he had in the four previous games combined.

- His 4.3 yards per rush against Miami is more impressive when you factor in that three of his attempts came from the Miami one-yard line, and his four-yard loss came on a sack. His other 15 carries netted 83 yards for a 5.5 average.

- In the eight closest games, he averaged 38 yards rushing per game; in the other six games, each decided by at least 18 points, he averaged 12 yards rushing per game.

- His three games with the highest rushing yards came in games decided by 11, six, and zero points in regulation.

- The five games in which he had at least 10 carries were all decided by seven points or less.

- In the seven games decided by seven points or less, he passed or ran for nine of the 14 offensive touchdowns, including all of the first seven.

- He had more rushing yards than the opposing quarterback in 13 of the 14 games, and in each of the last 12 games.

- In the games against Texas Tech, Washington State, San Jose State, and Miami, he ran for more yards than the opponent did as a team.

- Two of his three rushing touchdowns came in the national championship game. His other rushing touchdown also came away from Columbus, in the dramatic win against Cincinnati. Two of them were in the fourth quarter or overtime, and the other one was on a fourth down play against Miami. In the two games against Miami and Cincinnati, his combined passing numbers were only 21 for 50.

- In the Miami game, he passed or ran for 76% of the team's total yards. His six next highest percentages, in the range of 53% to 72%, were in the six other games decided by seven points or less, and his eighth highest percentage (51%) was in the eighth-closest game, Northwestern.

- In the Miami game, he ran for 56% of the team's rushing yards. His highest percentages and his most carries were in the eight closest games.

- In the wins over Cincinnati, Purdue, and Miami—where the combined scoring difference in regulation was eight points— he had the team's longest run. He also had the Buckeyes' longest run against Northwestern, an 11-point win. All four games were away from Columbus.

- His total offense of 2,478 yards was almost exactly twice the 1,237 of Clarett.

- Six of his top seven games for pass attempts came away from home. He averaged 22 attempts away from home and 14.6

attempts at home. Four of his five games with the lowest completion percent came away from home.

- He never threw interceptions in consecutive games, and had 10 games without an interception. He had consecutive game streaks of four, three, and two without an interception.

- Thanks to his ability to avoid interceptions, the team decreased its interception rate from 4% in 2001 to 2% in 2002.

- He was the first quarterback to run for two touchdowns in a championship game, to be followed by Vince Young of Texas in the 2005 season and Stetson Bennett of Georgia in the 2022 season. Both Young and Bennett played in winning games against Ohio State in their championship seasons.

In the 2003 season, he extended his streak to 16 (matching his jersey number) games where he had more rushing yards than the opposing quarterback, and in 20 of his last 25 games, he had more rushing yards than the opposing quarterback. In his last game as a Buckeye, the 2004 Fiesta Bowl against Kansas State, he surpassed the 5,000 yard mark in total offense.

In March of 2003, he received the *Sporting News* Radio Socrates Award, which is given to a college athlete who best embodies the Socrates Creed of "a strong mind in a strong body." His strong mind was pursuing a degree in Molecular Genetics. The ceremony was held in, ironically, the Fox Theater in Detroit. Other finalists for the 2003 award included Kliff Kingsbury of Texas Tech and Matt Walters, the defensive right tackle of Miami. It was Walters who flushed Krenzel out of the pocket on the play in the fourth quarter where Kelly Jennings's hold on Gamble's jersey was not called. He had five tackles of Krenzel in the Fiesta Bowl, with Krenzel gaining 23 of his 81 rushing yards on those plays.

The 2001 Michigan game was a pivotal point for Ohio State in his four years. From 2000 through 2003, the Buckeyes had a record of 14-8 BCS (Before Craig Started) and 26-3 ACS (After Craig Started).

He won the Vincent dePaul Draddy Award in 2003 as college football's premier student-athlete. With Bobby Hoying winning the award in 1995, Ohio State was the only college to have multiple winners in that nine-year span. He was also named to the College Sports Information Directors of America (CoSIDA) Academic All-America second-team in 2002 and first team in 2003, being named the Academic All-American of the Year by CoSIDA in 2003. He was named a second-team Verizon Academic All America in 2002, along with Ben Hartsock. He received a National Football Foundation and Hall of Fame Scholarship in 2003. In 2003, he was a recipient of the NCAA Today's Top VIII Award, recognized for "successes on the field, in the classroom and in the community", illustrating what Coach Tressel said on the day of his hiring, "I can assure you that you will be proud of your young people in the classroom, in the community, and most especially in 310 days in Ann Arbor, Michigan."

He was drafted in the fifth round by the Chicago Bears in 2004 with pick #16 (naturally) and wore jersey #16 (naturally). He was reunited with Tim Spencer, the Bears' first-year running backs coach who was the Ohio State running backs coach in the 2002 season. A fellow rookie was Alfonso Marshall, whose only tackle as a defensive back for Miami in the Fiesta Bowl was on Chris Gamble's 57-yard reception. The Bears' defensive coordinator was Ron Rivera, who had played for another team of Bears in college, at California; he and Krenzel may have shared stories about exciting finishes.

He won his first three starts, to run his record to 29-3 ACS. He had a touchdown pass in his first start, against the San Francisco 49ers, whose quarterback was Ken Dorsey. Krenzel was playing for a team located on Lake Michigan, while Dorsey was playing for a team near his home town of Orinda. Krenzel had a touchdown pass and a two-point conversion run in his second start, a seven-point win over the New York Giants. His third start was a two-point overtime win over the Tennessee Titans, a game that must have made Coach Tressel proud, as the Bears scored on an interception return, a punt return, a field goal with 52 seconds remaining in regulation, and the winning points on a safety. It was his fourth win in three years where his team did not have an offensive touchdown. His third and last touchdown pass in his career came in a 41-10 loss to Peyton Manning and the Indianapolis Colts.

He was with the Cincinnati Bengals in the 2005 season, but had no playing time in what turned out to be his last NFL season. He was released in 2006 due to an elbow injury.

CHAPTER 9

The Aftermath

LIKE MIAMI HEADING INTO its 2002 season, the Buckeyes seemed to have all the tools to repeat as national champions in 2003, with all 11 starters on offense returning, six returnees on defense, and Mike Nugent returning. Players with 44 of the 48 touchdowns would be returning.

The preview issue of *Sports Illustrated* picked the Buckeyes as Number 1, with Oklahoma at Number 2. The prediction on the Sooners would be spot-on, as they played in the BCS Championship game, but the prediction for the eventual champion was worse than in the 2002 season; they picked LSU at Number 20.

Buckeye fans were elated to learn that Will Smith, Michael Jenkins, and Darrion Scott elected to return for their senior season instead of opting for the NFL draft.

All the pieces seemed to be in place.

... until Maurice Clarett's legal issues that ended his Buckeye career after one season put a crimp in the offense.

With Smith, Tim Anderson, and Darrion Scott returning on the defensive line, the rushing defense improved from 77.7 yards per game to 62.3, second only to USC. LSU was third in the category; LSU was the national champion by winning the BCS game, and USC was the national champion in the Associated Press poll.

The Buckeyes continued to win close games, with one exception.

After a 28-9 opening win over Washington, they had three more wins—consecutively, to boot—by seven points or less, over San Diego State, North Carolina State (in three overtimes), and Bowling Green. That raised their pattern to nine such wins in the span of 11 games. The three-overtime win over NC State had the Buckeyes leading 17-7 in the third quarter, as the Miami game had. That streak and a 19-game winning streak ended in a 17-10 loss at Wisconsin, a game that was tied at 10 before the Badgers scored with 5:09 remaining. The Buckeyes had to play Wisconsin in Madison for the second consecutive season.

With a 16-13 win over San Diego State (interception and three field goals) and a 19-10 win over Iowa (punt return, blocked punt return, safety, and a 53-yard field goal), the Buckeyes had won for the third time in less than a year without scoring an offensive touchdown, after not having such a game in the 1986 through the 2001 seasons.

As Krenzel missed the Bowling Green and Northwestern games with a hyperextended right elbow, McMullen was solid. He was 10-for-16 with a touchdown pass in the 24-17 win over Bowling Green and 16-for-25 in a 20-0 win over Northwestern.

At Penn State, Krenzel was knocked out of the game before halftime with the Buckeyes trailing 17-7. McMullen threw two touchdown passes to Michael Jenkins, including a five-yard toss with 1:35 remaining for the final score in the 21-20 win.

A 16-13 win over Purdue in overtime raised their all-time record in overtimes to 4-0 and marked the second straight season where they had an overtime game the week before the Michigan game.

As in 1969 (a 24-12 score)—following their championship season— the Buckeyes lost in Ann Arbor by double digits, 35-21. They rallied from

21-0 down to make the score 28-21 and had the ball following a Chris Gamble interception, but could not score again. Krenzel had to leave the game with a shoulder injury, but did return.

The Buckeyes returned to the Fiesta Bowl in Tempe, beating Kansas State, 35-28. Compared to the tight game against Miami the season before, where their biggest lead was 10 points and they trailed twice, they had a three touchdown lead twice and never trailed. However, they did rely on their Fiesta Bowl formula of being outgained on offense and out-first-downed (10 fewer). They recorded their sixth score of the season from their defense or special teams—including one safety—when Harlen Jacobs (wearing jersey #13) blocked a punt and John Hollins returned it seven yards for a touchdown. Again, the defense contained a spectacular running back, the Wildcats' Darren Sproles, holding him to 38 yards for a 2.9 average on the ground and three catches for five yards. He averaged 132 yards per game and 6.5 yards per carry in the season. Like the win over Miami, the Buckeyes had four touchdowns on offense, except that all four against the Hurricanes were on the ground, and all four against the Wildcats came on Krenzel's arm.

Tressel and Kansas State's coach Bill Snyder would be inducted into the College Football Hall of Fame in 2015.

Without the services of Clarett, the rushing yards were only 126 per game, compared to 191 per game in 2002. The rushing touchdowns for the season were only 14, compared to 31 in 2002.

Krenzel had passed for at least 200 yards twice in 14 games in 2002, but did so seven times in 11 games in 2003. He averaged 25 passes per game in 2003, compared to 18 in 2002. His most completions in a game in 2002 was 14; he topped that five times in 2003. He had a combined six passing touchdowns in the Michigan game (two) and the Fiesta Bowl game (four), compared to none in the 2002 season. The six touchdowns in consecutive games marked a personal high, having had five in consecutive games in 2002.

Despite Ohio State's reputation as a ground-attack offense, Jenkins finished his career with 2,898 receiving yards, the most for any Buckeye. The passing attack was boosted by the emergence of Santonio Holmes, who was a redshirt freshman and had two touchdown receptions against Michigan and two against Kansas State.

Chris Gamble was used significantly less on offense, dropping from 34 plays for 548 total yards in 2002 to four receptions for 38 yards (all in a three-game stretch in games eight, nine, and ten) and three carries for 19 yards in 2003. He tied Jenkins for the lead in punt returns with 20 (none after the sixth game), and had six kickoff returns for 115 yards.

CHAPTER 10

In Their Words

BAM CHILDRESS, Andy Groom, Maurice Hall, Craig Krenzel, Donnie Nickey, and Mike Nugent graciously supplied their input for this book.

ON THE COACHING TRANSITION

Childress: I think the team took maybe a month to get really settled in and understand where Tress was coming from, what he wanted from us, what he expected from us. But once we got settled in and understood this is the goal, this is the standard, it was cool. Like you have a lot of athletes that's high level guys, but we just want to know what you expect, and we're going to go out, we're just going to try and make it happen. He's big on respect, big on representing Ohio State the right way. We did some good team building stuff, too, like a three-on-three basketball tournament that we did to have fun.

Nickey: It took that first year of Coach Tressel setting up the infrastructure and just the way we communicated. Coach Tressel communicated character and life skills, and football and X's and O's came secondary. Because we did embrace the spiritual part of selflessness and character strengths, we became a closer team, and we became a better team because of that. The football would just reveal your character every day. So, it was just the paradigm shift in our thinking.

WHEN DID YOU KNOW THAT THE TEAM HAD THE POTENTIAL FOR A NATIONAL CHAMPIONSHIP?

Childress: On the first day of practice and camp, I knew we would be special, because it was all this fuss about Reese [Clarett], right? Like, all this fuss about, is he going to be good? Is he going to live up to the hype? We met Reese before that. He was hanging out, lifting weights, just talking, laughing, joking, all that stuff. You can get a vibe of how people are, and Reese wasn't some cocky dude coming in. He wasn't an arrogant guy. He was just normal freaking nature, "I can lift anything, I'm fast." But he was just humble, down to earth. And that first day of practice, it was like two linemen. Reese went against Doss or Will Allen and the sounds that they were making when they were hitting each other, you knew our offense is going to be good, our defense is going to be good, but everybody put a lot of emphasis on Reese. Like, can he handle the Big 10? Can he handle all of this physical stuff? As soon as he and Doss or Will kept hitting each other play after play, I knew this was going to be special. It's going to be special because he's going to run over everybody. He's going to run by everybody and he's big enough, he's blessed with like just freaking nature of talent. He's going to handle all of the stuff that everybody's saying. Craig is going to be a good quarterback, Jenkins is going to be a good wide receiver, Doss, everybody, they're going to take care of their stuff on defense. But at that practice, I knew that we would be special.

Groom: We had winter conditioning that was super hard, I think it was at 5:30 or 6:00 in the morning. We really felt it started there and then into spring but summer, once we started our workouts and our outdoor activities through the summer. Obviously, we didn't do what we wanted to do, especially at the end of the season losing to South Carolina. But we felt like we had a lot of guys coming back at key positions, guys coming in, obviously like Maurice Clarett that were going to be able to contribute right away. And, it's funny, my pops was telling me after the South Carolina game, just wait till next year, you guys are going to win it all. It's crazy, I thought for him to say that. But he's the one that said that from the beginning, and then I obviously started to see that throughout our workouts, and I thought we had something very special that we could make a run out of. I know it's going to be super tough and very challenging, but I think it all started with that summer getting together, getting our work in, and really bonding as a team.

Hall: I think our minds had changed when Mike Doss said he was coming back to school, he was not going into the draft, he was going to come back to school for a national championship. And I think for us, that changed a lot of the players' mindsets, simply because we had the same team, we had just gone 7-5. For someone to say, I'm going to forgo millions of dollars, because I want to come back to school because I think we can win it all, despite that we just lost five games, and we have the same players. That for us was, so he sees something in us that we don't see. And, I really think it motivated the coaches as well. I feel like the coaches stepped up, and I feel like all the players mentally started to believe at that moment. And then as we continued to go through summer conditioning and winter conditioning, we were operating in a championship mentality. We had some great additions that year. Obviously, Reese was probably the biggest one. He came in the winter, as well. He jumped right on the same mental board as the rest of the team, as far as us being able to really make some noise and actually win a national championship. So, that's kind of how we prepared the whole off-season.

Nickey: After the South Carolina bowl game, we knew that we had something. The freshman class hadn't come in yet, but that was really when we knew, when Maurice all those freshmen came in. The kids were good. In the spring, Coach Tressel sent me to Ohio State's LeaderShape Institute, a camp on leadership and vision-setting, attended by members of all different groups on campus, but no sports. I was sent there to be the representative for our football team, and my job was to bring that home and teach my teammates what I learned, and it was all about vision setting. We set a vision for that season. My vision was to win national championships—with an "s". I went over it in camp, and everybody just bought into it, "We can do this. This program is the best program in the country, let's start winning, and let's start acting like it's the best program in the country." It's amazing what can happen when you don't care who gets the credit, and you have a belief in something greater than yourselves, the team. When you believe in your team and have faith that things are going to turn out in your favor, and you play for each other, you're unbeatable. Tressel planted the seed in my brain, then facilitated it for me to plant the seed in my teammates' brain. Mostly, it was the senior class.

Nugent: I know we started off and did pretty well, and you're undefeated through a few games. Okay, let's keep this going. It was just such a good locker room and a good group of guys. And we had really, really, really great leadership on the player side. Jim Tressel, just his resume and his character just speaks for itself. He is the kind of guy that absolutely every single person respects. You don't want to disappoint him or make him upset, but you also want to make him proud, kind of like a parent. And that was just a very cool thing to have the fact that you're away from home and get to be around these coaches every day. You care about the players so much. It was just on such a good positive personal level, you just love the guys so much you want to win for them. And then you start putting some games together. I think what really, really catapulted us forward was every

250

one of those games that we should have had bigger wins. We really kind of pulled through at the end and that brought us together a lot. Certain games like Purdue and in Paul Brown Stadium against Cincinnati really brought us together

AS THE SEASON PROGRESED

Childress: I got a little bit hesitant about a national championship at the Purdue game, because we knew, if we lose a game, it's going to be so hard to be in a national championship game. But that fourth down play with Mike, it kind of sealed the deal for me. We're going as long as we do what we do. It didn't matter who we play, but we are going.

Hall: Going into the season, we knew the teams that we had to beat. At the end of the day it was going to come down to us against Michigan. And that was something that we had been prepared for all year. As you know, we played a lot of close games that we ended up pulling out right at the end, so it was a never-say-die attitude.

Krenzel: You have to be so good. You have to be well-coached. You have to be disciplined. You have to be mature. And we were all of those things. But you also have to catch the breaks here and there. If you look at any national champion team, there's going to be a handful of plays all season long where the ball bounced the right way, they made the play, that's a big play in that moment. And I think we certainly had more than most. Cincinnati early in the season, Purdue, later in the year, Illinois in overtime … those were moments, as I look back, that tested our resiliency, and in January of '03, against Miami, you saw it all pay off.

Nickey: After the Cincinnati game, we knew we had something special.

ON POSITION CHANGES

Childress: I came in on defense. In a practice, Doss needed somebody to go with in one-on-ones. All the receivers were down, and I told Tress, I'll go over there, I'll play receiver. So I went over there, did real well against Doss. Tress said, we're going to put you on offense, we want you to learn the playbook. It's so much that you have to learn at receiver, but you can use a little bit more athletic ability on defense. But to see how Chris handled it and to see how Chris excelled at it was freaking awesome.

Nickey: I'm a linebacker [size-wise, but played safety]. In high school, I played every snap except for kickoffs, I was a punter and the returner for everything else. I have to feel like I was in a car wreck the next day. But it was never like that in college, but everything was more intense. So, an appreciation for what Chris Gamble did, for Cie Grant, for him to go from corner to linebacker, I don't even understand how he did that. It shows how good of an athlete he was. By recruiting design, it was supposed to be Cie and Mike Doss at safety, but somehow I kept Cie on the bench, but he was so good we had to put him on the field.

WHY WAS THE TEAM CONFIDENT
GOING INTO THE MIAMI GAME?

Childress: Our confidence was high. Like super high. And the only reason I think it was super high was because they never really faced a team like us. They faced a lot of teams that were fast. They faced a lot of teams that were just a little bit physical. But we had everything. We had physical, we had speed, obviously, we had good coaching. They had everything, too. I don't think they had as much physicalness on offense, but their defense was really good. Their offense was talented, fast. But we had a lot of confidence just because, looking at the film, they haven't faced an animal like us.

Groom: It was just what we've been able to do throughout the season through 13 games. We could have easily gone seven and six. We always found a way to win, our defense was phenomenal, our offensive squad got the job done, always gave us enough points to win, and we believed we had the best special teams in the country, so we had a lot of confidence. We knew Miami is one of the best BCS teams ever to play the game, and we were going to have to play a perfect game to win because, obviously, they had firepower at quarterback, at wide receiver, and specifically at running back, and their defense was fast and lit people up.

Hall: We were confident because, literally, there was nobody on TV that said they thought Ohio State would win the game, and, arguably, they were right, because we were playing against, we still say, the greatest show in college football. You look at all the players that came off of that team, and you say, how did anybody beat that team, but for us, we knew they were going to underestimate us. We knew, because it was leading up to it, it was like, "Oh, we're faster than them, we were quicker than them, we are winners", and that just continued to fuel us, and they didn't realize that we were just as fast, we're tougher, probably, because we are playing in the Big Ten versus the BIG EAST, and we have the mentality, and we've been battle-tested all year. So we're not a team that, if we get down, we're just going to give up. We know what it looks like to be down, we know what it looks like to play in close games and pull it out. So for us, that was our mindset going into it. We knew it was going to be a fight, we knew everybody was going to have to play their best game, and that's what we did.

Krenzel: Because we were 20-year old, 21-year old kids. Nobody expects more out of a team than the players in that locker room, not the coaches, not the fans, not the parents. The players themselves expect more out of their performance than anybody. They also have the confidence to go out there and make that happen.

Nickey: We had nothing to lose, it was: play with reckless abandon, like there's no tomorrow, and I think every player on the team did that and stuck together. We had a strong faith at that point that we were winning a close game that was galvanized by all the wins that we had that season. So, when it came to playing Miami, the pressure was on them, like we didn't have any pressure. We weren't even supposed to be there. So I think that let us relax and just take it to Miami. Leading up to the game, Dustin Fox and I both wrote notes to each other, and each of us wrote "2002 National Champions". I gave the pregame speech and ended it with me kicking a whole tray of food at the hotel, and I said, "We've got to kick them in the mouth." I remember just getting an adrenaline rush, and then waiting outside for the bus, the whole team was ready to go.

Nugent: I think we were in that really scary position. We were the team that it's scary to play, because we had absolutely nothing to lose. Miami was so unbelievable, looking back at their roster. It's just like, you've got to be kidding me. These guys are on the same team. They're coming off a national championship, and these guys are so phenomenal, they were a great team, and they were coached very well. But, we just came in thinking like, hey, we have nothing to lose. Like why not? Why not give it everything we've got and just see if we can make a run for it. I can't speak for them or how they felt on the other sideline, but I feel like they probably came in thinking, oh, that's a Big 10 team, they don't pass much, they only run the ball. And, I think after a few plays, maybe there was a little surprise there. Like, oh my gosh, like these guys are good, this is not going to be a cakewalk.

THE MIAMI GAME

Groom: We weren't perfect, but we played a very good game, and I think our defense and a few key plays on offense, specifically, Maurice stripping that ball. Everything aligned, and it was meant to be, and who knows how many times we beat that team if we play them ten times. But it was our night that night.

Krenzel: Minimizing risk was Tressel's model, especially early on in his career at Ohio State. That was probably the game plan when we knew what we were going to get defensively. We were going to get a lot of two-man—two safeties over the top playing zone coverage with linebackers and defensive backs playing man-to-man underneath—which was why I had to run the ball so much. It was kind of part of the game plan, because you are a little susceptible to the quarterback run when you're in that defensive coverage. We knew our defense was among the best, if not the best in the country. Coach Tress always said we had to play mistake-free, opportunistic offense. You can imagine, as a quarterback, that's not necessarily the best thing we want to hear, but it is what it is.

Hall: We had so many players step up that game, between Doss, Mike Jenkins, Chris Gamble, to obviously Reese, and Craig Krenzel made a tremendous amount of plays with his feet that got us first downs. All those little things play a huge part in the game and us eventually winning it. We knew it was going to be hard, we knew it was going to be tough, but we were like, hey, you know, we're going to win this game.

Nickey: It was a battle, it was the hardest hitting game that I had in college. In both the 1999 game and the Fiesta Bowl, the team speed was amazing. Bubba Franks was my headache in the first game, but then Kellen Winslow was the guy that I covered or the guy that gave me headaches in the second game. On that first punt, I was the personal protector, and I was trying to release in the middle, and Sean Taylor came out of nowhere and hit me in the head, helmet-to-helmet. I was on my feet, and I was awake, but I was knocked out. I probably shouldn't have been playing, but in games like that, I wasn't about to come out for anybody. Maurice made the play of the game.

Nugent: And sure enough to come out on top was just, I mean, something I get to be able to say for the rest of my life, which is just, I'm lucky to be able to say that we won that game.

THE FAKE FIELD GOAL

Childress: Groom is such a crazy athlete. I think, knowing him, he probably thinks he can do anything.

Groom: I was lobbying for the fake field goal that we talked about and worked on all year. I talked Coach Tressel into it. We talked about it as a field goal unit, and, unfortunately, the smartest guy out there who is now a very good surgeon, Simon Fraser, did not block for the fake. He blocked as if it was a field goal. He was supposed to pull out instead of drop back, and I had one guy to beat. Unfortunately, it was Sean Taylor, who I ended up playing at Washington with, one of the most athletic, fast, aggressive safeties ever to play the game. I had the option to pitch, but we were not getting out of that one. Nugent wasn't in the position to be able to pitch to and not get killed, and I thought about who could take a hit better and who was more valuable to the team. I thought Mike Nugent was at the time, and I decided to take the hit. After the play, I'm a little fuzzy, but I think I was yelling at Simon for not pulling. Simon's a big dude, I don't know if he'd have got to him, but I could have still cut under him to make that extra yard or two that I needed to get the first down. I think if I was jawing somebody it would most likely be Simon, because I still jaw at him to this day for that. He disagrees with me, but I know what was called, and we have fun with it to this day, because at the end we still won.

Krenzel: When it comes to fake field goals, fake punts, when to punt, when not to punt, that was something that you have to leave in the hands of the coaches. When you have a kicker like Mike Nugent, it's kind of automatic points. But, at the same time, we knew what we were up against, which was a team that hadn't lost in 34 games, and they were loaded with talent. We had the utmost confidence in our defense, but, at the same time, common sense tells you, you're going to have to score some points. Sometimes you make decisions that work, sometimes they don't. I coach little kids in baseball and football, and I tell kids from the youngest age, you're going to make mistakes, so make them aggressively. Don't make mistakes trying not to lose, make mistakes trying to go win. And, you know, that's what we did. We didn't execute, but, had we executed and punched in for a touchdown, it's a whole different conversation.

Nugent: Everything kind of was lined up. It was the look we were looking for and something they were setting up that we really liked. Andy made the call, and we were ready to go. I think it might have been Ben Hartsock and Simon Fraser, but it was so loud, I don't think those guys heard the call, and it was just kind of a broken play at that point. I know that I got the call, but I was only about two and a half yards from Andy, and Simon was probably about seven or eight. You don't want to call it miscommunication, because nobody messed up, I think it was just, they just didn't hear it and we weren't able to execute it. And Miami, they read it like a book. After the play, I was like, oh, I wish you would have pitched it, just because it would have been fun to run the option with Andy. But, sure enough, after watching film, I think there's two guys ready to absolutely destroy me if I got the ball. So, I guess we'll never know what would have happened.

257

THE PASS TO GAMBLE THAT
WAS RULED INCOMPLETE

Groom: I was on the sideline right there. It was real tight for him to catch it, he did end up catching it, it could have gone either way, but if you look at the play and freeze it, he was held twice. It should have been pass interference, defensive holding before that, so whatever anybody wants to say about the last call [the pass interference by Glenn Sharpe], he was held and he was held twice, and he ended up making a phenomenal catch on the sideline that, if we had instant replay, could have gone the other way.

Hall: It was clearly complete. But, you know, it was a lot of plays like that, and, a lot of the people I know from Miami, they always bring up the pass interference, but there were so many other plays that didn't go our way. But it was like those things that didn't go our way, things that could have put the game in a totally different light, where we might not even have to go to overtime.

PARRISH'S PUNT RETURN

Childress: It's one of those 50-50 calls on whether A. J. Hawk was blocked in the back.

Groom: I punted away from him to the right the whole game, and it went really, really well. I had one of the best games in my career, specifically in the first half. But it ended up that he was starting to really cheat on the right side. So I punted out left, kicked it right outside the numbers or on the numbers and right on the numbers right where I want to. I thought it was a 44 or 45-yard punt. And my guys were there to make the tackle. Roscoe made a couple of jukes and then went up to the sideline. It really should have been a 42-yard net, but he ended up getting by our guys.

That's what his specialty was, obviously, he played for a while in the NFL doing that. And I came up the sidelines, and I'm the last guy, and I don't want to be a regular punter who can't run or is not athletic. so I took the angle to make sure that he doesn't come back, and then I made a wonky tackle, and Doss came in and finished it off. Obviously, I had tunnel vision on where the blockers were coming for me, so I did not get in a bad position for him to make a cutback. All I wanted to do was make sure that I contained him to the outside and then put my body in a place to where I could potentially stop him. So I did my job, but I guess that was part of the game that made it very interesting at the end. I'm glad it all worked out, but that was a very stressful part of the game, and it worked out.

Nickey: No question, A. J. Hawk was blocked in the back. There were lots of questionable calls.

THE PASS INTERFERENCE CALL

Childress: Most people say that the official should have thrown it a little bit sooner. But with everything that's going on, we don't know when he threw it. The pass was incomplete, and then it was just chaos after that. But I think it was fair. I think it was a fair call. They rushed the field and threw helmets. And, we were like, wait a minute, dude. It's a flag. Why are you so happy? It was a little bit of new life, and then that kind of changed it a little bit as far as just momentum.

Groom: Freeze-frame, and if you look at it now, he was held, his jersey was held, he was beat up prior to making his cut. Obviously, the official threw it a little bit late and ended up calling it holding in the beginning and then pass interference. You can play it in slow-mo and watch his jersey being held and then him being pushed around. If you had today's technology, they said that the official got it right. He was saying that he didn't want to throw it right away, he was processing it. But at the end of the day, he wanted to get that call right, because it was at the end of the game, a very tight game, obviously. But I'll say this, going through the emotions of their whole team going out there, thinking we lost and thinking that we were going 13 and one. Going from that pure devastation, something we worked on all year, win a national championship, to see their team dancing in the middle of the field, and then the flag came out, it was like we were reborn, and nothing was going to stop us, and it was just a drastic change of emotions that I've never felt before in my life to this day, going from one to the other like that, that quickly.

Hall: Even when that flag came out, it was almost like non-belief for us, because we were so confident that we were going to win that game, that it didn't even register, at least in my head, it didn't even register that that was it. So, it was ironic and fair that the flag did come out, because it was pass interference and giving us an opportunity to move forward and ultimately win the game.

Nickey: We lost the game, then that flag came in late. They started celebrating on the other side, and I felt demoralization, dejection, followed by rebirth. Once we got that call, we had another chance, I saw them celebrate, and then they called the penalty, and then they came back on the field, everybody went back to the sideline, then I knew we had them then. I think that everybody on the team thought that same thing.

Nugent: I actually couldn't really see it too well, I was always one of the kickers, I was taught by someone a long time ago, I like to stand really far away from the uprights, and when it's my turn to go in, I'm running towards the upright. They're just getting bigger and bigger. So I was pretty far away. All I really saw was what was on the screen, but it was just one of those things where you can make arguments for days whether it was the correct call. I always had joking arguments with Jonathan Vilma when we were in New York together, and I told him "hey, it's a great call, he was in his face, can't do it." So, he was never a big fan of me.

HOW TO SUM UP THE SEASON

Childress: Perfect ending to I would say one of the best seasons in Ohio State history. I think that's a testament of all of us together, but that's all the coaches, all of everybody just coming together for one common goal. And we made it happen. It wasn't easy. It's a lot of blood, sweat, and tears that went into that. And not just that one game.

Groom: Just magical. We put in the work, just non-stop; I know a lot of teams say they put in the work, but it went from winter conditioning to spring ball to summer conditioning to football. It was a whirlwind that got us ready, the coaching staff did a phenomenal job getting everybody ready. And you know the little cliche, take it one game at a time, but we did. And we had to. It all started with that Cincinnati game and us able to overcome that adversity and then go on and continue to do that game in and game out. We didn't have too many barn-burners, they were all very close, and we always found a way to win. We had great leaders on that team, and that offense that was able to put up enough points to win, that defense that was one of the best ever to play at Ohio State, a lot of NFL people on that defense, and having our special teams the way they were. It was the perfect year, it was destiny, it was one of the greatest feelings in my life, and I cherish it to this day and will forever.

Hall: It was memorable, it was inspirational. And, for us, I would say it was a redemption story. Because, coming from Coach Tressel's first year, we played decently, but, ultimately, lost four games during the regular season, then had an opportunity to beat South Carolina in the Outback

Bowl and ultimately lost against them for a second year in a row. That was very disappointing. Coach Tressel, everyone was saying, "Oh man, he shouldn't have been hired. He's coming from one double A, and why didn't we get a coach that has already been big time and Division I, and all that stuff to, where we ended up 14 and 0. So that was a big moment. It was a moment about faith. And we had faith that we could do it, the whole thing. And it came true, to put in the work that we had faith in. And our goal came true.

Krenzel: Every kid that comes in that type of scenario, every kid coming out of high school, you had that dream of winning a Big 10 championship, winning a national championship, playing in for now, it's the college playoff, back then, the BCS title game. When that game was over, just being able to celebrate the accomplishment of reaching our goal as a team. A lot of people don't understand that you win that game in January, but preparation for that game started the February before. It's a year-long process that never ends, and it's a lot of work and conditioning and lifting and practice and film. It's blessed to be a part of, but it gets to be a grind. For all of that to finally pay off was just a dream come true.

Nickey: The main theme was the whole team was so close, we really cared about each other, which is what made it different, and how we were able to win close games. There was never any finger-pointing, it was all selfless play. The thing that was consistent was how hard we worked in the weight room, at practice, every day was a battle. There's a saying in football, the game is won in practice, so you play the game in practice before, that's how you win, and we battled each other, and we go as hard as we could every day, and that's how it became so great. It's just that iron sharpening iron on a daily basis. Coach Tressel really was the one who, behind the scenes, kind of set the stage for us to take control of the team and then build on it every week. And then with the spiritual part, and the mental and the character part being inserted, that was the winning formula, because the work ethic was there, the toughness was there, we just had to have that character part and that spiritual part, and then, once that happened, it was fun.

Nugent: I think the biggest thing I would say is just perseverance, just everyone just stuck with it, stuck together, didn't quit. A lot goes into the leadership we had. I remember, just distinctly, Mike Doss leading some workouts leading up to it. I think school was out and we were just getting ready for the game and just hearing Mike Doss kind of pushing us a little bit in a very, very positive way. I mean, if this guy thinks we can do it, like why not? This guy's a three-time all-American, just an unbelievable athlete and an even better guy character-wise, and everyone's just like, if he's buying in, I don't see why we shouldn't. Watching those older guys is like, this is our chance, how often do you get this opportunity? Really just the positive thing that really kept us together the fact that we were going through all those close games, it's like oh, here's another one, here's another one, but we still just kept pulling them out and coming out on top, which we should just always look back on and without a doubt, feel so proud of that.

PHOTO MEMORIES

Freshman sensation Maurice Clarett. *Photo courtesy of Buckeye Sports Bulletin*

Senior linebacker Matt Wilhelm made numerous big plays in tight games against Cincinnati, Purdue, and Miami. *Photo courtesy of Buckeye Sports Bulletin*

Chris Gamble, the defensive back/wide receiver/kick returner/punt returner, makes a 56-yard kickoff return with a block by Bobby Carpenter against Northwestern. *Photo courtesy of Buckeye Sports Bulletin*

Craig Krenzel in action in the "Holy Buckeye" game at Purdue. *Photo courtesy of Buckeye Sports Bulletin*

Michael Jenkins (#12) is mobbed by teammates after the "Holy Buckeye" play at Purdue. *Photo courtesy of Buckeye Sports Bulletin*

Darrion Scott brings the pressure that Ken Dorsey and the Hurricanes offense were unaccustomed to. *Photo courtesy of Buckeye Sports Bulletin*

Big play receiver Michael Jenkins, making the last reception of the season before Clarett's game-winning touchdown. *Photo courtesy of Buckeye Sports Bulletin*

Cie Grant's blitz of Ken Dorsey closed out the championship game. *Photo courtesy of Buckeye Sports Bulletin*

Two men who could be called "Mr. January", Mike Doss and Jim Tressel. *Photo courtesy of Buckeye Sports Bulletin*

Andy Groom, Cie Grant, and David Thompson at the celebration in Ohio Stadium, exactly two years after Coach Tressel's "310 days" speech. *Photo courtesy of Buckeye Sports Bulletin*

ABOUT THE AUTHOR

STEVE BASFORD'S first two books are *"Buckeye Memories: From the Couch, the Stands, and the Press Box ... and a Few Fun Facts"* and *"2001 Games (And Counting): A Sports Odyssey"*.

He has been a statistician for OSU football for Time Warner Cable in 1978 through 1980, for WOSU-TV from 1981 through 1990, and for the official stats crew for home games since 1993.

Not improbably, he lists the 2002 season as his favorite of all time, and attending the win over Miami on January 3, 2003 as his all-time favorite sports moment, followed by the 14-9 win over Michigan.